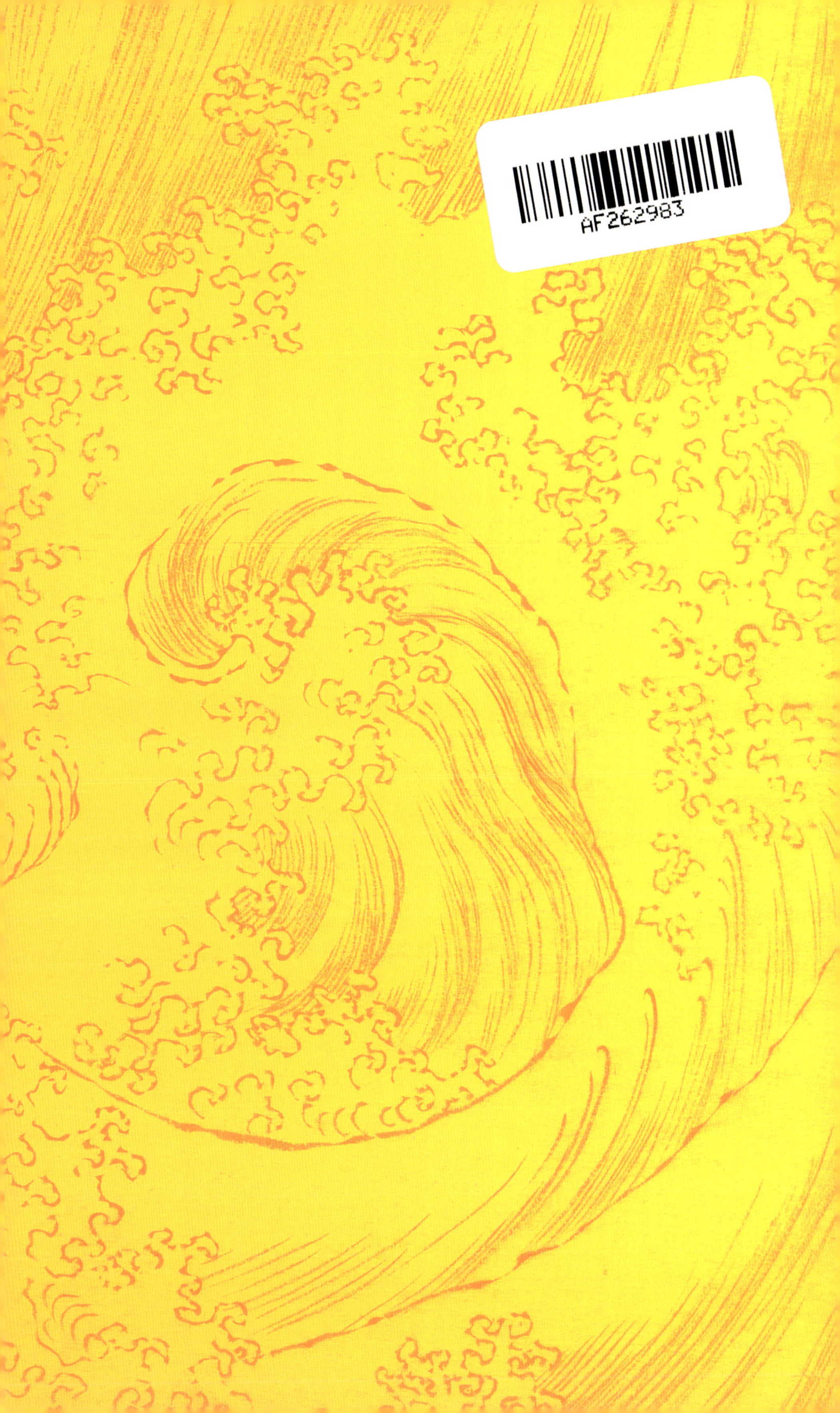

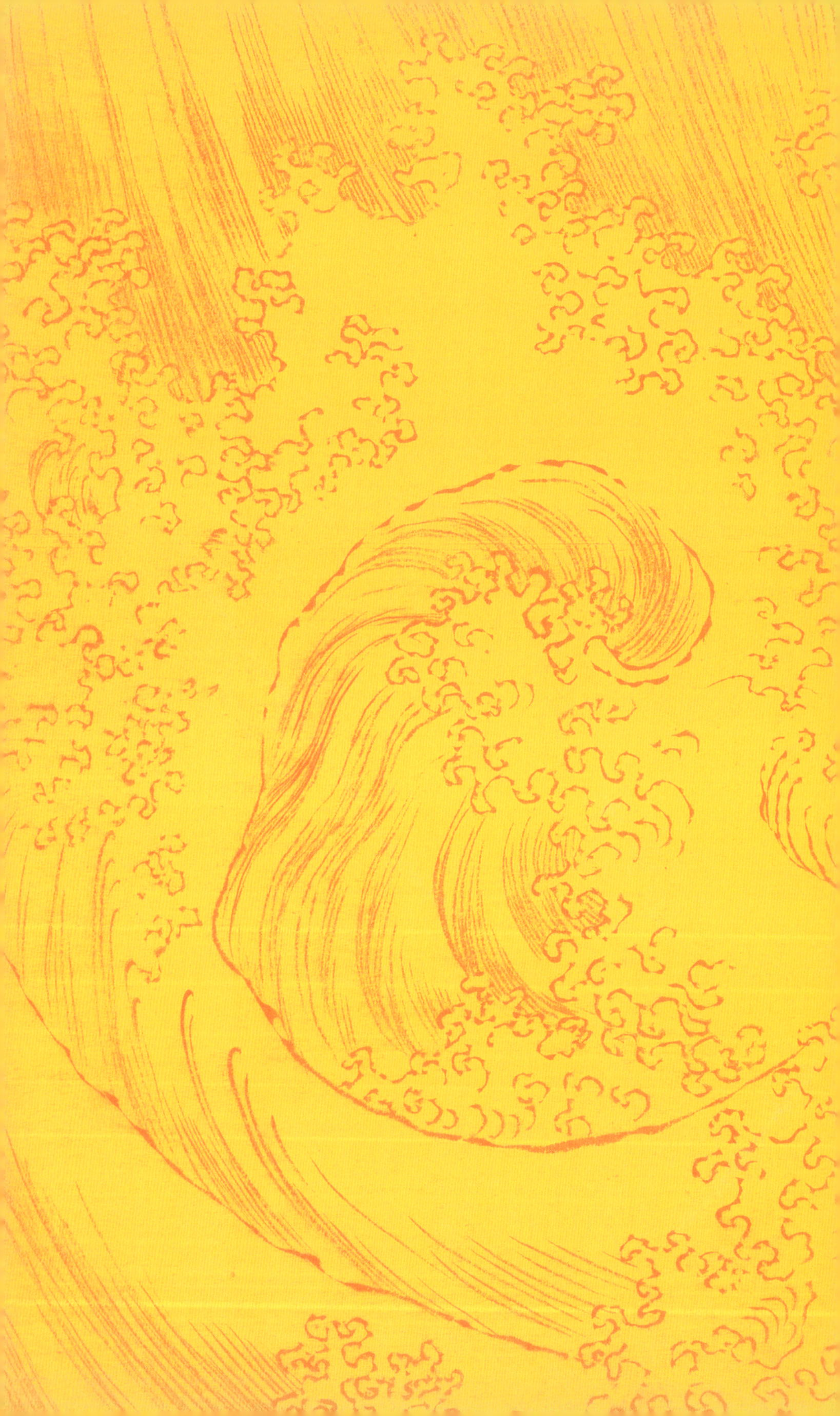

THE STORY
OF DRAWING

THE STORY OF DRAWING

An Alternative History of Art

SUSAN OWENS

YALE UNIVERSITY PRESS

NEW HAVEN AND LONDON

For information about this and other Yale University Press publications, please
contact:
U.S. Office: sales.press@yale.edu yalebooks.com
Europe Office: sales@yaleup.co.uk yalebooks.co.uk

Set in Sabon and Trajan Pro by IDSUK (DataConnection) Ltd
Printed in China

Library of Congress Control Number: 2024933068

ISBN 978-0-300-26047-2

A catalogue record for this book is available from the British Library.

10 9 8 7 6 5 4 3 2 1

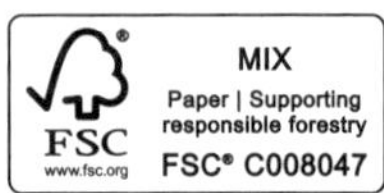

CONTENTS

Introduction   1

1. Scribes, saints and sinners   7

2. The wide world   19

3. In the Renaissance workshop   30

4. Discoveries   39

5. Shows of emotion   49

6. Close encounters   58

7. Enchanted landscapes   66

8. Virtuoso performances   74

9. Culture and colonisation   87

10. Peculiar ground   96

11. Searching for the self   105

12. Places of the mind   113

13. Marbles and models   122

14. Observation and imagination   130

15. New subjects, new methods   141

16. Mediums of modern life 149

17. Rethinking the body 160

18. Mapping the mind 170

19. The human span 179

20. Bearing witness 189

Glossary 199
On the bookshelves 216
Notes 219
List of illustrations 235
Index 244

The subject of drawing is both huge and human-scaled. Men and women the world over have drawn for thousands of years on rock, papyrus, parchment and paper, and today the medium is more popular than ever. And yet we experience drawings intimately, one to one. When you look at a drawing in a gallery or a museum's study room you are taking a step closer to its maker because, for centuries, artists have thought with chalk, pen or pencil in their hands. If you think of the painting or sculpture as the public performance, then drawing is where you can encounter the artist at his or her most unguarded: trying things out and wondering whether this or that idea will work, experimenting, looking, dreaming, planning – catching ideas on the wing. As Grayson Perry has put it, 'I lasso thoughts with a pen.'[1]

Drawing has long been the engine room of creation. It is not necessarily the most beautiful place, kept swept and arranged for visitors. For me, though, the more hastily a drawing is dashed onto the sheet, the more enthrallingly immediate it is. Before the invention of photography, the fastest and most efficient way of recording the visual world was by sketching it. Look at Leonardo's lightning-fast scribbles of a child embracing a struggling cat or Delacroix's fluid, inky study of a tiger in a Parisian zoo: this is to get exhilaratingly close to what – and how – these artists saw.

The word drawing can mean anything from the lightest sketch to the most complete, fully realised work of art. Ever since the nineteenth century drawings have been regarded as autonomous; even so, it was many decades before they approached the status of painting or sculpture. And because drawing has often been below the radar – where in some ways it remains even today – artists have appreciated the licence it offers and used it as an arena for experiment and candid expression. The French Impressionists loved pastels, chalks and watercolour because of their immediacy: dragged and dabbed rapidly onto the paper, these materials could keep pace with ballet dancers and the strobing of sunlight through leaves. Odilon Redon, on the other hand, drew not to record the real world but to probe the shadowy corners of his imagination. Käthe Kollwitz chose to be a graphic artist because the provocative and challenging things she had to say seemed better suited to democratic paper than expensive canvas. Louise Bourgeois drew to pin down the visual thoughts that drifted through her mind before they vanished, Henri Michaux to record the disturbing visions conjured up by his mescaline dreams.

This directness and informality is reflected in the cheapness and ubiquity of drawing materials. Drawing is democracy. You don't need expensive marble or oil paints. The market will want to sell you specialised kit, but in truth you don't need to buy it. Tools for drawing can be found in every home, school and office: a pencil or biro and a scrap of paper. Or outdoors: you can draw with a stick on a sandy beach, or, as Richard Long demonstrated in 1967, by walking up and down in a field. It has been felicitously described as 'the art of making do'.[2] Children instinctively draw; adults sketch and doodle. Even writing the words makes me want to pick up a pencil.

Where does the story of drawing begin? Drawing itself begins with the telling of stories. In the British Museum is a piece of water-smoothed limestone about the size of a paperback book, small enough to hold comfortably in your hands (fig. 1). Around 13,000 years ago someone took in their hand a hard-edged stone – in my mind's eye I see a flint arrow-head – and began to draw on its surface, the newly revealed stone showing up paler. This person drew four animals, each superimposed on the other: three horses and a reindeer with a feathered dart in its throat. Even seen under reduced museum light, the lines create the impression of movement; the animals seem to merge, one swiftly moving leg hard to distinguish from another, like a modern cartoon of someone pelting along. Because

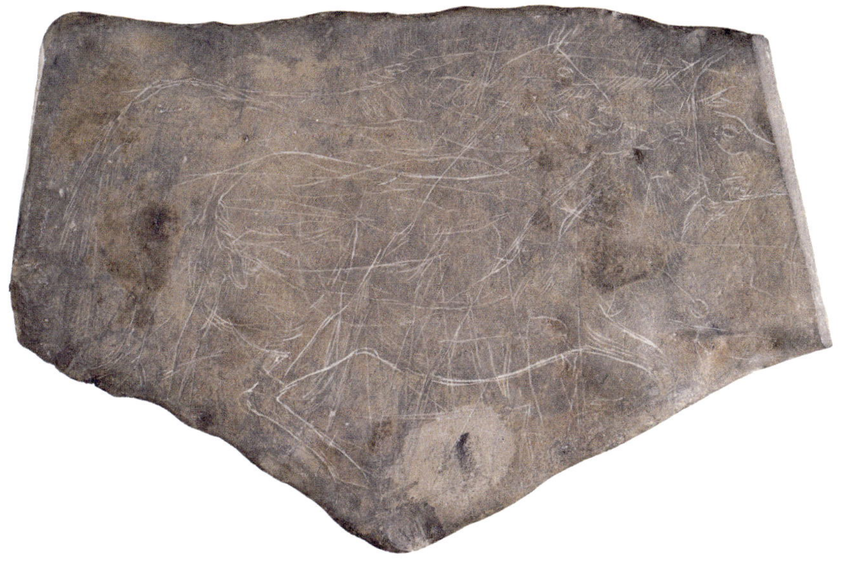

1. Engraved plaquette found at Montastruc, France, *c.* 11,000 BC. Stone.

of discoloration that tells us that the stone was exposed to fire, not only on this example but on others too, it is thought that when the image was first made it was intended to be seen by firelight. The stone was perhaps first held by the storyteller and moved in his or her hands, then put into the fire itself, men and women sitting around and watching as flames and shadows flickered across its images of cantering horses and stricken reindeer, the hunting scene brought to vivid life.[3]

Around 50,000 years ago a change in the human brain made people capable of imagination and artistic expression.[4] After that, at different places all around the globe, individuals and communities were inspired to draw representations of animals and hunters on the walls of caves, sometimes ingeniously incorporating the contours, bulges and hollows of the natural rock formations into their designs. The makers of these images rummaged in the remains of fires for usable charcoal sticks and dug out natural pigments from the land: usually iron oxide (haematite) for red and manganese dioxide for a blackish-brown colour along with earth and clay, grinding them with stones and mixing them with water and animal fat to make their marks. Why did they feel compelled to do this? Was it part of a religious ritual? Was it sympathetic magic, to ensure future success in hunting, or to commemorate successful expeditions? What seems certain is that the images were made for communities to forge connections with the world and its creatures, literally to inscribe themselves and their stories into the land. Perhaps artists are doing something of that kind even today.

The purpose of this book is to tell stories about men, women and drawing. In my imagination I have set out to meet around 100 individual artists – give or take – who at different times and places have sat down to draw. I have asked each one: how do you draw? And what, and why? I wanted to move across cultures and to spend time with individuals, taking a good look around their rooms and peering over their shoulders as they worked, whether they were scrutinising the natural world or diving into their imaginations. I wanted to find out what changed, and what stayed the same. Just as important to me was the effect of drawings on their audiences. I wanted to explore how individual works make us, their viewers, feel. How do particular drawings engage us emotionally and imaginatively? What do they ask of us? To answer the second question: it can be a great deal. While some drawings delight and bring joy, others discomfit. Some refuse to let us look away.

My focus on drawing as an intrinsically human activity suggested the book's unusually wide scope: it tells a peripatetic tale that begins with Amenmes, an ancient Egyptian scribe, and concludes with artists at work around the world today. Taking the long view has its advantages, offering unexpected angles on a familiar scene. One such that struck me forcibly as I was planning this book is that drawing can be regarded as the shadow side of art, a private arena for expressing ideas and emotions that are rarely explored in other media in quite the same way. If you step back and survey the long history of drawing, an alternative history of art emerges. Art forms such as painting and sculpture that have traditionally been more dominant often rely on someone else, usually someone with money and influence; through the centuries, artistic creation has been meshed into complex networks of patronage and expectation. Drawing has always offered creative latitude.

                    THE STORY OF DRAWING

Artists have often turned to the intimate medium of drawing to express emotion – some to mourn; some to confess; others to stay sane. They have used it to explore fantasies and traumas, to record unguarded reflections as well as to make grand statements. Their drawings can be extreme, direct and intensely personal. During the coronavirus pandemic, many who normally work in other media, isolated, found themselves turning to drawing as both touchstone and outlet.

The story of drawing dances and loops around the established history of art, sometimes staying close, at other times diving into darker and altogether less familiar territory. This book traces its route, both along broad paths and down narrow byways.

Can drawing be defined? In my opinion, the most realistic answer is: not entirely – and nor should it.[5] Once upon a time one could have pointed to traditional graphic media of charcoal, chalk, graphite, ink, pastel, crayon, watercolour and bodycolour, and common surfaces of parchment or paper. Today, drawing is being reimagined. Artists draw with fire, wire, pinpricks and neon. Cornelia Parker draws with rattlesnake venom and ferric oxide from dissolved pornographic video tapes, Andy Goldsworthy with leaves, twigs, slates and sticks. Shirin Neshat draws on the body, David Hockney on his iPad. Drawings have leapt from the page to hang from ceilings and spill down walls.

The edges of the territory upon which we might collectively agree shade imperceptibly into other areas: painting, sculpture, video, performance or conceptual art. The selection of material that follows will probably not be particularly contentious in this respect, and yet I have had to make difficult choices – with not all of which you might agree. I have excluded British landscape watercolours of the late eighteenth and early nineteenth centuries, for example, because they have always seemed to me to be in a category of their own, at a distinct tangent to drawing. But I decided to include a recent work by the Pakistani artist Imran Qureshi which is rooted in a context of Mughal miniature art and, as such, could traditionally be categorised as a painting, on the grounds that the materials with which it is executed are also associated with graphic art. In the end, I believe it is fruitless to police drawing's boundaries, to blow a whistle when a certain density of pigment has been reached and hold up a white-gloved hand to excessive use of liquid media, issuing a permit here and a penalty there. If I undertook the quixotic task of devising a definitive list of rules and regulations, artists would doubtless transgress them before I could close my laptop – and rightly so.

The great alternative artist William Blake – who, naturally, was an exponent of drawing – once wrote, 'Let a Man who has made a Drawing go on & on and he will produce a Picture or Painting but if he chooses to leave off before he has spoild it he will Do a Better Thing.'[6] If the medium of drawing is often speculative and open-ended, then those are qualities that I hope I have brought to this book.

CHAPTER 1

SCRIBES, SAINTS AND SINNERS

THE SURVIVAL OF humble objects can move us disproportionately. Things that are unusually large or precious demand to be preserved; it is the tools of everyday life that we often throw away and replace with barely a thought. That a small wooden palette and pen case from the thirteenth century BC survives at all is astonishing (fig. 2). But we even know to whom it belonged: Amenmes, royal scribe at the time of Ramesses II. It has nine neat hollows for the mixing of colours – there are splashes of red and black pigment marking the surrounding wood – a small chamber to hold water and an angled recess carved into the centre of the palette to hold reeds and brushes.[1] If you were to take Amenmes's simple, functional palette in your hands just as he took it in his and turn it over, you would see a small drawing of a human head in profile; the determined set of the lips suggests that it represents a particular individual rather than being a simple doodle. It is tempting to imagine this rather shrewd face as belonging to the artist himself.

Many ancient Egyptian drawings themselves should, by rights, not have survived. Those that have come down us have often done so by accident. This is not to say that drawing was not central to the visual culture; it was. But its role was not to shine in itself, but to underpin the other arts with its precise, elegant line. Before a sculpture was created, its contours were drawn on the block of stone to guide the sculptor's chisel and disappeared as the form took shape; a painting

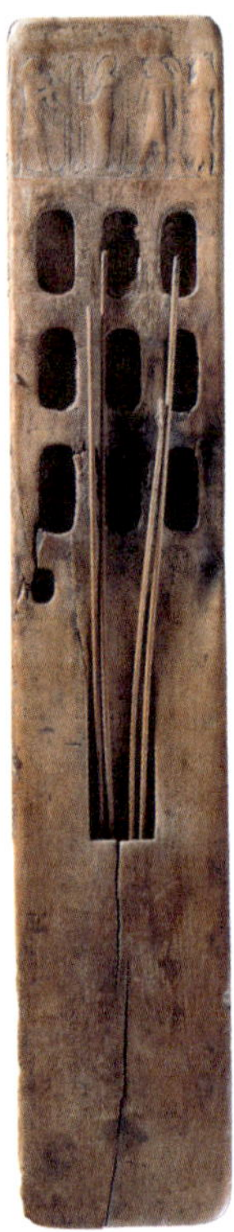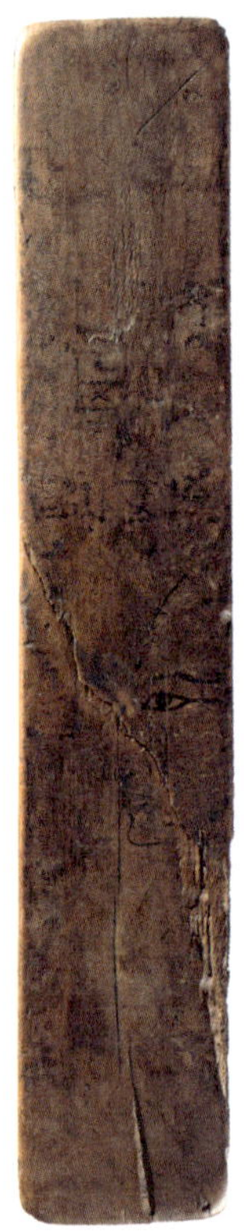

2. Palette belonging to the scribe Amenmes,
Egypt, 1279–1213 BC (front and back). Wood.

on the wall of a tomb would first be set out by an 'outline scribe' before pigment was applied. In both processes the drawing was obliterated as the work of art was completed. Occasionally, though, when a work was abandoned before it was finished, this first layer remained visible. A spectacular example dating from Dynasty V in the Old Kingdom – some forty-four to forty-five centuries ago – can be seen today at Saqqara, just south of Cairo. Within the tomb chapel of Neferherenptah, the king's principal hairdresser and keeper of the royal wigs, a flock of pigeons is drawn on the wall – the intention had been to carve the birds to create a low-relief sculpture, but this never happened. What is evident is the immense care and precision with which the outline scribe delineated each bird as he stood in front of the limestone wall in the cool of the chamber, with a brush simply made from a rush that had been beaten or even chewed at one end

     THE STORY OF DRAWING

in order to separate the fibres. This precious survival is no rough sketch, but the precise coordinates for the work of art.

Most surviving drawings from ancient Egypt only exist today because they were discarded. The exceptions were those drawn on papyrus, made from the pith of a wetland sedge. This material was precious, so was reserved for official documents such as the funerary manuscripts commissioned for individuals known as Books of the Dead. Placed in coffins or burial chambers, highly formalised religious and magical papyri were designed to serve as guides to the underworld; an example in the British Museum shows the jackal-headed Anubis weighing the heart of a kneeling supplicant. The demon Ammit is poised close behind, ready to snap it up in her crocodile jaws if it proves to be heavier than the feather of Maat, who personifies truth, justice and the cosmic order. The ink lines picturing this moment are uncompromisingly perfect and unbroken, reflecting the absolute authority of the gods and their system of retribution.[2] More often, however, scribes and draughtsmen picked up the smooth flakes of limestone that were a plentiful by-product of tomb construction, and used them as today's artists might use sketchbooks. On these fragments, called ostraca, they practised and doodled, tried out ideas and even sketched for their own amusement. They drew vivacious dancers and musicians, bulls

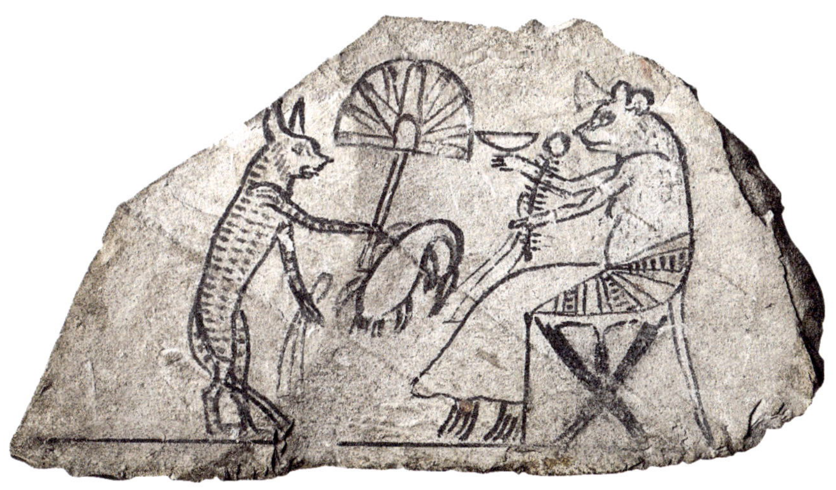

3. Ostracon figure of a cat and a mouse, *c.* 1295–1075 BC.
Limestone and ink

and lions in fierce combat, climbing monkeys and nesting birds. In preparatory sketches for formal portraits they bring us face to face with individuals who have an animation that has often been painted out in more finished works of art. Perhaps most surprising are their humorous scenes, in which animals often impersonate people: in one, a cat waits on a mouse, bringing him a fan to keep him cool and a fowl for his dinner (fig. 3). Is it a parody of a scenario often represented in tombs, in which the deceased, setting out on their journey to the afterlife, are served at a banquet? Or could it illustrate a long-forgotten fable? No one can say. But these surviving limestone scraps, little valued by their makers, allow us to peep through the eyes of these ancient scribes at a witty and informal visual world.

The land itself was used as a drawing surface many hundreds of years before Richard Long trod the grass of a field to create *A Line Made by Walking*.

Sometime between 1380 and 550 BC, people of the late Bronze Age living in south-central England decided to make an image of a horse. We don't know why: perhaps it represented their tribe or maybe it was a way of marking a sacred place. But it had to be big. Not just big: enormous, many times the size of an actual horse. The only surface available to these people that was large enough for such an image was the land itself, and to create it they needed picks and flints to cut and dig down into the turf to make lines and contours. Into these trenches, up to a metre deep and wide, they emptied pigment: carts of crushed chalk mined from the ground and hauled up the hill, designed to show up startling white whether against the vivid green of spring or the dull khaki of autumn. It was only in the frosts and snows of winter that the horse lost its definition and hibernated, a creature sheltering under its winter coat.

The white horse was built to last, and last it has. We can imagine how it was made, visualise the teams of workers digging and excavating, breaking up chalk, filling carts and barrows, pausing and looking on with satisfaction as the trenches were filled and the lines took shape. But how was it conceived? Was the image time-honoured – had it been chalked onto wooden planks or stones for hundreds of years, an instantly recognisable symbol of

                    THE STORY OF DRAWING

group identity? Or does it record the vision of a single artist – a shaman – a seer? And who was intended to see it? The horse was evidently meant to be viewed from a distance: close up, it breaks up into individual lines that disappear as the land undulates; walking on the hillside is a disorienting experience. It only gallops into focus for eyes looking from the other side of the vale – or, perhaps, from a vantage point up among the stars. This drawing might have been intended as a message to other tribes – or, equally, as one to the heavens.

Hundreds of years later and more than 6,000 miles away, the Nazca people made gigantic drawings, or geoglyphs, in the Peruvian desert for their gods to see. They delved twelve inches or more beneath the rust-coloured rocks and pebbles of the hot ground to expose the contrasting lighter sand beneath and used it to create outlines. Then they scaled up drawings they had devised of plants and creatures, pacing out the length of a vast hummingbird from tail-tip to beak, looping round the spiral of a monkey's tail and trudging up and down each leg of the biggest spider in the world. The gods, however, are not the only ones with a bird's-eye view. It has been suggested that at least some of these geoglyphs may have been created as part of a ritual designed to bring rain: many of the birds drawn on the earth are inhabitants either of distant rainforests or of coastal regions and would have appeared in the sky as they migrated in the late autumn, harbingers of the rainy season; perhaps the Nazca people believed they brought the weather with them. With these geoglyphs, drawing is deployed as powerful magic. The faith they demonstrate is all the more astonishing when one considers that those making the images would never see the full effect of their finished work.

The faith that led people to create these vast land drawings was immense; the drawings themselves, however, are fragile. England's National Trust, which looks after the White Horse of Uffington, organises a regular scouring day when volunteers carrying hammers and buckets of chalk gather to re-whiten its lines – without which the figure would soon grow dim and fade back into the hillside. The Nazca lines, which have survived because there has historically been so little wind and rain in the desert to erode them, are especially vulnerable to the unpredictable weather of a fast-changing climate.

In medieval Europe, drawing revolved around faith. Even so, it is rare to find as personal and heartfelt an expression of devotion as one created around 950, when an artist sat down to draw a large image of Christ on an otherwise blank sheet of parchment in a grammatical textbook (fig. 4). The book belonged to Abbot Dunstan, an important figure in the tenth-century English Church and a man who would become one of the most venerated of Anglo-Saxon saints. He was eventually to rise to become archbishop of Canterbury, but the drawing was probably made when Dunstan was at Glastonbury Abbey. Did Dunstan draw it himself? He was admired as an artist and embroiderer, so it is possible, although it remains an open question.[3] Whether it was Dunstan or another cleric, whoever drew Christ was determined to create an icon radiating calmness and stillness. Every line speaks of authority, from the unbroken contour describing Christ's shoulders and arms to the downward swooping folds of his robe. So definite and solid is his physical form that it seems to project forward from the page, more like a relief sculpture than a drawing. The artist has found a way of suggesting a presence too vast to be bounded by the sheet, or flattened into two dimensions.

It is easy to overlook the other figure in the drawing, so insignificant does he appear in comparison. But see: there in the lower right-hand corner is Dunstan himself, a small, touching figure – rather stout – prostrating himself in prayer by the fluttering hem of Christ's garment, the expression on his face earnest and beseeching. While Christ's robe falls in graceful folds, Dunstan's habit, drawn with a finer quill, creases and wrinkles in tight folds at his knees and elbows: it looks uncomfortably constricting. Above his portrait Dunstan himself has added a two-line verse in Latin, which reads: '*Dunstanum memet clemens, rogo, Christe, turere, / Tenarias me non sinas sorbsisse procellas*' – 'I ask you, merciful Christ, that you watch over me, Dunstan, that you not allow the Taenarian storms [the *Taenarum* being the stormy entrance to the underworld] to swallow me.' If Christ hears his worshipper's entreaty, however, he gives no direct sign, but inclines his head and turns his solemn gaze to an infinite spiritual world somewhere beyond the scope of the page. Even today, the taut lines of Dunstan's self-portrait seem

                                              THE STORY OF DRAWING

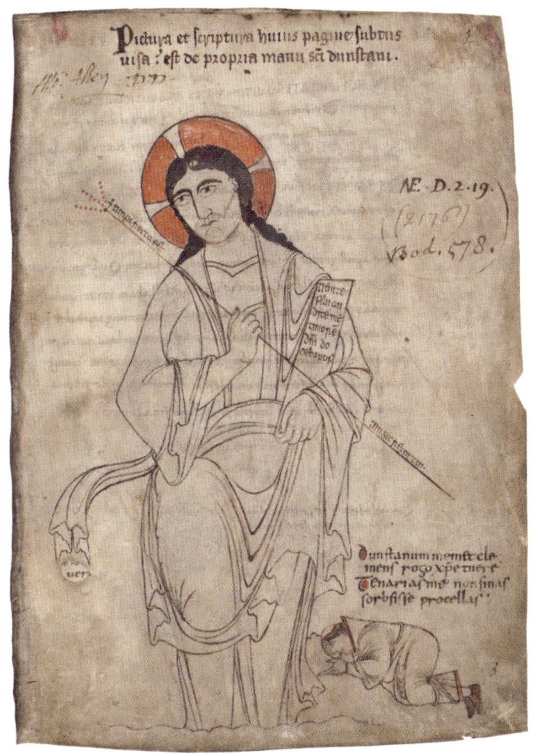

4. Christ and St Dunstan
in St Dunstan's Classbook,
c. 950.

to quiver with spiritual longing. It is not so much a drawing as a
prayer in visual form.

Words and images were intimately connected in medieval
manuscripts. Some manuscript leaves are so densely decorated it
can be hard, indeed, to tell where text ends and image begins.
Initial letters, in which the two were interwoven, played an important
role on the page because they pointed out to the reader where a
new biblical verse or a psalm began on a leaf crowded with words
and otherwise hard to navigate; parchment was expensive, and
every scrap needed to be filled in. But they also offered the
opportunity for creating images that were beautiful, playful or profound – images that prepared the reader for the sense of the text
to come.

The scribe's preparatory outlines for initials were often hidden
when rich colours were laid over the top. But in others, the artists
have revelled in the shared ground of drawing and writing and the

opportunity for witty linear flourishes. Some of the most inventive initial letters were drawn in a book of psalms and canticles (sacred songs, hymns and chants) made around 800 at the Benedictine monastery of Corbie, in northern France. When the scribe and the illuminator were separate people, the former, in charge of lettering, would complete the text, leaving room for the initial letter on the manuscript leaf, which would then be passed to the artist. For this psalter, the artists (it is thought there were two) wove letters and imagery together with hybrid initials so engaging they must have caused the sacred text's readers to linger (fig. 5).[4] To make the first vertical and diagonal of the letter N, for example, two hounds stand on their hind legs, leaning into each other so that their muzzles cross, while a brave duck forms the right-hand upright stroke. Two plump and scaly fish collide with a bishop's mitre to form a letter T. To make the G of *Gloria*, Christ stands in the centre of the curve, hand raised in blessing, while below, forming the letter's tail, a figure seems to sail in space, supporting the letter O in his hand and opening his mouth in a song of praise. Drawing has seized the upper hand; on a roll, high on its own exuberance, it pushes text into ever more extravagant and hilarious fancy dress.

Who were these artists who drew portraits of saints, decorated initial letters or enlivened margins with creatures and foliage? Who – on occasion – had such fun with pen and parchment? Until the end of the thirteenth century in medieval Europe, most books were made within religious houses. These complex organisations were able to take on the whole system of production from preparing the parchment to the eventual binding of individual leaves. Some of the larger monastic institutions had dedicated scriptoria with tables and benches where scribes worked, while others provided separate cells; go into the south side of Gloucester Cathedral's cloister today, and you will see a row of twenty stone cells, built in the late fourteenth or early fifteenth century, that were intended to be used for reading and writing.[5] As time went on, scriptoria tended to be placed near the kitchens – not so much for the comfort of the monks as in an attempt to keep the materials dry. In some institutions monks were assigned particular tasks: one would be expected to prepare parchment by rubbing it smooth with a pumice stone

                    THE STORY OF DRAWING

5. Zoomorphic initial from the Corbie Psalter, early ninth century.

and removing odd hairs still attached to the skin; this would then be handed over to the scribe, who, when he had ruled lines and written the text, leaving space for initial letters, would hand it to the illuminator. The scribe's and illuminator's tools were simple: ink, a quill pen and a penknife for mending the nib; parchment; an awl (a needle-like tool for pricking guidelines) and perhaps a ruler for marking lines with lead to keep the script from inadvertently sinking or rising on the page. Those producing books were not always in holy orders; it was common for itinerant skilled laymen to work alongside monks in scriptoria, and by the thirteenth century tasks were often carried out by professionals who set up their businesses outside the abbey walls – the beginnings of the modern book trade.

Writing was not easy work, and nor was illuminating. 'Only try to do it yourself,' grumbled one tenth-century prior, 'and you will learn how arduous is the writer's task. It dims your eyes, makes your back ache, and knits your chest and belly together. It is a terrible ordeal for the whole body.'⁶ Nonetheless, the task demanded more patience and fortitude than physical strength, and there is evidence that female scribes and illuminators were not uncommon. While many, like their brother monks, were copyists, we now know that others were creating the most prestigious of decorative manuscripts. In 2011 a group of researchers decided to study the teeth of a nun who had died at a German nunnery sometime between 1000 and 1200. Expecting to gather data about her diet, instead they discovered something quite different: lodged behind a front tooth was a deposit of the pigment lapis lazuli, the intense blue used to illuminate the most precious manuscripts and which was as valuable as gold. For it to have got there, this nun must have been in the habit of shaping the tip of a loaded brush with her tongue before applying it to the parchment: she could only have been a skilled illuminator.⁷ In an age in which most manuscript illuminations went unsigned, with this visceral detail she seems almost to appear before our eyes, sitting at her desk, taking a breath and hesitating a moment with her brush suspended in the quiet air before beginning.

Sometimes art changes direction so suddenly that to experience it is like being buffeted by a gust of wind. In most medieval drawings, figures appear indoors – and even if there are few visual clues, they have the air of being in a calm and controlled environment. But in the early ninth century, at a monastery in Reims – now in northern France – draughtsmen rethought the relationship between figures and their surroundings with such originality of vision that even today a distinctly unsettling atmosphere hangs over their drawings. The manuscript folio now known as the Utrecht Psalter is illustrated with an image for each psalm, each drawing taking up the full width of the page (fig. 6). These images are full of men, women, saints, sinners, angels, devils and soldiers who crowd together, brandish spears, climb hills, tumble into the mouth of hell, preach, utter anguished cries or offer thanks unto the Lord in a bleak and seemingly unstable landscape of hills, rocks and rivers. Whipping lines suggest it is all going on in a high wind; those describing the volume of little hills give the discomfiting impression that they are spinning. The figures'

     THE STORY OF DRAWING

hands are disproportionately large and their gestures exaggerated, as though they are actors in a twentieth-century Expressionist play. There is detail, too, for those who care to linger over the images: even toes are eloquent in the way they bunch up or cling to the earth. The figures seem exposed and vulnerable on the face of this strange, blustery land as they act out the pleas, laments, praises and expressions of faith of the psalms; the artists had to delve deeply into their powers of invention to find visual images that would represent each phrase with a literal faithfulness. Because the meaning of the whole psalm has to be worked out from individual visual components, the effect is as strange and fractured as a half-remembered dream, especially as most psalms have little narrative structure.

Most illuminated psalters – certainly on the lavish scale of this one – would have been illustrated in colour, with pigments derived from earth, stone or insects ground up, mixed with a binder and applied as watercolour. No one knows why the Utrecht Psalter remained monochrome, but the effect is to give a cosmic dimension to the landscapes as though the action is taking place under

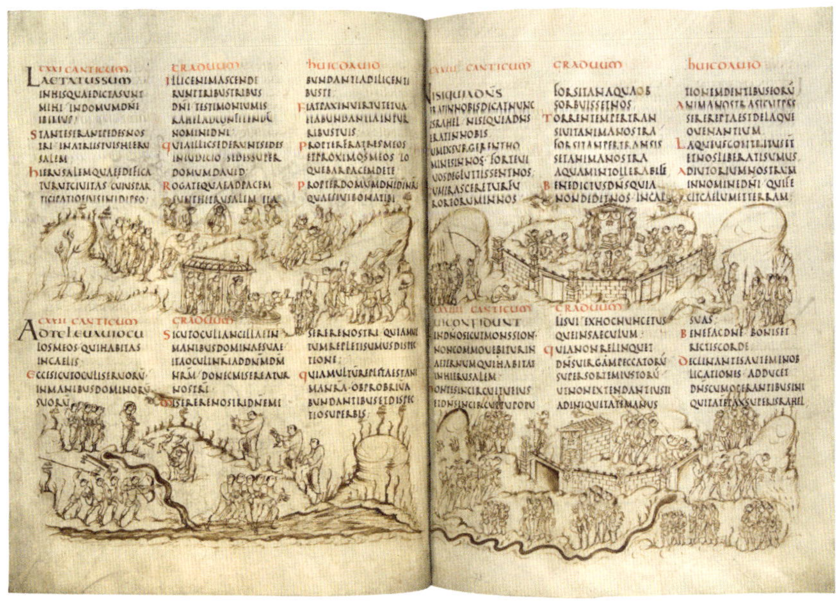

6. Psalms 122–4 from the Utrecht Psalter, *c.* 820–45.

an eclipse of the sun that has drained colour from the land. Because it was an anomaly, this strange and unconventional work had an electrifying effect on other artists: by 1000 it was in Canterbury, where copies were made and circulated, so that its strange, intensely linear vision of the world, and the place of men and women in it, flooded Anglo-Saxon art with its influence.

CHAPTER 2

THE WIDE WORLD

Viewing a landscape drawing made on a Chinese handscroll requires patience, attention and dexterity. First one must take it out of its box, remove its silk cover and undo its toggle fastening. Only then can one prepare to unscroll the picture, proceeding section by section. There is no option to consume the image in one go, as one might a painting hanging on a wall; instead one must view it sequentially, as though watching a film – although one can set one's own agenda, scanning some sections quickly and lingering over others, scrolling backwards or forwards. Viewed for the first time, it unfolds a sequence of surprises. Above all, it is an interactive process. The drawing demands from its viewer an engagement that is both physical and imaginative – while holding it in the hands and unscrolling it, using weights to keep a section open on a table, he or she is also asked to become a mental traveller through the artist's landscape.

In the early Song dynasty (960–1279) what we might now call drawing – the making of largely monochrome works, often spare and linear – began to be practised by amateur artists, scholar-officials rather than professional painters. It was partly because many chose to live in the country, away from the political turmoil of the town, that landscape became increasingly important as a subject. From their rural retreats artists contemplated the beauty of the natural world and tried to find order there instead. This is not to suggest that they rushed out into the country with their sketchbooks and faced the breezes, rains and mists. The landscapes they drew, though inspired by close study of nature, were often constructed within their imaginations – or were responses to evocative lines of poetry, which the artist might inscribe on the drawing itself. We know about the extreme fastidiousness with which an artist of the eleventh century, Guo Xi (*c.* 1020–1090), approached the act of drawing because his son recalled how he would prepare by sitting down at a clean table, by a bright window, with incense burning on either side of him. 'He would choose the finest brushes,' his son wrote, 'the most exquisite ink; wash his hands, and clean the ink-stone, as though he were expecting a visitor of rank. He waited till his mind was calm and undisturbed, and then began.'[1]

Not all Guo Xi's landscapes were created under such controlled conditions; he was drawn to the plastered walls of buildings, liking a rough surface because it suggested landscape forms to him. According to tradition, when working in this way he would even ask for more layers of plaster to be applied to the surface of a wall, and then turn the lumps and bumps into mountains, hillsides and trees.[2] For the room's inhabitants, these murals would have created the illusion of being surrounded by poetic scenery. 'Without leaving your room,' Guo wrote of landscape art in general, 'you may sit to your heart's content among streams and valleys . . . Could this fail to quicken your interest and thoroughly capture your heart?'[3] These wall paintings do not survive, but Guo's subtle and atmospheric approach can be seen in a handscroll, *Old Trees, Level Distance* (fig. 7). As viewers unrolled the scroll they would first see a river valley in hazy evening light, then the first of three gnarled old trees; their branches frame a pavilion on a hill, within which a figure can be seen making preparations. Next, servants carrying cushions come into view, hurrying up to the building, and then, finally, two old men cross a bridge as they make their slower way towards it. With subtle brush strokes that emphasise some elements while allowing others to remain shadowy, Guo unfolds a touching story of old friends meeting – it is thought that the drawing might have been made for a colleague on his retirement, and perhaps represents a farewell gathering.[4] In this case the trees take on another, symbolic role, as they could be said to stand for the central figures:

　　　　　　　　　　　　THE STORY OF DRAWING

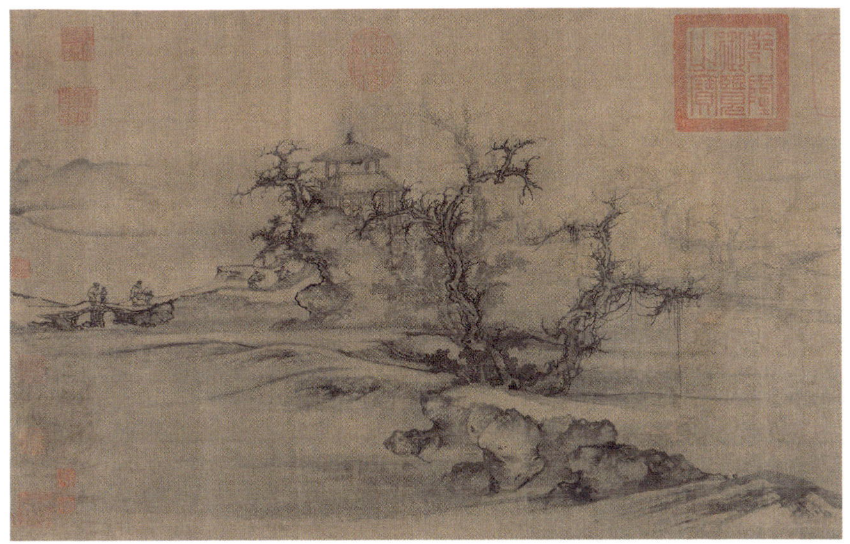

7. Guo Xi, *Old Trees, Level Distance*, *c.* 1080.
Handscroll; ink and watercolour on silk.

weather-beaten, yes; old, certainly; but still standing. It is a drawing
that describes an inner state of mind – wistful and nostalgic – every
bit as much as the external world.

Guo Xi and artists of the later Song dynasty such as Xia Gui (active
c. 1195–*c.* 1235) and Ma Yuan (*c.* 1155–after 1225) were masters
of mist and connoisseurs of cloud who could remake the world as
an insubstantial, nebulous place. The contemplative scholars they
so often included in their compositions gaze out over landscapes in
which it is unclear how – or even whether – one towering outcrop
of rock or group of trees is connected to another. Drawing offered
a means of thinking about one's place in nature and of reflecting
on the vicissitudes of life.

Drawing was versatile. If it could be used to evoke the most subtle
emotions by capturing fleeting effects of evening light, it could also
frame the world in the opposite way, imposing strict order on units
of time, space and forces of nature. Medieval Europe was an engine
room for explanatory diagrams of varying degrees of complexity
that merged text and image in attempts to explain the world in
clear and elegant forms.

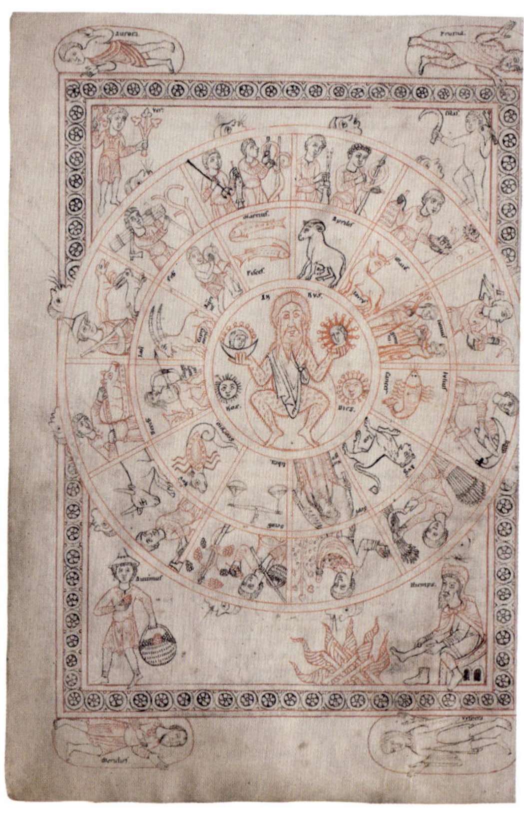

8. Cosmological representation of the annual cycle, from *Annals, c.* 1162.

A wild man squats at the very centre of one such diagram, made around 1162 in Swabia, southwestern Germany (fig. 8). Supporting the sun in one hand and the moon in another, he represents the year. Night and day hover by each hairy knee. Around him is a circular border, drawn with the aid of a compass, and beyond that a broad margin bearing the twelve zodiacal signs. Around that, in a further deep border, the artist has drawn the months, each in a neat box and identified by its associated activities: in January there is hare coursing and in February pruning. In August the corn is cut and in September the fruit gathered; and if November means slaughtering acorn-fattened pigs, then December brings feasting. Around the outer border are faces in profile, pushing out their lips and blowing: these are the twelve winds. Beyond them can be seen the four seasons: spring flourishes a bunch of flowers, summer waves a sickle and autumn pauses to catch our eye as he hurries off with a basket of grapes, while well-wrapped winter sits down, pulls off a boot and

                                    THE STORY OF DRAWING

warms his foot by a cheerful fire. Finally, outside a decorative border, human figures, each encompassed by his or her own oval border, personify the four times of day from dawn to evening. None of these figures is newly invented; rather, each reflects a time-honoured way of thinking about days, months and seasons. No one looking at this chart in the twelfth or thirteenth centuries would have expected to learn anything new from it. Its value lay in setting out what was already known in as clear and complete a way as possible.[5] The creator of this diagram has tried to encompass everything: not just the earth but the heavens too, and all the different ways in which time passes, from a single day to the cycle of the year with its seasonal tasks. Even the apparently unruly winds are contained within the system, as though drawing them would render them governable: to the medieval Christian mind, all natural phenomena, however wild, inconvenient or unexpected, were part of God's plan and must therefore conform to harmonious rules. The artist's firm, confident pen lines, concentric borders and use of ruler and compasses enact his drive to pin it all down. When we notice the times of day breaking through their borderlines with stray hands or feet, it feels almost subversive.

Spare linear drawings, lying on the page with such a nothing-to-hide air, could also provide information about the strange and marvellous creatures that, although one may never meet them, assuredly lurked somewhere in the world. Bestiaries were among the most popular medieval books, especially in France and England. These compendia of folklore and fable, which contained moralising tales about familiar beasts as well as fabulous ones, offered rich opportunities for illustration. The texts were often in the vernacular rather than Latin, so that they could be enjoyed by a wider audience, but even those unable to read would have been entertained and possibly even instructed by the drawings. One of the strangest of the creatures depicted in these books was the Aspidochelone. An English bestiary of the twelfth century vividly illustrates this amphibious creature's treacherous behaviour with confident and characterful ink lines (fig. 9). Men land their little boat beside what appears to be an island; the crew drop the mast while a bearded man raises his hands and thanks God for their safe haven. What they are unable to see – but the artist makes sure we, the readers, do – is that the 'island' is

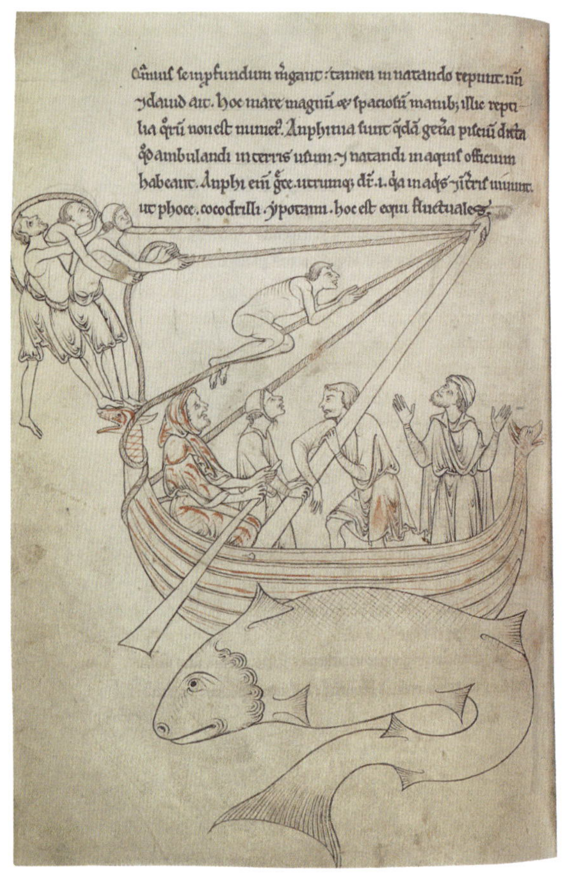

9. The Aspidochelone, in
a bestiary, twelfth century.

actually the back of a giant fish. The Aspidochelone eyes its victims
from the water and slowly swishes its tail, patiently waiting for
the men to step out of the ship, at which point it will sink to the
depths and drown them. The supple lines, which describe individual
character so acutely through facial expressions and gesture, draw
the reader right into the story at this dramatic moment; we hardly
need the text to describe the dangers of being misled.

For the monk Matthew Paris (*c.* 1200–1259), drawing was indis-
pensable if you wished to make sense of the world and its history.
Matthew spent most of his life within the walls of St Albans Abbey
in the south of England, but his imagination whisked him to far-flung
countries and sent him soaring back into the past. He was in his
mid-thirties when he became the abbey's historian, and among the
numerous chronicles and saints' lives he was to write there, the most

important was a capacious universal history: the *Chronica majora*. Matthew wanted his readers to know as much as he could possibly assemble, so he began with God's creation of the world and came right up to date – he was still adding contemporary events in 1259, the year of his death. It was an ambitious undertaking. What made it more extraordinary still were the drawings with which he illustrated his own text, outlining with ink and tinting with watercolour washes.[6] Matthew thought in visual terms: in his works the act of showing keeps interrupting the business of telling like a garrulous person eager to add colour and drama to a friend's story. He drew portraits of British kings beginning with the legendary Brutus, a descendant of the Trojan hero Aeneas, and pictured key events in their reigns: it happened like *this*. In the margins and occasionally interrupting the text he depicted dramatic battles and the grisly details of martyrdoms. He included astonishing creatures such as the elephant that had been given to Henry III, because his readers wouldn't know how to begin to imagine them themselves (Matthew attempted the elephant twice, anxious that the sheer physical magnitude of the beast should be appreciated). He even included little graphic icons of some of the official documents he had seen – a papal bull, for instance, with its seal – to prove that he had actually clapped eyes on his source material. Look: evidence! Sometimes he drew from memory and observation, and at other times he resorted to his imagination, which was probably one of the most active and well equipped in England.

Matthew's drawings were not just designed to enhance the reader's understanding of an event or to underline his own authority as a reliable chronicler – some reached out into stranger territory. Although his own travels were limited (apart from a trip to Norway he made in 1248), he was able to visualise the world in a way that would help other people to navigate it. As well as making no fewer than four maps of Britain, he cast his mind overseas, creating visual itineraries explaining how to reach pilgrimage sites in Italy or the Holy Land. For these, he imagined the route as a straight line punctuated by major sites and stopping-off points. A pilgrim en route to Naples, for example, would begin in London – symbolised by the Tower – and head to Dover, where they would cross 'La Mer', indicated by a wavy green line, and, once safely at the other side, proceed through various ports, abbeys and cities until they reached their destination. Some road maps were more elaborate than others. Matthew's itinerary of the route between London and the Holy Land concludes with a magnificent double-page plan of Palestine showing Jerusalem, the coastal stronghold of Acre (with a camel patrolling the city walls), the Dome of the Rock, Mount Sinai and tiny Bethlehem with its star still hovering above it (fig. 10). And if he then remembered something he had left no room for on the sheet, he drew it on a flap of parchment and sewed it to the edge. Matthew imagined himself hovering over Palestine, looking down at its city walls, castles and towers, its coastal towns and its inland waters, working out the best and clearest way to communicate what he saw in his remarkable mind's eye – though whether any of his readers saw his maps as practical guides, had them copied and slipped them into their pockets when preparing to set out on pilgrimage, or

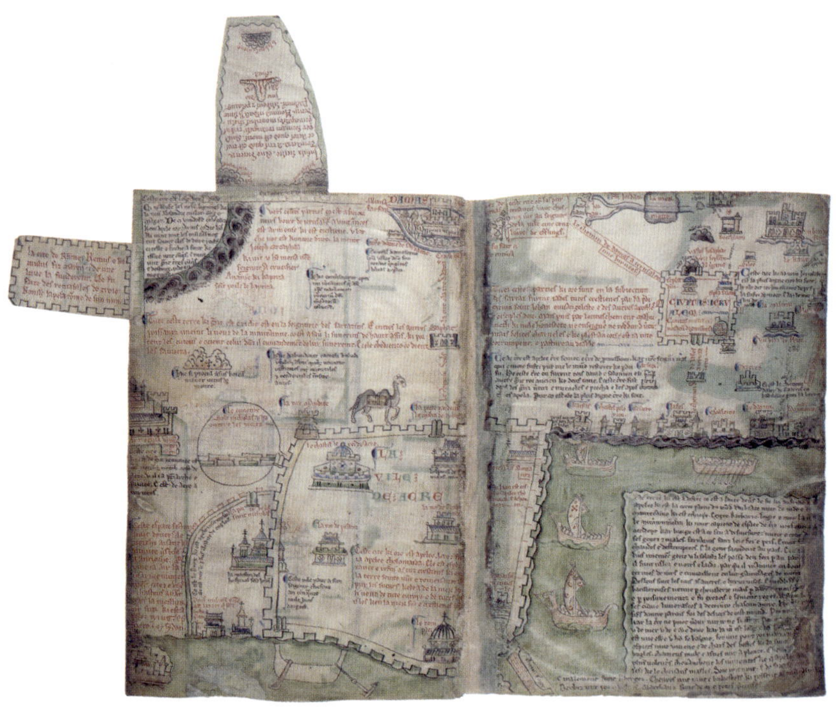

10. Matthew Paris, *Map of Palestine*, c. 1250–9.

                                    THE STORY OF DRAWING

whether most undertook the journey in their own imaginations as a spiritual exercise, is another matter.[7] One suspects that for Matthew, both ways of using his drawings were equally valid.

Matthew's teeming and innovative visual imagination was one thing. But most medieval artists had no desire to deviate from time-honoured ways of representing saints, apostles or Christ on the cross: drawing had a job to do, less glamorous than describing elephants and kings but vital all the same. It excelled at underpinning artistic creations in other media. What are now known as model books (although most were likely to have been unbound sheets gathered together in a portfolio) were circulated to supply artists about to embark on an unfamiliar subject with useful visual formulae. On these sheets were drawn outlines of biblical figures, or decorated initial letters, or scenes from the New Testament – often crudely drawn, or upside down and sharing a sheet with an unrelated subject – but that hardly mattered. They were not intended to be works of art in their own right. What was important was clarity, which made for ease of copying. These schematic models were used by artists producing images for anything from small personal items such as a psalter (sacred songs from the biblical Book of Psalms) to large surfaces, such as a wall in a church interior or a painted banner to be carried on feast days. Those charged with creating public images needed to replicate motifs that were both clear and familiar, so that people could recognise and understand them from a distance. Model books could travel some distance, carrying motifs between counties, countries and empires.[8]

At roughly the time Matthew was composing his chronicles and imagining distant places from the vantage point of St Albans, a draughtsman from Picardie in northern France called Villard de Honnecourt (active *c.* 1220–40) was looking at the world in a different way. He assembled a portfolio of some 250 drawings, sprawling over both sides of thirty-three sheets. Working at first in leadpoint – the precursor of the modern graphite pencil that leaves a fainter, softer grey mark – and then mostly reinforcing his lines with ink, he drew figures in bold outline: there are knights and bishops, insects, birds and snails, nude male figures, faces made from green leaves, apostles, Christ and the Virgin Mary.[9] He has ruled triangles or rectangles inside some of his figures, demonstrating natural laws of proportion and geometry. But most of all, Villard – who some have speculated could have been a mason or other craftsman involved with great building projects – was fascinated by architectural detail: his pages contain the plan of a cathedral's apse, the tracery of a rose window, elevations of Reims Cathedral.

He certainly thought of his book as an aid to others. On the page with the twelve apostles, he has written:

> Villard de Honnecourt greets you and begs all who use the devices found in this book to pray for his soul and remember him. For in this book will be found sound advice on the virtues of masonry and the uses of carpentry. You will find strong help in drawing figures according to the lessons taught by the art of geometry.

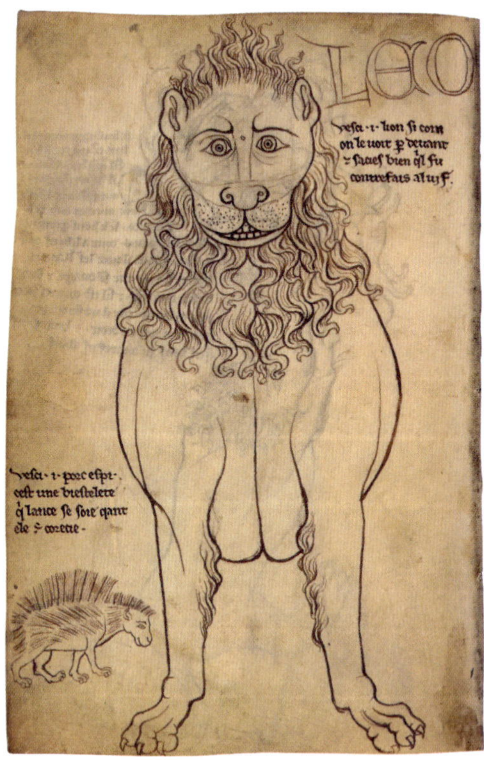

11. Villard de Honnecourt, *Lion and Porcupine*, c. 1240.
Leadpoint, pen and ink on parchment.

On a drawing of an elaborate tower he gets more specific: 'This is a clock tower. Whoever wishes to build a clock tower should study this one that I once saw.'[10] And while many of his drawings are formulaic representations of faces or figures designed to be scaled up or down according to need, there are others that have the air of being inspired by particular objects or creatures that caught his attention as he travelled from place to place. Even these, however, are not the spontaneous sketches we think of today, but were channelled through the conventional methods of representation for which Villard habitually reached. It was, simply, the visual language he knew, and in which he drew. A splendid but – to our eyes – distinctly unrealistic lion glares at us from one sheet (fig. 11). 'Here is a lion seen from the front,' explains Villard, adding: 'Please remember that he was drawn from life.'

In time, though, what drawing from life actually meant was to change as artists found radically new ways of observing the world around them – and of recording what they saw.

CHAPTER 3

IN THE RENAISSANCE WORKSHOP

IMAGINE YOU ARE walking down a street in Florence around 1450. You pass a door standing open, and hear sounds of industry from within: curious, you turn back and look inside, and find yourself on the threshold of an artist's workshop. The master himself does not seem to be present, but the room is busy with *garzoni*: assistants and young apprentices learning the business. As your eyes adjust from the bright street you see that one is kneeling on the floor by a low table topped with a slab of porphyry, using a stone to grind pigment that will later be used for painting; another is making brushes from squirrel hair, deftly tying the bunches with thread and sticking them into goose quills.[1] A third is preparing a large wooden panel so it will be ready for his master to paint a commission for a wealthy client, while a fourth is sitting on a bench, drawing with a metal stylus on a wooden tablet balanced on one knee; there are some loose drawings on a table and he is evidently copying one of them. It might at first seem as though he is idling while the others are hard at work, but in fact he is diligently fulfilling one of the tasks of his apprenticeship. Drawing was at the heart of an artist's training. As the writer and painter Cennino Cennini wrote in his *Libro dell'Arte*, a practical treatise on workshop practice he composed towards the end of the previous century, 'you begin with drawing'.[2]

Artists' workshops were places where not only paintings and sculpture were created but also designs for metalwork and textiles that were produced elsewhere: trade signs and coats-of-arms, costumes for tournaments and decorations for festivals. Mastering the art of drawing was thought to be essential for all of these. Paper and parchment were both far too expensive to be given to apprentices for their practice, and Cennino recommends instead reusable panels of hard boxwood which should first be washed, dried and smoothed down. Then he suggests looking under the table to find discarded bones of fowl, putting them in the fire until they turn white, then grinding them as finely as possible.

> And when you need some for priming this little panel, take less than half a bean of this bone, or even less. And stir this bone up with saliva. Spread it all over the little panel with your fingers; and, before it gets dry, hold the little panel in your left hand, and tap over the panel with the finger tip of your right hand until you see that it is quite dry. And it will get coated with bone as evenly in one place as in another.[3]

To draw on this surface, the apprentice then needed to take a stylus with a silver tip – the hard metal would leave almost no trace on a sheet of paper, but on the slightly abrasive bone it made a mark that quickly oxidised in the air to a grey-brown colour. Drawing with the stylus, known as metalpoint, was an exacting business. For one thing, it encouraged precision: once made, a mark cannot be erased. It is also an unresponsive medium in that it does not produce a thicker or darker line when more pressure is applied; to model or give the impression of shade, the artist needs to add closely-spaced strokes. Metalpoint left nowhere for the apprentice to hide; no flourish with the pen or distracting wash could be slyly deployed to divert attention away from weak draughtsmanship. But no matter how good it was, once finished the drawing was considered to have no intrinsic value. It was, in fact, fit only to be swept up with the dust of the workshop floor: the young man would rub the panel down, take out his wrapper of powdered bone, spit onto his fingers and reapply a fresh ground for the next attempt. This part of the training, says Cennino, could be expected to go on for over a year before the apprentice was permitted to use a quill pen on a sheet of paper. This more advanced discipline would, he states optimistically, 'make you expert, skilful, and capable of much drawing out of your own head'.[4]

The human figure would have been front and centre of this mid-fifteenth-century apprentice's training. If he had not been copying an existing drawing, he might have been studying the sculptural folds of drapery as it fell over the shoulders and knees of a wooden lay figure, set up for the purpose; sometimes the fabric was dipped into liquid clay so that, once arranged, it set and stayed put. The drawing of drapery was a serious matter because most figures in paintings and frescos were clothed, so the ability to describe convincingly the way fabric behaved on the body was vital. Or perhaps the apprentice was getting one of the others to pose for him. In the mid-1480s the Florentine artist Filippino Lippi (1457–1504) made just such a drawing, although as an established master his was on paper prepared with an attractive bluish-grey ground, and was preserved – or, at least, it survived (fig. 12). Two male nudes

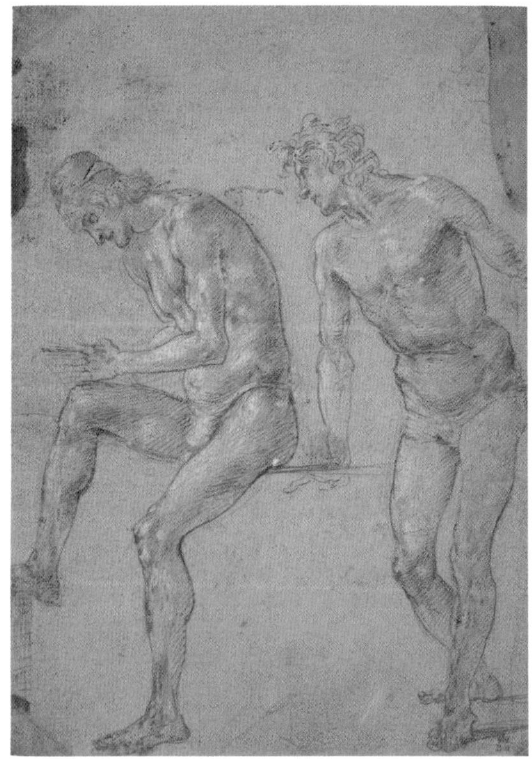

12. Filippino Lippi, *Two Nude Men*, c. 1485–8. Silverpoint (left figure) and leadpoint (right figure), heightened with white (partly discoloured), over blind stylus, on grey prepared paper.

THE STORY OF DRAWING

appear on Filippino's sheet: the left-hand figure is evidently busy with his own drawing, while the other appears to be looking over his shoulder – although it is clearly the same model, whom he has drawn twice over. He might have made the drawing in the course of planning a composition, or as a model for his workshop assistants to copy – perhaps, in the end, it served as both.[5]

Great changes happened in Italy over the course of the fifteenth century as new currents of thought transformed the way people looked at the world. Artists began to recognise that conventional methods of representation failed to match up to reality; they developed new ambitions to draw and paint the natural world as it appeared to the eye in all its complexity. The human figure gained in significance in the visual arts – partly because of the magnificent examples of ancient Greek and Roman sculpture that began to be discovered at this time – and as a result it was studied with a keen new focus. Drawing was not just part of this change; it was one of the factors that helped to drive it. Where previously its role had largely been confined to planning works in other media, now its job description was radically overhauled. Artists began to realise drawing's vast potential for exploration, expression and creative thinking. The stagehand was discovered to be a star.

None of this happened overnight, however. Throughout the fifteenth century, among the most precious items in an artist's workshop was a model book, the descendant of the medieval pattern book. Usually composed of durable vellum sheets, this was the workshop's visual archive, and it contained drawings of animals, birds, figures and other useful motifs. If, for example, the artist wanted to add a hunting dog to the painting he was composing, he would open the model book to find reference images of hounds in a variety of poses: running, standing, sitting and lying. Typically, the pictures would be distributed two to a page in order to convey the information most clearly. These drawings, often coloured with watercolour to enhance their lifelike appearance, may have been studies of actual creatures, but in the case of rarer animals they were more likely to have been copies of pre-existing images.

There was a lot to be said for model books. Why start from scratch when you could take a ready-made, purpose-built image off

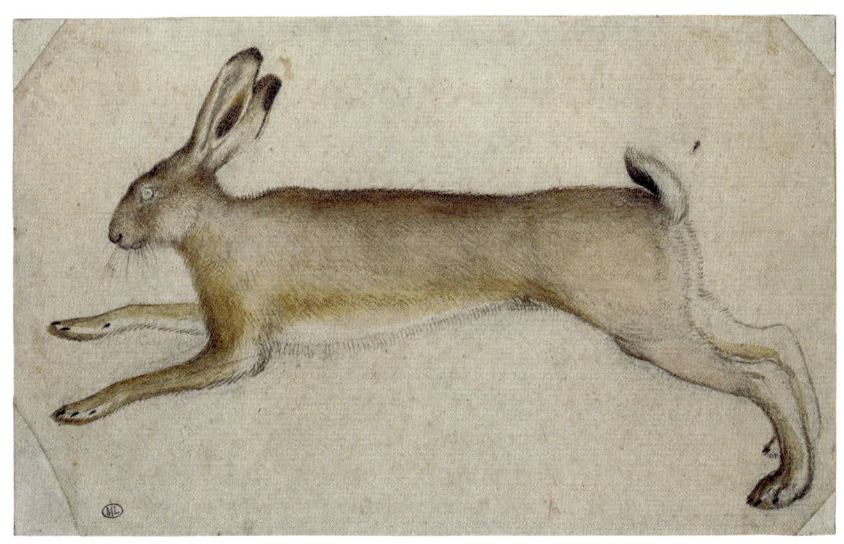

13. Pisanello, *Hare*, *c.* 1430–2.
Watercolour over black chalk.

the shelf? Time was money in a busy artist's workshop. There was, however, an artist in northern Italy, Antonio Pisano (1395–1455) – known as Pisanello – who, in the first half of the fifteenth century, began to make his own model drawings. We don't exactly know why. Was he dissatisfied with the images available to him? Had his own model book met with an unfortunate accident? For whatever reason, he decided to take specimens of creatures, some living, some dead, and to sit down to draw them himself. Picking up a stick of black chalk, he described greyhounds sprawling across sheets of paper, plump partridges and horses (a favourite subject) from all angles, returning to their soft and expressive muzzles on sheet after sheet. He drew monkeys and peacocks and someone's right foot. He drew a dormouse with as much fascinated attention as he lavished on the head of a cheetah. At first sight many of his studies resemble examples in model books in their careful placing on the page, but look more closely at the hare, stretched out as though running: something has changed (fig. 13). Pisanello has used the finest of brushes for the hairs of its pelt and the whiskers of its snout, drawing with such delicacy that we are given the illusion of a nervous, twitching animal. In his hands, creatures become

                                          THE STORY OF DRAWING

individuals, not types. Many of them made their way into his painted work.

For Pisanello, drawing was not just a medium for meticulous studies; he also made rapid, often summary sketches on paper. He might take a pen and draw a profile in connection with his work as a medallist, or jot down details of costume or architecture that caught his eye. Drawing, for him, became a means of fixing something in his memory, of making a series of notes to which he could refer later.

It is easy to talk of currents of thought, but sometimes change occurs for quite mundane reasons. Over the course of the fifteenth century in Italy more paper began to be manufactured than before, and while still far from cheap it became increasingly available. As a result, artists felt able to use it, and to experiment in ways they had not previously been able to do. In the British Museum in London is an album of drawings on paper by the Venetian artist Jacopo Bellini (1400–1471), executed with soft, grey leadpoint.[6] It was a book in

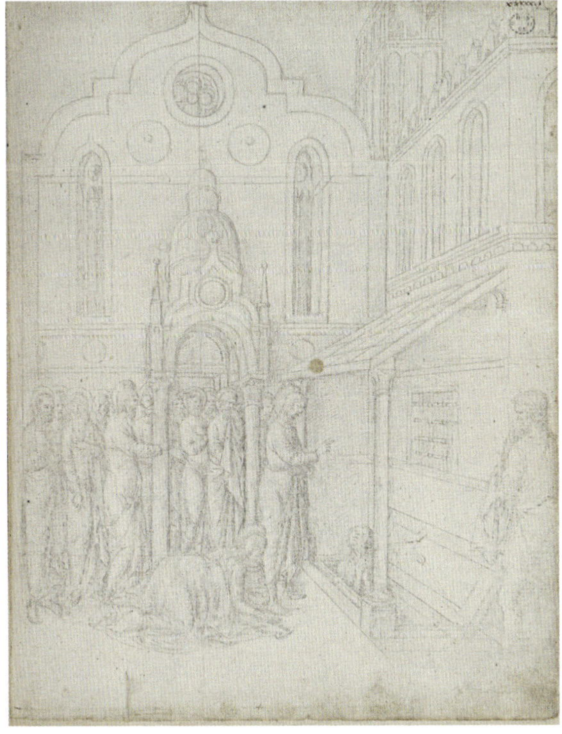

14. Jacopo Bellini, *The Raising of Lazarus*, c. 1440–70. Leadpoint.

which he drew designs he could show to prospective patrons. It is easy to imagine him turning the pages to impress with the range of his inventiveness: here is the Annunciation of the Virgin; the Crucifixion; the city walls of Jerusalem; riders winding round a mountainous road; an echoing courtyard setting for the beheading of John the Baptist; Jesus raising Lazarus, who sits up in his tomb with an awestruck expression (fig. 14). Each scene is steeped in its own distinctive, haunting atmosphere; the spaces ring with imminent drama. Bellini loved to draw architecture, and his dramas take place against a splendid backdrop of domes and towers, tall staircases and arched recesses which allowed him to demonstrate his grasp of perspective. Over time the leadpoint has rubbed and faded to the palest grey, testimony to the number of times the album's pages have been opened, the number of hands that have touched the paper, indicating this or that detail; but Bellini's patrons would have been intensely aware that this artist was showing them something sharp and fresh. Here was an artist who saw the potential of paper to try out ideas – and to demonstrate his skill as an inventor of pictures. What was new about these drawings was that Bellini and many others after him thought of them as works of art in their own right.

Sandro Botticelli (1444/5–1510) is best known today for works such as *Primavera* (*c.* 1478) and *The Birth of Venus* (*c.* 1484), pictures that have become such common visual currency that they are recycled in popular imagery around the world. They are remarkably linear, his figures in particular so firmly defined by crisp contours that the paintings can appear more like vast coloured drawings, an effect magnified by Botticelli's use of the quick-drying medium of tempera, which demands greater delicacy and precision than slicker, more expressive oil paint. In his own time, however, the artist was well known as a prolific designer. Imagine being in town on a day when the friars of Santa Maria Novella were processing, and seeing a banner painted by him, a Botticelli hoisted aloft and swaying down the street. He designed everything from ecclesiastical vestments and furnishings to glorious decorations for Florentine civic festivals. But for one of his most ambitious projects he pushed his visual imagination into an alternative world to explore the mysterious and fantastic topographies

　　　　　　　　　　　　　　　　　　THE STORY OF DRAWING

of Hell, Purgatory and Paradise. In the 1480s Botticelli began work on illustrations to the *Divine Comedy,* a narrative poem by the fourteenth-century poet Dante Alighieri, making unusually large, full-page drawings: the text was added to the reverse of the sheets rather than, as was conventional, sharing the same visual space. It was a formidable undertaking – and one that the artist never finished. If the ninety-two drawings he created remain in various stages of completion, however, they fascinatingly reveal the processes by which he worked. Taking sheets of fine-quality parchment, Botticelli first planned his compositions with metal styluses to make preparatory marks and faint lines that, in many cases, he strengthened afterwards with ink of two different shades: a light brown ink and a darker iron-gall ink.[7] Although most illustrations remain in outline, he perhaps intended each to be fully coloured, like miniature paintings – although in the end only four were worked up in this way.

Botticelli's illustrations for the *Divine Comedy* picture the soul's journey through the realms of the dead. His task was to capture

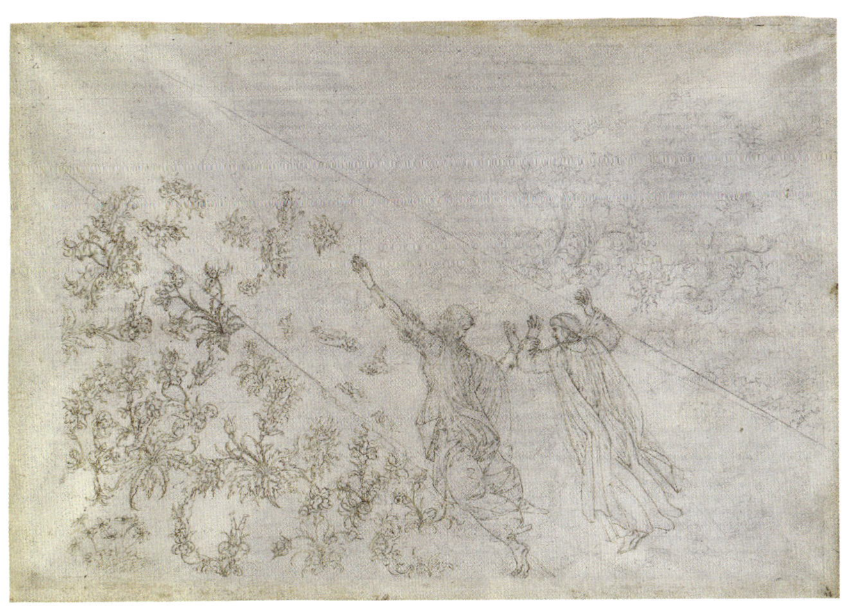

15. Sandro Botticelli, *The Empyrean: Beatrice and Dante in the River of Light, Paradiso* XXX, drawing for Dante's *Divine Comedy, c.* 1480s. Pen and ink and leadpoint on parchment.

Dante's complex and often abstract imagery with his elastic, descriptive lines: he shows us the figures of Dante and Virgil crossing a rocky bridge over a sea of flaming souls; the spirits of those who did violence to others simmering in a river of boiling blood; the devil himself as a huge shaggy beast, each curl of his hair executed with an exuberant flourish. Botticelli drew a chart of Hell itself as a vast and terrifying funnel tapering downwards. He added colour to this one, the strong pigments giving it a three-dimensionality that makes it appallingly real. But if this chart feels like the culmination of the complex systems by which medieval draughtsmen imposed order on the world, a new spirit animates Botticelli's drawings of Paradise. In one of the final illustrations he shows Dante's guide to Heaven, Beatrice, taking him to the river of light that leads to the Empyrean, the heaven of pure love and intellect (fig. 15). When Dante bathes his eyes in the river he is granted the ability to see angels and transfigured souls and to withstand the dazzling, glittering, sparking light around him. But how to go about drawing a spiritual vision, a scene that could not be witnessed by earthly eyes? Here, in a drawing more elusive than descriptive, Botticelli achieves it with lines of such delicacy that the ethereal figures of Dante and Beatrice seem to float gracefully from the sheet.[8]

CHAPTER 4

DISCOVERIES

THE FLORENTINE ARTIST Paolo Uccello (*c.* 1397–1475) placed a chalice on the table in front of him, took a sheet of paper and prepared to draw it. His hand moved over the paper, marking points here and there, as he looked repeatedly up at the chalice and then down at the drawing. But if anyone had quietly entered his room and peered over his shoulder, they would have been thoroughly baffled. Uccello's drawing was, at first, all but invisible. Taking enormous care, he was marking the lines he intended to make with a stylus, using a ruler and compasses as guides as he pressed it into the paper. The indentations he made had to be precise; there was no room for vagueness. Uccello may have appeared to be examining the surface of the chalice, but he was using his imagination and knowledge of perspective to picture it in its three-dimensional form. When he finally took his pen, dipped it into the inkwell and began to join up the points, the structure of interlocking facets and volumes became visible. Slowly and painstakingly he built up a perspectival, three-dimensional chalice on the page so modern looking that it is hard to believe it was not created by a computer program (fig. 16). You almost expect it to rotate through 360 degrees on its sheet.

Not everyone appreciated these extraordinary visual innovations, however – much later, the artist and biographer Giorgio Vasari (1511–1574) dismissed them as *ghiribizzi*, capricious things, while Uccello's

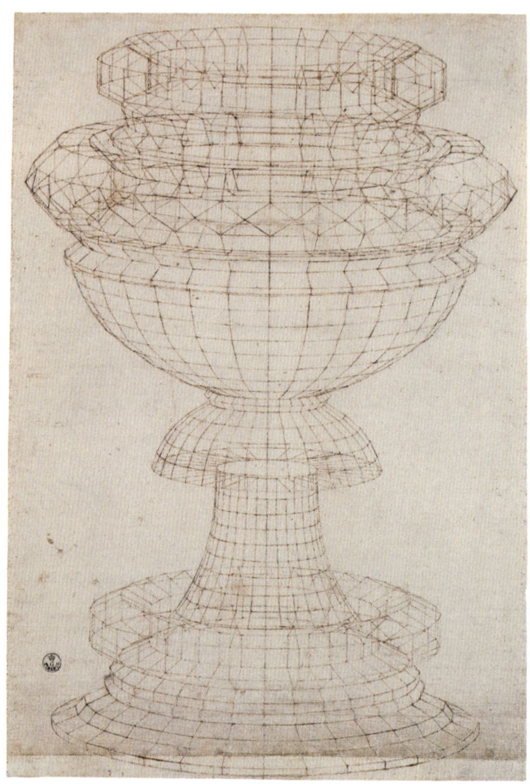

16. Paolo Uccello, *Study of a Chalice, c.* 1450–70. Pen and ink over ruled stylus and compass.

friend Donatello thought his geometrical designs fit only to decorate furniture like the ingenious intarsia (wooden inlays) they superficially resembled.[1] Why, they both wondered, was such an ingenious artist wasting his talents on this arid science? But what appeared to be an obsessive interest in perspective and geometry – and perhaps was – had another dimension. The chalice drawing represents not a narrow interest but a wide one. In the planes, interstices and spatial depths of Uccello's extraordinary drawings can be glimpsed a profound desire to discover the mathematical rules that governed the world.

Another kind of exploration, no less profound, was conducted by Andrea Mantegna (1430/1–1506). Mantegna married Nicolosia Bellini, the daughter of Jacopo, and so had presumably spent time browsing through the pages of his father-in-law's drawing albums and absorbing his ambitious approach to composition. But the younger artist's focus is different. If Bellini conjured atmosphere from city squares and rocky mountain paths, the younger artist

      THE STORY OF DRAWING

found it in concentrated form in the human figure. There is a sheet of paper now in the Courtauld Gallery in London upon which Mantegna worked out a composition for an engraving (fig. 17). It was to show the Flagellation of Christ, an event described in each of the gospels in which, prior to his Crucifixion, Christ was bound to a column and beaten by Roman soldiers. From the artist's point of view, it was a difficult subject. How could you show the suffering reflected in Christ's face, and the flogging itself, without awkwardly contorting his figure? Looking at the sheet today, you can watch as Mantegna thought through the possibilities: first he took pen and ink – good for rapid, fluid strokes – and sketched a figure bent over in pain (he probably began with the side shown on the right here). Then he tried the pose another way, with the muscular tormentor in the centre and, to the right, Christ shrinking from the coming blow. It still did not satisfy him, though, so he turned the sheet over and began again. This time he drew Christ standing upright but bowing his head in agony, and then again in a more resigned

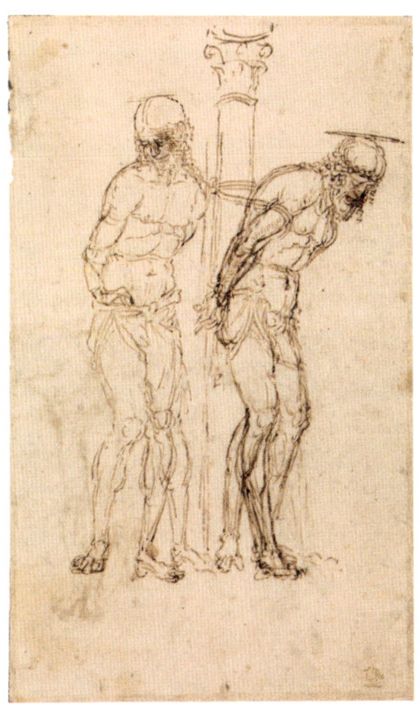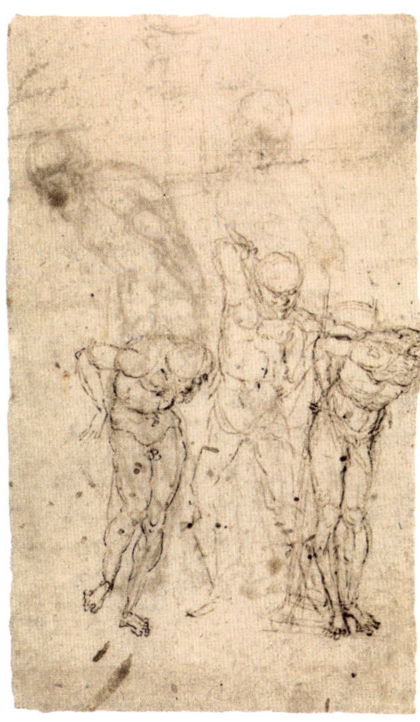

17. Andrea Mantegna, studies for *Christ at the Column*, early to mid-1460s. Pen and ink.

position, eyes shut and mouth open as though gasping for breath. Mantegna could not decide where his legs should go so he drew them again and again. When he knew he had got close to the figure he wanted, he took his pen and went over the lines again to refine the pose, asking: what angle should the back make? How should the arm be? In both figures he darkened Christ's face to underline the intensity of his suffering. The resulting engraving of Christ in a grand interior surrounded by soldiers and generals is a powerful work of art; but the messy working drawing, with its intense focus on a single figure and with all its try-outs and changes of mind and inky scratches, reveals a deep pool of humanity that is mopped up somewhat for the finished composition. When Mantegna made it, was he aware that he was around the same age as the man he was depicting, who was shortly to be put to death?

Christ did not appear to Mantegna's mind's eye straight away: at first he was a figure with uncertain outlines. The artist used his pen to find him on the page, and through repeated inky strokes, he persuaded him to take shape. This idea – that the act of drawing itself could be a dynamic process of invention and discovery, as well as one of recording – was taken to a different level by an artist of a younger generation, Leonardo da Vinci (1452–1519).

Throughout his career Leonardo got through a staggering amount of paper. Around 6,000 sheets survive, and it has been estimated that these are only about a fifth of the pages upon which he wrote and drew, the rest having since been lost.[2] From the time of his training in the Florentine workshop of the sculptor Andrea del Verrocchio (*c.* 1435–1488) in the early 1470s, when like other apprentices he studied draperies arranged on lay figures, to his final years at the French court before his death, drawing was at the heart of Leonardo's creative and intellectual life. His surviving drawings are windows into his mind, showing us the manner and range of his thought. But they are also windows through which we can look outwards, at the dazzling worlds he discovered and imagined. As a painter, sculptor, designer, theorist, anatomist, cartographer, architect and engineer, Leonardo drew to plan compositions, to record the natural forms that fascinated him, to map the landscape, to devise weapons and flying machines and to understand the mysteries of the human body. Drawing took him to places no one had dreamed of.

                                    THE STORY OF DRAWING

To make his unparalleled drawings Leonardo pushed materials and techniques to their limits. Early in his career he quickly mastered the two drawing techniques commonly used at the time, pen and ink and metalpoint. Pen and ink were the most versatile. The way the nib glided smoothly over the paper allowed him to design with great freedom and fluency. A sheet of drawings shows him pouring out ideas for a composition of the Virgin and Child with a cat (fig. 18). His pen dashes over the paper to describe how, in pose after pose, the boy ecstatically reaches for the cat to embrace it as it struggles to free itself from his grasp or rubs against the Virgin's leg. This is not the cautious and painstaking development of a pose, but a dynamic stream of invention so rapidly and summarily skimmed onto the page that some areas are hard to interpret. A study of 1508–9 for the cartoon of *The Virgin, St Anne, the Christ Child and St John*, takes this to an extreme: it is formed of a scribbled superabundance of lines so densely layered the subject is all but obliterated in a sooty mass.[3] In

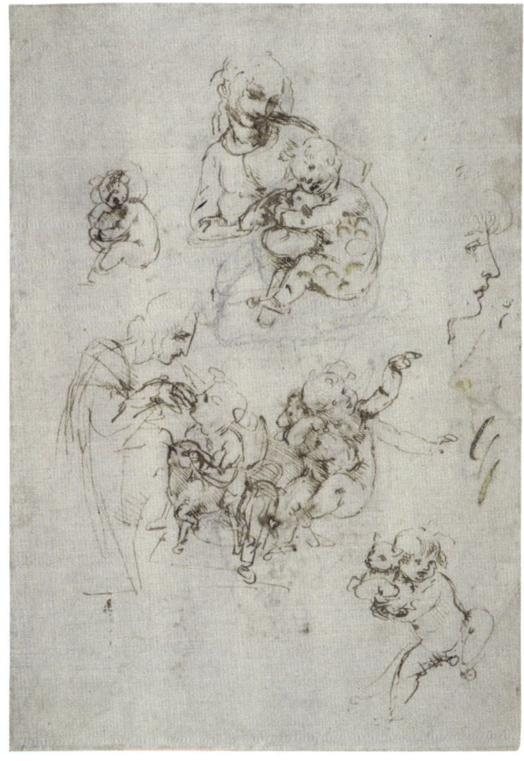

18. Leonardo da Vinci, *Studies of the Virgin and Child with a Cat*, c. 1475–82. Pen and ink over black chalk and leadpoint.

sheet after sheet of these 'brainstorming' drawings Leonardo allowed his creativity to gallop across and down the sheet, the pen barely keeping up with his ideas as one was abandoned and another begun.

As well as enabling these exuberant outbursts of creativity, quill pens were capable of producing exceptionally fine lines (Leonardo was evidently skilled at cutting nibs), suggesting a more controlled and sensitive approach. In the late 1480s Leonardo became interested in anatomy; an inscription on a study of a human skull made in 1489 reads 'Book Entitled On the Human Figure', suggesting that he envisaged a lengthy treatise on the subject. In this, and a related drawing of a bisected skull in the margin of which he depicted and described teeth (fig. 19), Leonardo draws with the tightest of discipline, building up the illusion of three dimensions with precise parallel strokes in order to render every detail legible and annotating the image in his characteristic mirror writing (he was left-handed, and seems to have got into the habit of making notes to himself in this way). Some years later, in the winter of 1507–8, he returned to his anatomical studies with renewed energy when he had the opportunity to dissect the body of a man who had died at the age of 100 – it was the first of many human dissections he would carry out in which he researched the muscles and the bones, the organs, the movement of fluids and the growth of the embryo in the womb. The pen and ink drawings Leonardo made to set out his discoveries were fair copies, rather than those made in the room when his papers would surely have been splashed and stained with fluids. As he ruefully noted on one sheet, 'If you have a love of such things, you might be deterred by your stomach, and if this did not deter you, you might be deterred by the fear of living the night hours in the company of these corpses, quartered and flayed and disgusting to see.'[4] There was no established method of drawing anatomical specimens, so Leonardo devised his own visual vocabulary to describe what he saw, his incisive mind imposing an astonishing degree of clarity and precision on the messy and sickening mass of decaying flesh on the table in front of him. For these pioneering studies he adapted the architect's practice of making drawings in plan, section, elevation and perspectival view, rotating a body on the sheet or cutting it in half in his imagination in order to observe the internal workings. Sadly, the treatise he planned

   THE STORY OF DRAWING

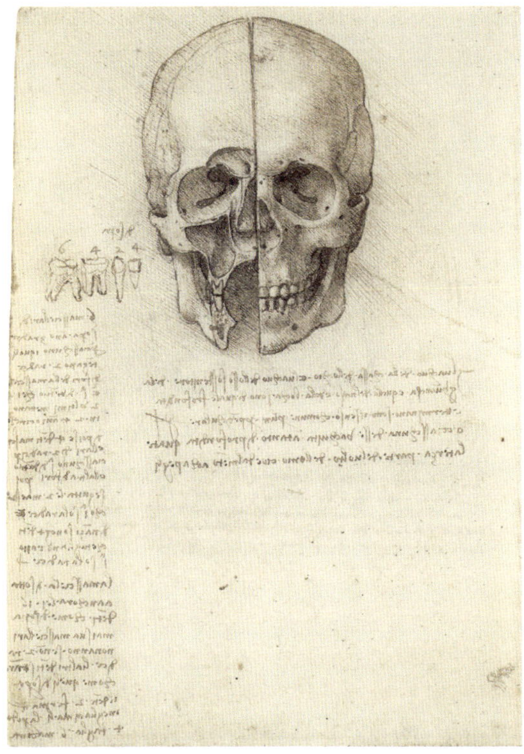

19. Leonardo da Vinci,
The Skull Sectioned, 1489.
Traces of black chalk,
pen and ink.

on anatomy never took coherent shape. The discoveries set out in drawing after drawing remained among his private papers after his death in 1519, and were not fully published nor their astonishingly accurate contents appreciated until recent times.[5]

Just as Leonardo pushed the technical capacity of pen and ink to its extremes, when he used the more intractable technique of metalpoint he produced drawings of exceptional delicacy. Usually drawing on paper prepared with grounds tinted with attractively coloured pigments, he was able to achieve parallel shading so fine that in places it loses its linear character and becomes a pale brownish-grey tone. For an exquisite study of a woman's hands, which he probably made in preparation for his painted portrait of a lady with an ermine of around 1490, he added white pigment for the light-catching areas so that the hands, in the finished areas, become silky and all but three-dimensional, seeming to lie uncannily on top of the pinkish-buff ground.

In the early 1490s, however, Leonardo stopped drawing with a stylus on prepared paper. Having driven the modest car of metalpoint to the limits of its capacity, he now looked around for a vehicle with more power under the bonnet, and found it in naturally occurring chalk. At this point black chalk (in geological terms a soft carbonaceous schist) was only occasionally used by artists in Italy, and red chalk (iron oxide suspended in clay) barely at all. His innovation was to realise that each had distinct qualities that would enable him to explore avenues that had been closed before. Tonal effects had been difficult to achieve with the range of conventional drawing media available to him. There was charcoal, which was often used for roughing out preparatory lines, but it was dry and friable, all too liable to smudge and brush off the paper. Ink washes could be added to give the illusion of depth, but a wet medium was not precise enough. Chalk, however, had range and adaptability: as a material, it was dense and could be sharpened to a point and used for detailed linear work, but it was also soft enough for tonal shading and thus was poised to bring a new breadth and naturalism to drawing. When in the mid-1490s Leonardo came to make head studies for his great painting of *The Last Supper* in the refectory of the convent of Santa Maria delle Grazie in Milan, a commission from Ludovico Sforza, he had mastered chalk's capacity for subtle gradations of tone. He now used it to explore the expressions of individual apostles at the moment Christ tells them that one of them will betray him, exploiting the realism of its effects to emphasise the psychological drama of the moment. Leonardo retained his old interest in the effects of a coloured ground even when drawing with chalk, and for his study of the profile and muscular, contorted neck of the traitor Judas he used an earthy orange as a background for the red chalk, the combination of the two warm colours, tones edgily clashing, heightening the emotional tension of the drawing.

Leonardo was fascinated by details of the natural world and he channelled a great deal of his energy into their study. Sometimes he exploited the precision of pen and ink and at others he turned to the combination of contour and tonal gradations offered by red chalk. He drew plants in order to understand their pattern of growth: sedge, brambles, guelder rose, a branch of oak. Among the most challenging of natural forms to capture on paper was the movement of water, which fascinated and preoccupied him for many years. He sat by a stream and watched the patterns the water made as it fell

　　　　　THE STORY OF DRAWING

into a pool, and experimented by creating obstructions in a stream and observing the resulting circular eddies and spiralling ropes of running water. For the resulting studies he would often use a combination of red chalk and pen and ink in order to add warmth and lively depth to linear whorls and vortices.

Towards the end of his life, Leonardo tended to use chalk when he drew from his imagination. He had often experimented with techniques, adding washes and other colours to chalks in order to achieve subtle effects of shading. And yet for his last works he returned to the simplicity of pen and ink and black chalk. Around 1517–18 he was in Amboise in the Loire Valley where he was engaged by Francis I as 'first painter and engineer to the king' – a capacious job description that encompassed everything from designing a spectacular equestrian monument to party planning. Now in late middle age and experiencing some physical frailty, Leonardo made a series of eleven drawings depicting cataclysmic storms (fig. 20). No one knows why. Did the idea take root as he was planning a court masque with a

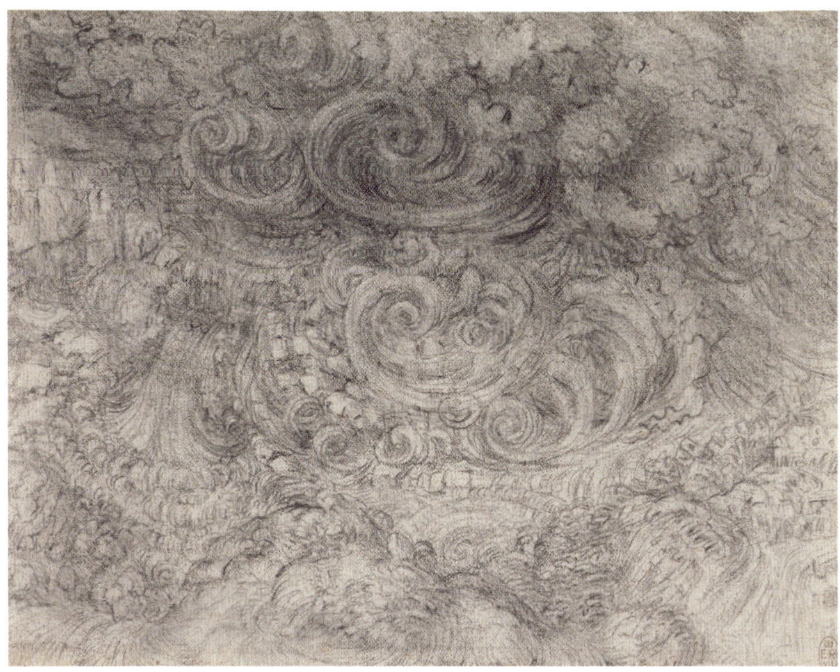

20. Leonardo da Vinci, *A Deluge*, *c.* 1517–18. Black chalk.

stormy theme? Other drawings that survive from his French period record his designs for theatrical costumes, so ethereal and fanciful that it is hard to imagine them being created even in the finest of silks. Do they reveal an inner pessimism and growing preoccupation with destruction and annihilation as his own death approached? Or, on the other hand, perhaps he simply became fascinated by storms as he had by so many other natural phenomena, and, characteristically, wished to explore them from every angle. Leonardo imagined cloudbursts, cyclones and torrents of water crashing down on the earth below, destroying the walls of a city. Great stones fly, feather-light, whirling against the dense clouds of the sky with their patterns of curls and vortices. In some areas he applied the pigment then rubbed it with his fingertip to create smoky depths, while in others he sharpened his chalk to a fine point and used it to outline details of lightning, debris, tumbling rocks and to dwell on the terrible sweeping onrush of wind and water, imagining what one would see if one stood in the storm's path. The drawings are small in scale, on average just 16 × 20 cm (6 × 8 inches), yet 500 years after Leonardo set down his visions of cosmic destruction they still seem to crack open the surface of reality to reveal vast and frightening dream-spaces and to rumble with distant thunder.

CHAPTER 5

SHOWS OF EMOTION

BEFORE THE SIXTEENTH century a large proportion of drawings were lost when artists discarded them, simply because these preparatory studies had served their purpose in the planning of a painting or sculpture and were no longer useful. But with drawing's new role, that changed. If a drawing transferred an artist's creative thought to paper, it followed that it was valuable evidence of his or her intellect at work – that it captured the essence of an idea before it was translated into paint or marble. By the early sixteenth century drawings began to be highly valued not just by the artists who made them but by others too, keen to collect and preserve them. Leonardo kept his drawings and bequeathed them to his pupil, Francesco Melzi. The biographer and proto-art historian Giorgio Vasari was the first to make a systematic collection of drawings by predecessors and contemporaries that he mounted in what he called *il nostro Libro de' disegni* – our book of drawings. As a young apprentice in 1528–9 Vasari acquired drawings from the studio of Lorenzo Ghiberti and artists of the fourteenth century, including some purporting to be by Giotto; over time he filled at least seven volumes with works by his predecessors and contemporaries alike, mounting each precious work with care and surrounding it with elaborate border decorations that he executed in pen and wash.[1]

In this climate, it comes as a shock to discover that Michelangelo Buonarroti (1475–1564) made bonfires of many of his late drawings.[2]

Perhaps he wished to guard his reputation as '*Il Divino*' (the divine one), the name his contemporaries gave him: Vasari suggested that he burned his drawings 'to the end that no one might see the labours endured by him and his methods of trying his genius, and that he might not appear less than perfect'.[3] Around 600 sheets from across his career have survived to this day – and although this seems a lot, it is sobering to think of how many more perished, and what these lost drawings could have told us about the mind of this remarkable artist, sculptor, architect and poet.

To understand Michelangelo as a draughtsman, compare him with Leonardo. Both artists were fascinated by the human body and both sought to reach a profound understanding of it through studying corpses. Here, as elsewhere, Leonardo's curiosity was boundless. He studied proportion and musculature and the articulation of the bones; and once inside the human machine he audaciously chased after every detail, from the workings of valves and vessels to the origins of life in the womb. His drawings hum with observations, reflections and wonderings. Michelangelo, however, was as single-minded as Leonardo was encyclopaedic. The nude human figure was central to his work as both a sculptor and a painter, and so he made detailed drawings of human musculature from écorché, or skinned, figures because they allowed him to study the interplay of muscles, bones and tendons without the obscuring veil of skin.[4] Any deeper investigation into the internal organs would, for him, have been superfluous. The human body was so important for Michelangelo because, in its range of poses and gestures, it was the vehicle for everything he needed to express: spirituality and sensuality; emotion and appetite; love and anger; strength and vulnerability; grief and joy.

Some of the drawings Michelangelo created between 1508 and 1512 when he was decorating the ceiling of the Sistine Chapel in Rome survive. Today they appear as works of breathtaking beauty, but they also provide insights into the mechanics of the project, and how the artist experimented with poses until he found ones that satisfied him. A study for the figure of Adam receiving life from God the Father zooms in on Adam's torso, which is drawn with a sculptor's concern for the three-dimensional form of the bones and muscles under the skin (fig. 21). So much emotional potential is packed in

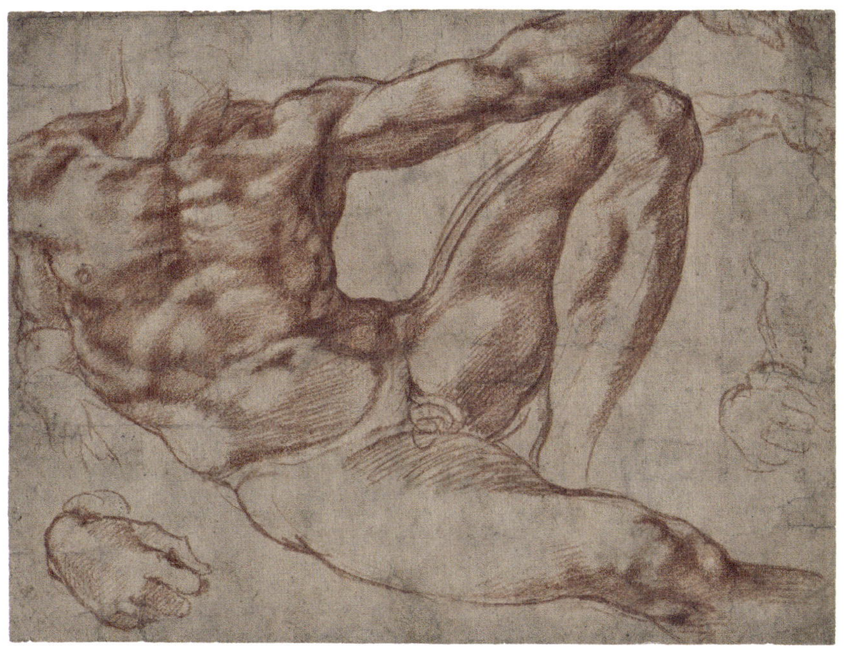

21. Michelangelo, studies for the figure of Adam in the fresco
The Creation of Man on the vault of the Sistine Chapel, *c.* 1511.
Red chalk over stylus underdrawing.

that rising, reaching chest that we hardly notice how much is missing: the head; most of the right arm and a bit on the left; part of the right leg. As a drawing it is rough and functional: Adam's right hand is drawn separately at the bottom left of the sheet, and tried out again on the right. The contour of his left thigh is attempted three or four times. And we hardly register that the pose would, in fact, be physically impossible to adopt; Michelangelo has exaggerated the bend and flex of the torso in order to achieve a greater dramatic intensity.

Michelangelo used red chalk for many of his studies for the Sistine Chapel, where before he had usually picked up black for drawing the human figure. Being denser than black, red chalk could be sharpened to a finer point so could produce crisper contours. The colour also brought a greater naturalism to the human figure, breathing vivid, urgent life into it. He probably made further preparatory drawings for Adam that no longer survive; other, more advanced studies have emphatic outlines and more polished shading. Also missing, apparently because the artist ordered them to be burned, are the scaled-up drawings which he used to transfer these designs directly to the ceiling itself.[5] These cartoons – a term deriving from *cartone*, the Italian word for a large sheet of paper – had small holes pricked around the principal outlines. The cartoons would then be held against the surface to be painted – this could be an awkward process, and it called for several assistants – and powdered chalk or charcoal, contained in a little cloth bag, would be tapped against the holes, sending enough of the pigment through to leave a dotted line to guide the artist.

For many, Michelangelo's powerful, sculptural drawings exemplified what became known as *disegno* – a concept that combined the act of drawing with the intellectual process of design. It was an idea that indicated the artist's rise in status from jobbing artisan. Yet as well as making drawings in connection with projects, Michelangelo drew in other contexts too, making highly finished drawings in black or red chalk – works of art in their own right – as presents for close friends. For Tommaso de' Cavalieri, a young nobleman described by Vasari as someone the artist loved 'infinitely more than any of the others', he created four of these: one represents a story in Ovid's *Metamorphoses*, with the giant Tityus chained to a rock in Hades, being punished for attempted rape by having his liver (traditionally thought to be the seat of lust) pecked out every day by a vulture; another shows Jupiter's abduction of the beautiful young shepherd Ganymede, an explicitly homosexual subject.[6] Two others, the *Fall of Phaeton* and *A Bacchanal of Children*, are drawn with such minute dashes and stipples of chalk that they give the impression of being three-dimensional, like relief sculptures.[7] With these drawings Michelangelo reimagined what the medium could be, and what it could do.

These robust forms seem to reflect Michelangelo's strength as a draughtsman. But towards the end of his life, then living in Rome, he made drawings that were the reverse of this, tentative and searching. The commanding statement changed to a questioning whisper. The artist became increasingly devout, describing his changing state of mind in a sonnet he sent to Vasari in 1554: '*Né pinger né scolpir fie più quieti / l'anima, volta a quell'amor divino / c'aperse, a prender noi, 'n croce le braccia*' (Neither painting nor sculpting can any longer quieten my soul, turned now to that divine love which on the cross, to embrace us, opened wide its arms).[8] Preoccupied with endings, he meditated on the Crucifixion of Christ by drawing the subject over and over again (fig. 22). While previously the artist had drawn the resurrected Christ as an athletic figure springing from the tomb, in these works his suffering body almost seems to dissolve in front of our eyes. In one drawing, the hunched and grieving figures of Mary and St John, infinitely sorrowful and powerless, stand on either side of the cross; though they are softly drawn, Michelangelo has sharpened the chalk to define their features and hands with precise lines. Christ, however, at the moment of his death, seems to be fading into veils of smoky vapour, the contours of his head and body uncertain and fuzzy. Michelangelo had spent his entire career exploring all the human body could express, with unprecedented depth and humanity. Now, in his eighties, it was as though he were quietly rubbing it out as he prepared for his own death.

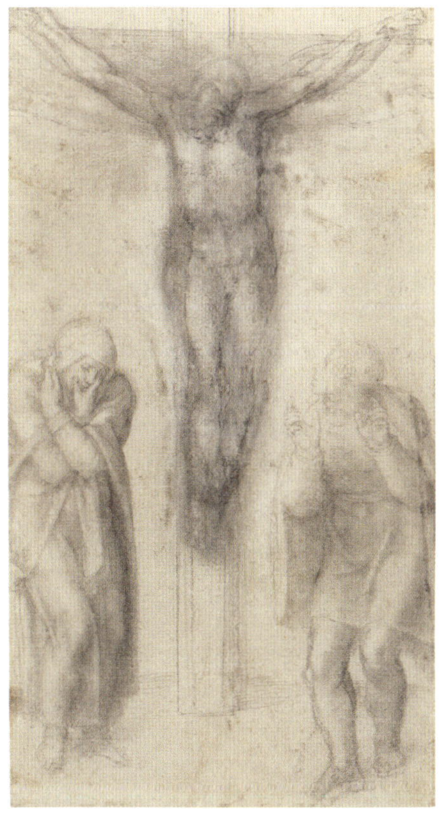

22. Michelangelo, *Christ on the Cross with the Virgin and St John*, c. 1560–4. Black chalk and white heightening.

There are some artists whose finished work is almost too perfect. It is as though the eye finds nothing to hook on to, no quirk or oddity, but instead glances off the smooth surface. The paintings of Raffaello Sanzio (1483–1520), better known as Raphael, can have this effect. While Leonardo's few surviving pictures fascinate with their undeniable strangeness, and Michelangelo's frescos sweep the viewer into their orbit by dint of their sheer power, Raphael's compositions were loved for centuries precisely because of their sweetness and affecting sentiment. But tastes change. Today his work generally evokes more admiration than passion and it can feel as though there is a barrier between it and us. But look at his drawings: this is where to find him.[9] This is where one can look over his shoulder and watch as his hand moves across the paper, hesitates and goes on. It is on paper that one can see him thinking, trying things out, changing his mind.

Raphael was a generation younger than Leonardo, and eight years Michelangelo's junior. As a young man he went to Florence and studied the works of both masters, in particular adopting Leonardo's 'brainstorming' method of exploring a subject, in which the momentum of the pen moving over the paper leads to further invention. A sheet now in the British Museum records his ideas for a Virgin and Child composition; it is a welter of inky lines rounding out the Virgin's attentive oval of a head and the Child's chubby arms and legs again and again; his pen swoops and circles as it captures ideas. And yet you would not mistake this sheet of summary studies for a drawing by Leonardo. Even when Raphael is drawing at speed and barely lifting the pen from the paper, the forms he imagines retain grace, poise and a concern for ideal forms, with little of the uninhibited exuberance of the older artist.

Many artists' commissions in sixteenth-century Italy were for religious subjects. But it was also a time in which wealthy families built villas away from the commotion of cities, and these buildings were often in styles that echoed ancient Greek and Roman examples with decoration based on classical mythology. One such, now known as the Villa Farnesina, was built on the banks of the Tiber in Rome by a Sienese banker, Agostino Chigi. Among a number of artists Chigi commissioned was Raphael, who was to paint the vault of the garden loggia with scenes from the story of Cupid and Psyche. The frescos were not a great success. Raphael ran a large studio, and some of the paintings, carried out entirely by his assistants, were coarse enough for Michelangelo's friend Leonardo Sellaio to write from Rome describing them as 'a disgrace for a great artist'.[10] Although this is not a story of the finished work of art being too perfect – quite the reverse – it is in a drawing Raphael made in preparation for the project that we see the brilliance of his idea before it was dulled in its execution (fig. 23). He was planning a scene in which the Three Graces sprinkle a libation over the married couple at the Wedding Feast of Cupid and Psyche. He made the drawing in stages: he used a single model in three different poses, moving across the sheet, and drew only what he needed; this was a working drawing, not intended as a finished composition. He chose red chalk because it could give warmth and luminosity to skin tones, and because it

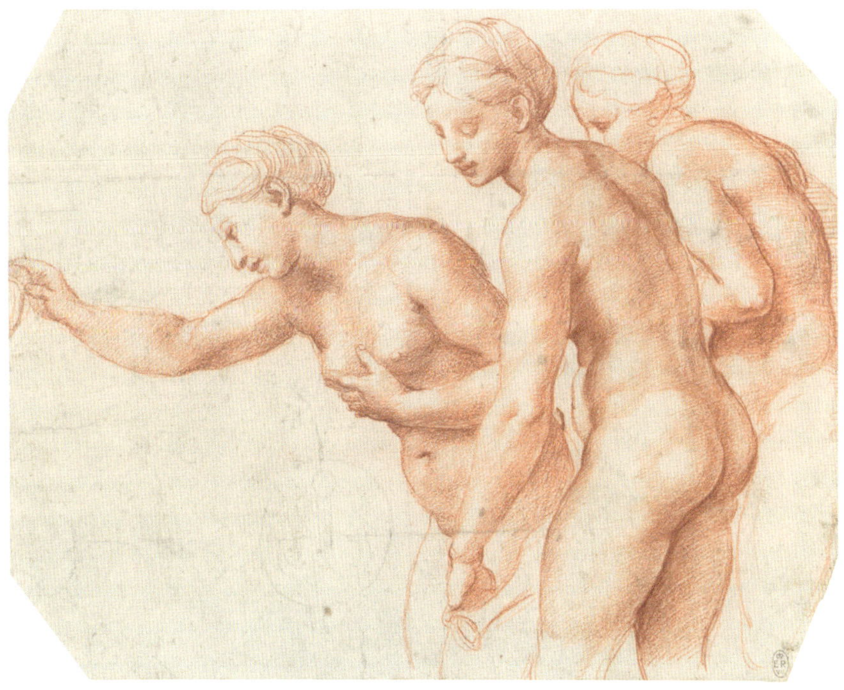

23. Raphael, *The Three Graces*, c. 1517–18.
Red chalk over some stylus underdrawing.

created a softer effect than black, more suitable for flesh. His contours and shading are gentle: the drawing shimmers with tender emotion. And there is another change, too; in an age in which most artists were obliged to pose male models for female subjects – so evident in the defined musculature of many of Michelangelo's drawings, for instance – there can be no doubt from the rounded thighs, buttocks and bellies here that Raphael was working with a female model. On this sheet a new naturalism can be seen in the making.

A single-minded focus on the human body was not, however, an option for everyone. Sofonisba Anguissola (1532–1625) was in a particularly difficult position in this respect: not only was she a woman, and as a result prevented from studying the human figure in the context of a workshop in the way an aspiring young male artist would, but her aristocratic background placed further barriers in her way. Other female artists of her era tended to be the daughters of artists who had grown up with the smell of paint in their nostrils, but not Anguissola. Still, she made the most of the resources available to her: she could look at her reflection in the mirror, so she painted numerous self-portraits; and she had siblings, whom she persuaded to model for her. And if she was barred from gaining the anatomical knowledge that would allow her to pose the human body in the way Michelangelo or Raphael might, there was no barrier to her looking closely at faces to study how shades of feeling were manifested in changing facial expressions. As a result she became a skilled portraitist who brought an unusual degree of psychological nuance to her paintings. But it was in scenes of everyday life that she could explore the more overt expressions of emotion that seem to have fascinated her most of all. According to Tommaso de' Cavalieri, when a drawing by Anguissola of a smiling girl was shown to Michelangelo, he said that he would have liked to see a weeping boy because it was a more difficult subject to draw. Michelangelo wrote to Anguissola to tell her this, a letter that put her on her mettle. She approached her young brother, Asdrubale, and asked him to pose – without perhaps telling him what she had in mind. In her composition, an older girl holds a basket full of crayfish, one of which has nipped the boy's curious hand, causing him to weep. Whether a crayfish was involved or, perhaps more likely, a sharp pinch administered at

                                        THE STORY OF DRAWING

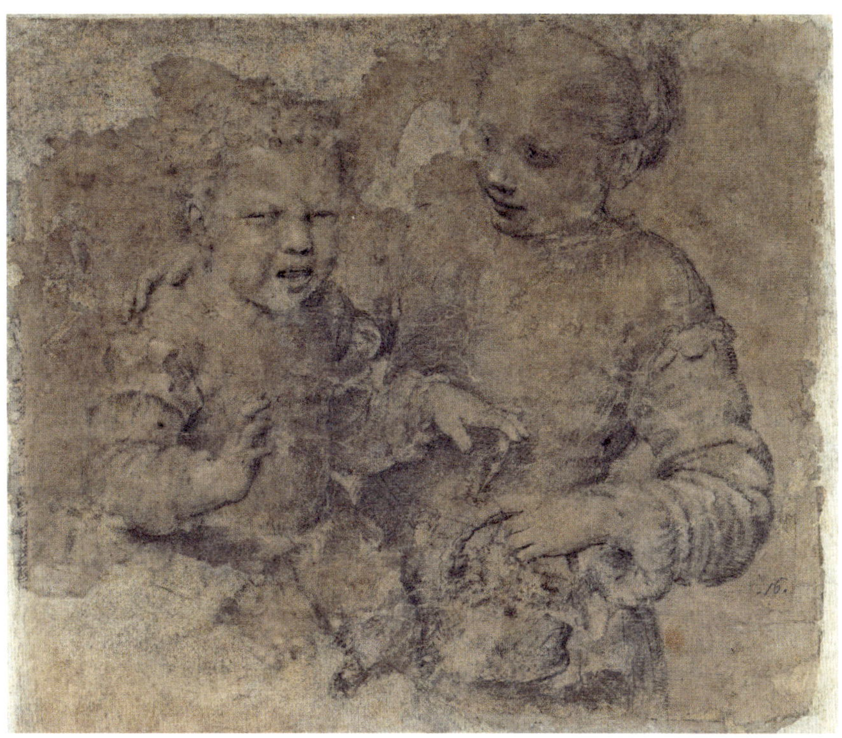

24. Sofonisba Anguissola, *Asdrubale Bitten by a Crayfish, c.* 1554.
Black chalk and charcoal with white heightening, reinforced
by a later hand in ink, on oxidised blue paper.

the right moment, as her young brother's face crumpled into tears
Anguissola took her black chalk and captured his expression of
anguish on paper (fig. 24). When Vasari saw the drawing, he said
that there was 'nothing more graceful (*graziosa*) to be seen in that
drawing, or more close to the truth (*più simile al vero*)'.[11]

CHAPTER 6

CLOSE ENCOUNTERS

O NE DAY IN 1484, when Albrecht Dürer (1471–1528) was just thirteen years old and apprenticed to his goldsmith father at their home in Nuremberg, he decided to draw a self-portrait (fig. 25). Rather than looking directly in the looking glass and confronting himself full-face, he arranged two mirrors so as to study his appearance from an unfamiliar, sideways angle. Perhaps he wished to see himself with as much objectivity as possible. Taking a sheet of prepared paper and a metalpoint stylus, this precocious boy carefully drew the image that appeared in the glass, using long graceful strokes for the soft waves of his hair and subtle little dashes to model his face. His cheeks are still childishly rounded, and his eyes have widened with the strain of the exercise. He points with his right hand towards his reflection in a determined gesture, perhaps even a challenge – though whether directed towards himself or others it is impossible to say. Here I am, it seems to say. I am now an artist.

Over the following years Dürer drew portraits of himself over and over again: he drew his own face wearing a quizzical expression, his raised hand and his crumpled pillow (he spends more time studying the topography of the pillow than his face, turning the paper over and drawing it again, six times over); he drew himself when unwell, pointing to his side to indicate the spot where it hurt; and fifteen years after his first self-portrait he drew himself naked, his long hair tied back and bundled into a net, leaning slightly towards

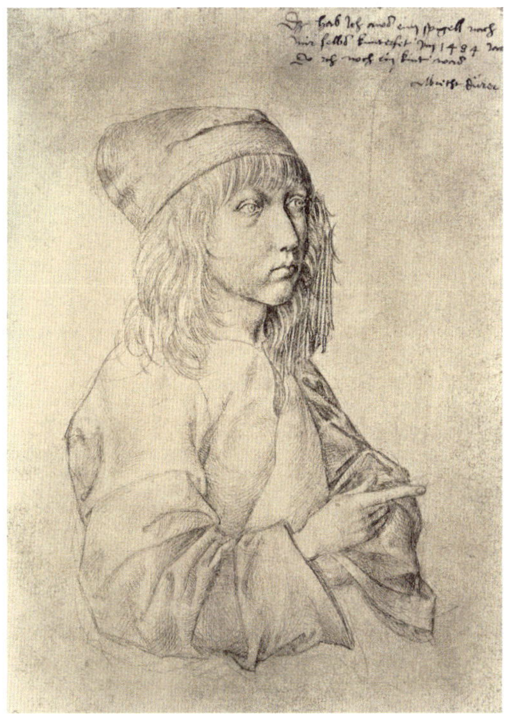

25. Albrecht Dürer, *Self-Portrait at the Age of Thirteen*, 1484. Silverpoint on prepared paper.

the mirror and fixing us with his right eye (slight strabismus means that his left looks off to the side).[1] It is discomfiting, even embarrassing, to witness this determined embrace of vulnerability and act of self-scrutiny. With his painted self-portraits Dürer dramatises his appearance, dressing up and presenting himself to the public view as a young lover, as a dandy, as Christ. His sketches are where he strips it all away.

The gaze Dürer turned on his elderly mother, Barbara, in March 1514, just two months before her death, is every bit as unsparing (fig. 26). To draw her face and neck he got close, close enough to see every line and shadow. Where other portrait sitters present a public face to the world, Barbara, who had lived in her son's household since 1504 and, long ailing, had recently endured a severe illness, seems indifferent to what her son is up to. She is content to sit still, gazing into the middle distance, absorbed in her thoughts. Taking a stick of charcoal, Dürer outlined her sharp cheekbones and sunken cheeks, the wrinkles of her forehead and the wormy vein at her temple, noting the way her skin stretched over the tendons

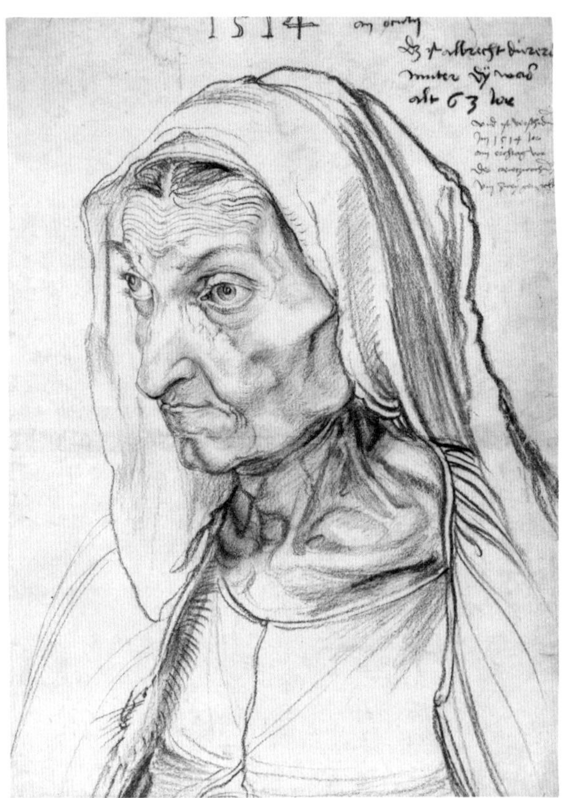

26. Albrecht Dürer,
*Portrait of the Artist's
Mother at the Age of
Sixty-Three*, 1514.
Charcoal.

and bones of her neck and shoulders with the same objectivity he might have paid to the gnarled root of a tree. If he had used another medium the portrait would not have such power: black chalk is too dense and smooth, metalpoint too delicate. Charcoal, however, leaves a crumblier, less certain line, and so is ideal for depicting papery skin. It is also easily broken, this carbonated remnant of a once-supple willow twig, and its powdery marks are just as easily swept off the paper; it is hard to imagine a medium better suited to depicting the fragility of human life. For some artists at this period the appearance of advanced age was a subject for farce, and the elderly were often depicted as grotesque caricatures of the younger men and women they once were.[2] By contrast, despite the uncompromising commitment to truth in the son's observation of his mother, tender understanding and humanity are present in every line of this drawing.

                    THE STORY OF DRAWING

The round, determined face of the fourteen-year-old Hans Holbein the Younger (1497/8–1543) appears alongside that of his older brother Ambrosius in a metalpoint drawing of 1511 by their father. Holbein the Elder ran a busy workshop in Augsburg, with as many commissions for altarpieces as he could cope with. He did not accept so many portrait commissions, although as religious compositions needed convincing human faces he made sensitive drawings of townspeople in a sketchbook that seems to have served him as a pattern book. He referred back to it when he needed to paint figures in saints' lives or in scenes from the Passion: the biblical folk in his pictures might as well come from Bavaria as anywhere.

The young Hans grew up to be a versatile artist. At first, working in Basle, he followed in his father's footsteps as a painter of altarpieces, and made portraits and designs for stained glass, woodcuts and title pages for books. In 1526 he travelled to England with a letter of introduction from the Dutch philosopher and theologian Erasmus to Sir Thomas More, secretary and personal adviser to Henry VIII and one of the most powerful men in the government. First, More commissioned Holbein to paint his portrait (fig. 27). Holbein sat More down, examined his face and made a preparatory drawing in coloured chalks that goes into such minute detail that it represents the sitter's stubble with tiny flicks of a sharpened point of chalk and every hair of his eyebrows. Pleased with the resulting portrait, More then commissioned a family group from the artist. The large painting is now lost, probably destroyed in a fire in the eighteenth century, although some of the artist's preparatory drawings survive. They show More's father in a fur collar; his daughter, Cicely Heron, a look of quick intelligence in her face and the ties of her bodice loosened because she was expecting a baby; and his son John consulting a book (More educated all his children, both boys and girls, in Latin and Greek, philosophy, theology, logic and mathematics). With delicate shading and subtle use of chalk, Holbein brought an astonishing warmth and liveliness to these drawings, seeming to capture some essence of the living person that still shimmers over the surface.

In 1528 Holbein was obliged to return to Basle in order not to lose his citizenship. Four years later, however, he was back in England, plunged into a fast-changing political world in which he

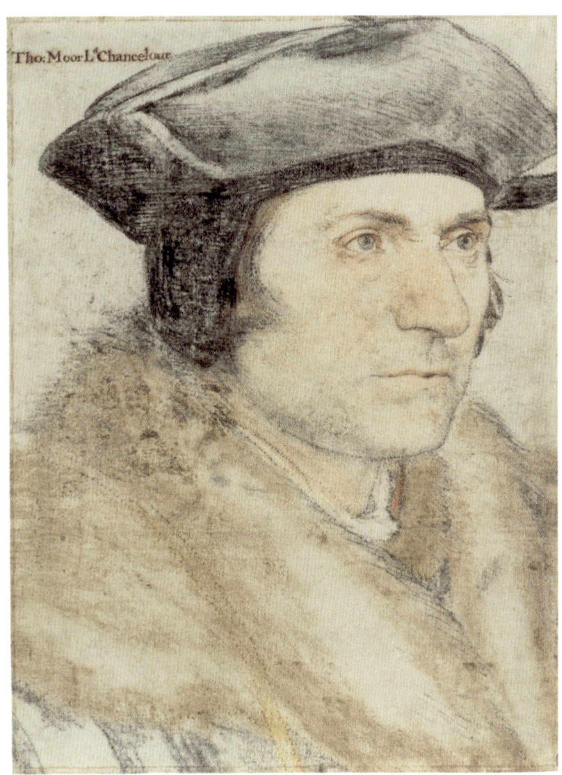

27. Hans Holbein the Younger, *Sir Thomas More*, *c.* 1526–7. Black and coloured chalks, the outlines pricked for transfer.

had to seek out new patrons close to the Crown to replace those who were either dead or in disgrace. The first of these was Thomas Cromwell, among the most powerful and influential men of the era, who was shortly to become Henry VIII's secretary; in 1536 Holbein was appointed King's Painter, a position that attracted portrait commissions from numerous members of the Tudor court.

Painted portraits get dispersed. They usually go to the women and men who commissioned them. In time they might be moved to less important rooms, taken down, stored, sold, forgotten about, lost or destroyed. But sometimes drawings, usually being of little interest or value to anyone save the artist, stay together. This – excepting a few escapees – was the fortune of Holbein's preparatory studies for his portraits, those he made in the presence of the sitters. He seems to have kept the drawings in his studio. After he died in 1543, the king acquired them and it was possibly at this point that they were bound into an album which descended to Charles I. Having little interest in

  THE STORY OF DRAWING

drawings, Charles exchanged them for a single oil painting by Raphael. His son Charles II eventually re-acquired the album, at which point it was remarked that 'The Book has long been a Wanderer, but is now most happily fallen into the King's Collection'.[3] The drawings, which remain in the British Royal Collection, were taken out of the binding as far back as 1730 and mounted individually.[4] Open the Solander boxes in which they are now kept: out come Queen Anne Boleyn, Queen Jane Seymour, Princess Mary and the future Edward VI as a small boy; the diplomat and writer Thomas Elyot; William Warham, archbishop of Canterbury; poets Henry Howard, Earl of Surrey and Mary, Lady Heveningham; Henry VIII's close friend Henry Guildford; and a host of ladies in waiting, courtiers, ambassadors and politicians whose images have kept each other company for not far short of 500 years. You find yourself half-listening for whispering voices to rise as you lift the lid. For many of these studies Holbein coated his paper with pink primer to simulate flesh tones and to give an additional warmth and naturalism, and annotated the sheets with notes about colour and texture: 'atless' (silk), 'dam' (damask), 'ora' (gold). What astonishes most, though, are the subtle details he notices and sets down, such as the slenderest of pins fixing a woman's fine linen headdress in place.[5] Seemingly insignificant, in their very everydayness these things collapse the intervening years and bring us face to face with individuals, many of whose names are still familiar to us today. Holbein captured them in the midst of life, many of their deeds yet to be done, their futures hanging in the balance.

The drawings of Matthias Grünewald (*c.* 1475/8–1528) can be disconcerting. With Holbein, when our attention is caught by the details of clothes it can have the effect of making us return to the faces of his sitters, to search individual expressions more closely for emotional states and to study casts of features for indications of character. With Grünewald it is the other way around. In a study for a painting of the Annunciation, probably for the left-hand panel of the Isenheim Altarpiece of 1515 that he made for the Antonine monastery a few kilometres south of Colmar, Mary kneels in front of a large prayer book whose pages she has been turning (fig. 28). Her features are drawn with fairly summary lines and as a result her expression is bland and hard to read – she has opened her mouth, perhaps in surprise (we have to imagine the figure of the Angel Gabriel who has just burst dramatically into her room), and she lifts one hand as though to shield her face, but the impression one gets is that she has yet to register fully the prodigious event that is happening to her. Nonetheless, Grünewald's drawing all but vibrates with emotion. Look at the pleated cloak she wears that fastens at her neck and cascades to the ground, which Grünewald has drawn in extravagant, almost fetishistic detail, exploiting the capacity of black chalk to create effects both bold and subtle. All the tension and astonishment of the moment are expressed in the structure and fall of the fabric. It has even become an extension of her self: the waves of Mary's abundant hair mingle with the folds of her cloak, making it hard to tell where one ends and the other begins. The contrast between the tightly wriggling pleats and the loose billows of the fabric as it touches the floor dramatises the contradictions she faces: of anxious resistance versus acceptance, even of the opposing states of virginity and pregnancy which Mary must embrace.

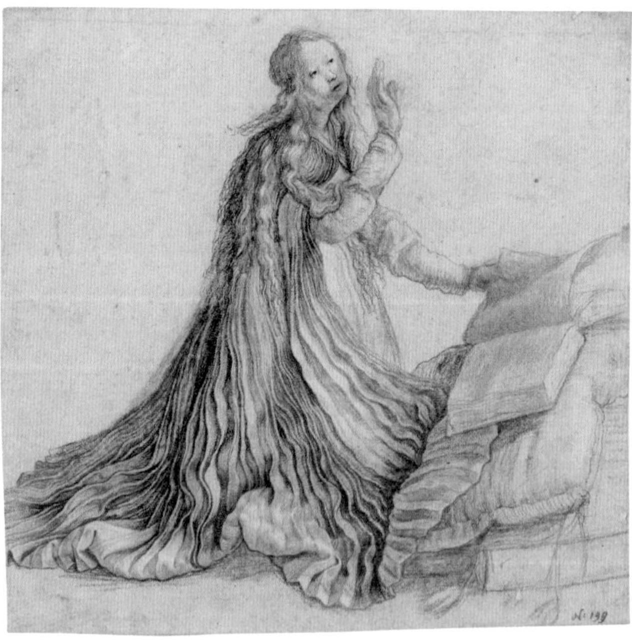

28. Matthias Grünewald, *Study of the Virgin for a Painting of the Annunciation, c.* 1512–14. Black chalk, heightened with white.

 THE STORY OF DRAWING

Grünewald – properly Mathis Gothart Nithart – was fascinated by the expression of emotion. He was also one of art history's great lateral thinkers. In a drawing for a scene of Christ's Transfiguration, in which Jesus's divinity is exposed in a blinding light, he works out the position of an apostle who is pushed to the ground with the emotional and spiritual force of the revelation.[6] The artist decides to draw the apostle – either James or John, it is hard to tell – from behind, in a pose so unexpected and undignified it could make you laugh the first time you see it. Enveloped in a shapeless robe, he awkwardly tumbles, bottom in the air and feet scrabbling, one hand about to hit the ground painfully, his face entirely hidden from the viewer. It is not how any of us would choose to be seen. And yet, as he falls, his back is illuminated by heavenly light, which the artist indicates with white highlights. Holy radiance, it seems, can fall upon us even at our most ridiculous and humbling moments. Highly unusually, Grünewald also made studies of crying children, perhaps in preparation for a painting of the Crucifixion in which they would be transformed into mourning angels. It gave him the opportunity to examine features contorted with extreme, unselfconscious emotion. One charcoal drawing describes in tender detail a small, curly-haired child with his head thrown right back in abandonment, eyes screwed tight, mouth wide open in a scream. Riveted and apparently oblivious to the noise, Grünewald gently shades the soft puffy skin of the face and the distended throat, delineates the bunched muscles of the forehead and even draws the interior of the child's mouth, carefully depicting his exposed teeth seen from below. Adult emotional states were complex and subtle; but here they are in the raw.

CHAPTER 7

ENCHANTED LANDSCAPES

Dürer looked at nature with roving curiosity and the same unflinching objectivity he brought to portraits. In 1494, while in his early twenties, he left Nuremberg for Venice, keen to learn what Italian artists were doing there. Along the way he did something new: at his stopping points he sat down to capture views of the places he was passing through, recording the shapes of the hills and the distribution of trees, the towns built on rocky outcrops, the castles and the quarries, noting not just topography but also how the light and the shadow fell on foliage and stone in these unfamiliar places. One can trace his journey through the drawings he created along the way. He used watercolour paints for these views, which allowed him to capture light, shade and the hues of nature. Watercolours – natural pigments mixed with a binder, usually gum arabic (the dried sap of the acacia tree) – were ideal for use on the move, as they were light and portable and needed no complex preparation. All that was required was water, paper and a brush. Although Dürer never made landscape a central subject in his art, when he returned to Nuremberg he looked afresh at his surroundings. A watercolour he made around 1497 of a 'weierhaus' or timber-framed building on a local lake on a calm evening with the gentlest of breezes to ripple the surface, the light just beginning to fade, communicates a potent sense of place, a feeling that the artist lingered, unwilling to leave the bank and turn from the sky as it darkened. And in

1503 he created a virtuosic landscape-in-miniature with his *Great Piece of Turf*, subjecting the grasses and dandelion to such fierce scrutiny one wonders that they did not wilt under his gaze. Rather than focusing on distant hillsides, here his eye made an insect-like progress, creeping up and down every stem and crawling over each overlapping leaf. He approached this seemingly insignificant clump of weeds and earth with an intellectual stamina to record the intricate details of nature in all its tangled disorder that was matched only by Leonardo da Vinci.

Ink and watercolour, pens and brushes: all could be tools for recording and understanding the natural world. But they could also be a means by which the world could be experienced in ways that had more to do with the imagination than with objective reality.

Albrecht Altdorfer (*c.* 1480–1538) lived in Regensburg, a Bavarian city on the Danube. He owned houses and vineyards. He sat on the inner council and represented the city on important business. He was a man of wealth and status: busy, civic-minded and respectable.

Albrecht Altdorfer had visions of enchanted forests. In his mind spruces towered through mysterious half-light, their branches like bony fingers draped with snaky foliage (fig. 29). They grew in woods that were wild enough to hide wodewoses and satyrs. If you walked there you might stumble across rapt lovers or woebegone corpses, undergrowth tangling into their hair. You would be hemmed in by jagged rocks and confronted by forbidding tunnels. Altdorfer's forests both frighten and spellbind – as much as you want to turn away, you find yourself tempted to wander in, half longing to lose yourself there.

In European painting, landscape was not a subject in its own right until Altdorfer made it one. Dürer's landscape watercolours of the 1490s, made on the road between Nuremberg and Venice, were not circulated in his lifetime. Sometime between 1520 and 1532 Altdorfer is thought to have painted the first picture in which landscape itself is the star – not just the background to a portrait or a Flight into Egypt. But it was not with oil paint but with his pens, inks and papers that this upstanding citizen with a double life delved into the heart of the wild woods of his imagination to create some of the strangest images of the era: only drawing offered sufficient freedom.

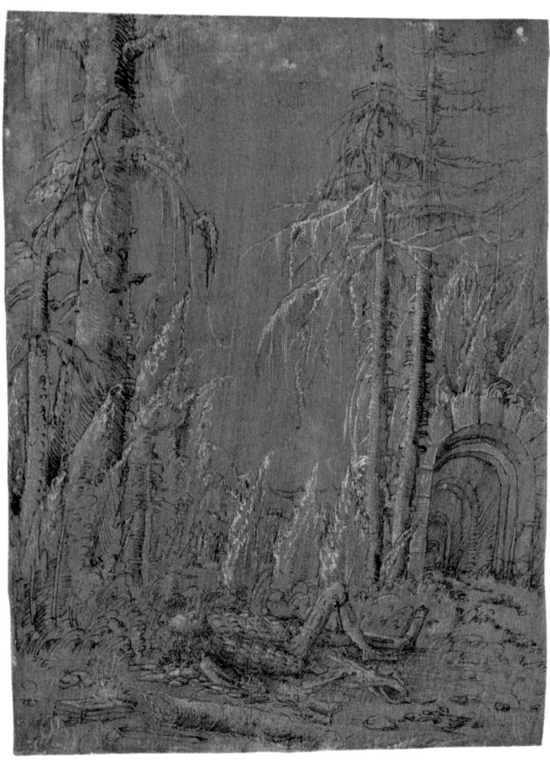

29. Albrecht Altdorfer, *Dead Pyramus*, *c*. 1511–13. Pen and black ink, heightened with white, on blue prepared paper.

Altdorfer made more drawings of this kind than paintings over the course of his career.[1] He liked to draw on coloured papers, choosing deep aqueous blues and rich reddish browns, sandy yellows and greys the colour of whale skin. After he had brushed his paint onto his paper and let it dry – you can see the sweeping vertical strokes – he cut his quill to a fine point and began to draw with black ink, first sketching in the knobbly tree trunks, then adding details and highlights with ghostly white bodycolour (opaque watercolour), his calligraphic and looping strokes making the stark branches and dripping foliage shiver with animation. In his drawings, the forest is every bit as alive as the creatures within it – sometimes rather more.

The strong tradition of printmaking in Germany fostered the development of landscape drawing alongside oil painting. Those attracted by the freedom and immediacy offered by drawing included Wolfgang Huber (*c*. 1485–1553), an Austrian artist who settled in Passau on the Danube. Throughout his life he made careful drawings of his surroundings, getting the particularities of south German and

　　　　　　　　　　　　　THE STORY OF DRAWING

Swiss rivers, bridges, hillsides and towns down on paper in precise lines of brown ink on soberly uncoloured paper, or filling in outlines with pale watercolour tints. On the face of it they are works of rigorous observation: informative travelogues to Altdorfer's strange melodramas. Yet as time went on, Huber's landscapes became more expressive. A drawing he made in 1552, towards the end of his life, captures a rocky landscape in the Prättigau valley that looks as though it is surging upwards in great destructive waves (fig. 30). Where previously Huber had relied on outline, in this dramatic scene he creates the illusion of three-dimensional form with grey washes. This is massive and dangerous topography, seething and unstable, poised to engulf any poor human figure who ventures into it. Were it not for the date hovering in the air, apparently recording the fact that Huber was in that place at that time, we might suspect it of being not so much an objective landscape drawing as the inspiration for a sombre German folk tale.

When Pieter Bruegel (*c.* 1525/30–1569) looked at the Netherlandish landscape he did not see it as a place echoing with emptiness or one criss-crossed with dangling branches in which the only human figure

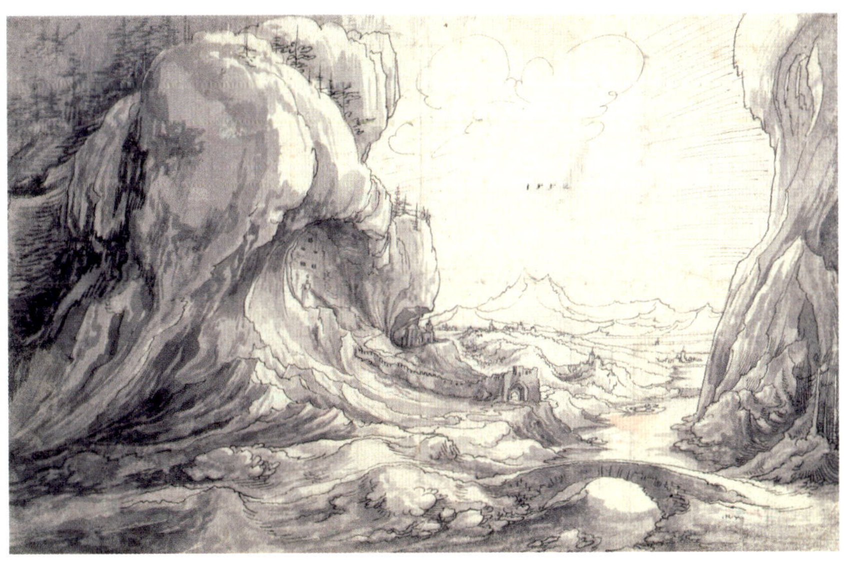

30. Wolfgang Huber, *Infernal Castle in a Ravine*, 1552.
Pen and ink with grey wash.

you might stumble across is a corpse. On the contrary, his landscapes babble with anecdote and teem with human detail. They are places in which nature is tightly managed: vines are pruned, vegetable beds prepared, corn harvested, honey collected from the hive. Bruegel's precise ink drawings depict sturdy human figures working the land, the controlled short dashes of his pen emphasising their capable bulk. Faces are often hidden by sun-protecting hats or bent towards their task, as though these folk are part of the landscape itself with no independent existence.

But things are not always in such harmonious balance. During his apprenticeship in Antwerp, Bruegel absorbed the visions of the older artist Hieronymus Bosch (*c.* 1450–1516) and learned to see the Netherlandish landscape through his eyes. He drew Boschian scenes for an Antwerp publisher, Hieronymus Cock, who sold engravings of them, capitalising on a keen local demand. One such is a drawing Bruegel executed in 1556, *The Temptation of St Antony* (fig. 31). There were plenty of visual precedents for this subject, plenty of paintings Bruegel could have seen in reality or through the medium of print. He decided, however, not to recycle the usual stock-in-trade of sexually alluring women and tormenting demons. What did he devise instead? Imagine what the end of the world might look like if it were overseen by a Lord of Misrule while under the influence of magic mushrooms. A giant human head, one eye of which is a broken window, floats in a pool. Some men are trapped in its open mouth, from which a plume of smoke issues, and another sails from an ear cavity on a canoe, arms wide and mouth open in the black 'O' of a shout. Balanced on the head is a giant fish with a gaping hole in its side, in which two figures tumble a third upside down while a strange beaked figure looks on. On the ground, rotund creatures fight, joust and crawl; another balances on a branch to perform an elaborate fart. Some play lutes and blow horns: the noise must be cacophonous. It takes a moment to spot the saint: oh yes, there he is in the bottom right-hand corner; this master of mindfulness has turned his back on it all and is patiently focusing on his scripture.

The Temptation is not an image that can be swallowed in one go. Chaotic and disjointed, it demands close and lengthy perusal, section by section. It is more like a story than a picture: Cock was giving good value to the purchasers of his engravings. What

 THE STORY OF DRAWING

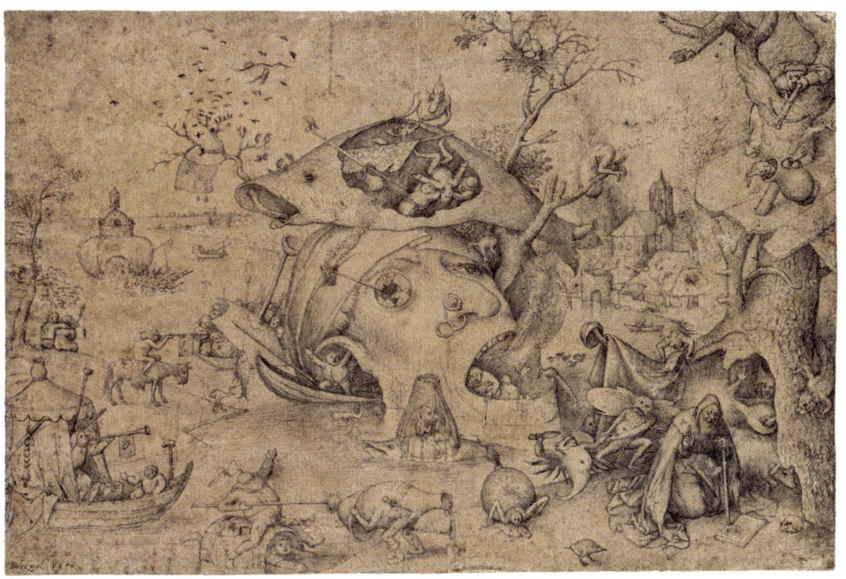

31. Pieter Bruegel the Elder, *The Temptation of St Antony*, 1556.
Pen and ink.

makes Bruegel's drawing even more sinister is the sheer control of his line, the lack of expressive flourishes describing this unnatural world. The lines needed, of course, to be precise in order to guide the engraver; but the contrast between the wild antics of Bruegel's Boschian creatures and the extreme finesse of the drawing style creates a disquieting effect in itself.

The moral lessons spelled out by Bruegel's precise lines might also be there in landscapes of the Veneto by Titian (Tiziano Vecellio, *c.* 1485/90–1576), though they are easier to miss. His imagination transformed the landscape into an enchanted place where episodes from myth, legend and poetry could quietly unfold, away from the bustling business of town with its commonplace concerns. Some of his landscapes, executed with pen and brown ink, are devoid of figures (apart from the odd goat), but with the expectant emptiness of stage sets; others are peopled, though his figures are a far cry from Altdorfer's wild men and Bruegel's sturdy peasants. As a young man, between around 1505 and 1515, he drew a pair of hairy satyrs entwined on a hillside outside a town, consulting an astrological disc, and lovers in an arcadian landscape, tending sheep and playing music beneath a graceful stand of trees. Baldly described, these scenes sound intriguing enough, but each has a mood that is as intense at it is allusive. In each, one figure looks into the distance as though they have heard or seen something dramatic or been struck with a powerful emotion – whatever it is, it seems as though they are arriving at some sort of crisis, terrible or piercingly sad. The long, curving pen lines with which Titian describes the landscape are poetry to Bruegel's neat prose. It is almost as though they create their own soundless music.

Much later in his life, Titian was commissioned by the future Philip II of Spain to create a series of large paintings based on classical myths, with subjects derived from Ovid. The six dazzling pictures he created, which included *Venus and Adonis* (*c.* 1552–4) and *Diana and Actaeon* (1556–9), became known as the *poesie* because Titian considered them equivalent to poems, with the same allusive approach to storytelling and appeal to the emotions. Around the time he was completing this commission in the first half of the 1560s, Titian took up his pen and drew an enigmatic landscape scene (fig. 32). We, the viewers, are given a more expansive vantage point than in his earlier, more focused drawings: first we look down over a peaceful hamlet among trees, then towards a town on the horizon from which smoke rises, more thickly than it would from chimneys: buildings must be on fire. In the foreground are animals: a goat, a boar and a flock of sheep. Two figures recline in the shade of trees – it is high summer; one is male, the other perhaps female, though it is hard to say. Strangest of all is the figure of a woman in the foreground, half-reclining on a bank. Bizarrely, she is not naked from the waist up, which would be unremarkable, but from the waist down and with her upper body, arms and head wrapped in a cloak. Like a poem, the drawing both invites and sidesteps attempts to fathom its meaning. What are we to make of it? Is it an allegory, with figures under the tree personifying Indolence and the female nude Lust? The presence of the goat hints at this, as does the erotic torpor of the summer-afternoon atmosphere. But what about the burning town? Does it indicate that the scene illustrates the biblical story of Lot and his daughters, who have fled from the

THE STORY OF DRAWING

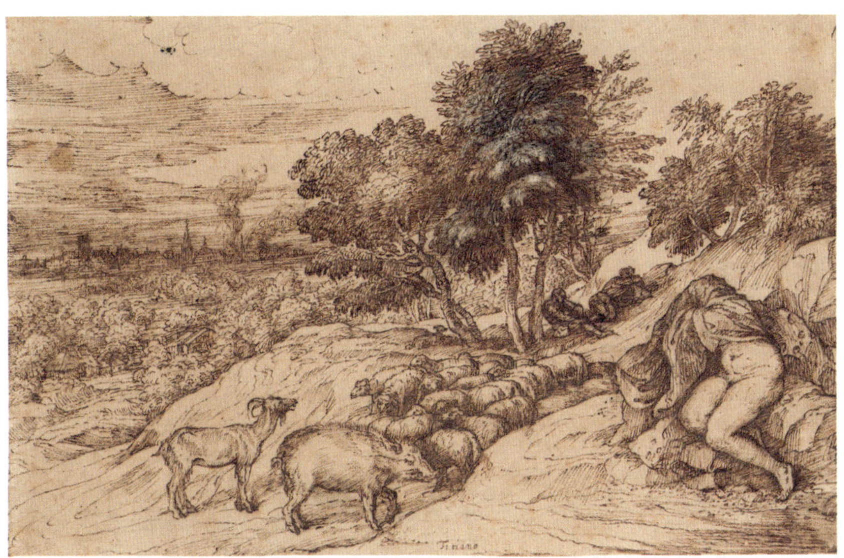

32. Titian, *Pastoral Scene*, c. 1565.
Pen and ink over black chalk, heightened
with white gouache.

sinful city of Sodom just before its destruction by God? Or did
Titian include these elements to trap us into attempting to decode
a drawing that he designed to be poetic, to resist interpretation? As
with his earlier drawings, he leaves the beguiled viewer wondering,
playing with pieces of a puzzle that cannot be made to fit together.

CHAPTER 8

VIRTUOSO PERFORMANCES

FROM A EUROPEAN perspective, the world itself had begun to feel like a puzzle that could no longer be solved. Religious upheaval had eroded the authority of the Catholic Church, while the discovery of the New World had undermined the Christian West's confidence in its centrality. New ways of thinking that prioritised observation and experiment over time-honoured dogma had gone so far as to dislodge the planet itself from the privileged position in the universe it had been assumed to occupy. Old certainties, it is fair to say, were crumbling. It was against this troubled background that artists began to create a new kind of art with an emphasis on subjectivity. Characterised by elegant artifice, sensual elongations and distortions of the human figure, it came to be called Mannerism from the Italian word *maniera*, meaning style. The daylit clarity of Renaissance compositions was replaced by the mistier light of partial and contingent experience; contorted poses and dramatic light effects created images that were exciting and emotionally intense. Between around 1520 and 1600 all kinds of art from altarpieces to portraits to the decoration of rooms were affected by this craze. All had their origin in drawing.

Perino del Vaga (Pietro Buonaccorsi, 1501–1547) was an artist who trained in an atmosphere conditioned by masters of the High Renaissance. Vasari recorded that as a boy he had practised drawing by copying Michelangelo's cartoon for his fresco of the Battle of Cascina, and on moving to Rome he made sketches of the master's

paintings on the Sistine Chapel's ceiling. He joined Raphael's workshop, where he learned to invent decorative 'grotesques': elegant
designs incorporating masks, creatures and scrolling acanthus leaves.
It suited him: Perino became so well known for his imaginative flights
of fancy that whether a wealthy merchant desired a magnificent pair
of candlesticks or the city wished to commission a temporary triumphal arch or festival barge, it was agreed that he was the man for
the job.[1] When he sat down to draw, his pen flowed over the page,
leaving in its wake a teeming company of gods, putti, sea horses and
winged creatures, each seeming to be in a perpetual state of joyful,
ingenious transformation, side by side with extravagantly leafy swags
and cornucopias overflowing with fruit. These brown and black
images were then translated into precious metals for private dining
tables and gorgeously painted decorations for the streets of Rome.

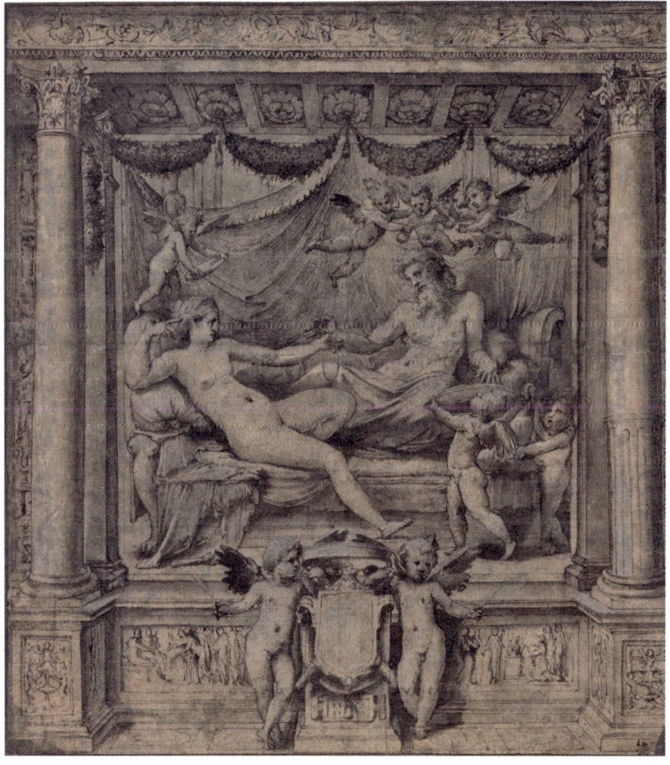

33. Perino del Vaga, *Jupiter and Juno*, study for the *Furti di
Giove* tapestries, *c.* 1532–5. Pen and dark brown ink with
brown and grey wash, heightened with white gouache.

When in the early 1530s the wealthy admiral-prince Andrea Doria came to plan the furnishings of the palace he had built outside Genoa he turned to Perino to design a magnificent suite of tapestries on the theme of Jupiter's erotic liaisons. These have long since disappeared, but surviving drawings hint at their splendour. In one design Perino draws the gods Juno and Jupiter reclining elegantly on their marriage bed surrounded by an attentive host of putti (fig. 33). He has imagined the bed itself set back in an architectural recess like a proscenium arch, framed by columns and hung with festoons. With intricate use of a fine quill along with grey and brown washes the artist has conjured up an intoxicating atmosphere of luxury and sophistication, both precise and dreamlike.[2]

The passion for extravagant decoration also flourished in France. When in the late 1520s Francis I began to build his magnificent chateau at Fontainebleau, southeast of Paris, he sought artists from Italy to decorate the rooms and galleries. Artists including Rosso Fiorentino (1494–1540), Francesco Primaticcio (1504–1570) and Niccolò dell'Abate (1509/12–1571) arrived at Fontainebleau and began to create exuberant decorative schemes that combined painting with relief sculpture, with rooms and galleries devoted to literary and mythological subjects – the story of Ulysses, or the history of Psyche. Some of the schemes themselves have subsequently been destroyed, but numerous surviving drawings can be pieced together to reveal the energetic dramas that once unfolded through the palace interiors. The court was, in the mid-sixteenth century, as enthusiastic about parties as it had been when Leonardo was the king's painter. No masque costumes survive, of course, being by their nature ephemeral; but designs, such as those by dell'Abate for a feathery bird-man and a scaly frog-man, give a sense of the inventiveness of these Franco-Italian artists who made the palace their canvas and members of the court whatever they wanted them to be (fig. 34).

Mannerist artists loved to blur the boundaries between art forms. Painted figures tricked the eye into believing them to be sculptures, while frames grew so extravagant they overshadowed the paintings they housed. Conspicuous displays of virtuosity were cultivated because of their capacity to astonish and delight. The Dutch artist Hendrick Goltzius (1558–1617), who was equally at home as a painter, draughtsman and printmaker, achieved these in a way that was

 THE STORY OF DRAWING

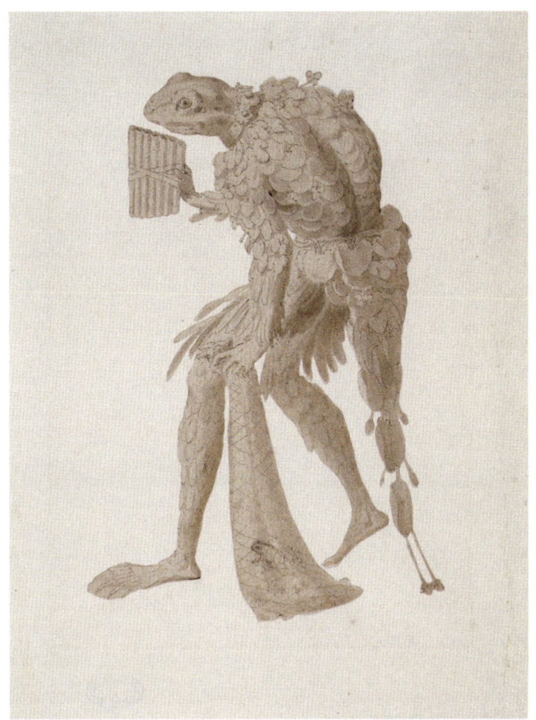

34. Niccolò dell'Abate, *Masquerade Costume: The Frog Man*, *c*. 1552–71. Pen with brown ink and wash.

as sophisticated as it was bizarre. He was among the most versatile and gifted of draughtsmen, so adept at making precise portraits in metalpoint, for instance, that his freely sketched, painterly chalk drawings almost seem to be the work of a different artist: chameleon-like, he could disappear into his drawings, leaving little trace of his authorship. But he also became adept at a kind of drawing known as *Federkunststück* – literally, 'quill artwork' – and when he practised it the results could hardly be by anyone else. Its origins were in the highly skilled profession of engraving. Goltzius, who trained as an engraver himself and became a publisher of prints in Haarlem, pioneered a new way of working with the burin, or engraving tool. He realised that by gradually exerting greater pressure then easing off when cutting a line into the copper plate, he could make it swell expressively and taper to a fine, elegant point.[3] Together, either in parallel or crosswise, these lines with their varying widths could create the powerful impression of rounded, three-dimensional forms; he demonstrated this memorably in an engraving he called the *Great*

Hercules (1589), a nude figure whose physique bulges so excessively with muscles that the Dutch laughed and christened it the *Knollenman*: the tuber-man. Goltzius became so fascinated by these serpentine lines and their capacity to create the illusion of form that in the late 1580s he began to emulate them with pen and ink.[4] In 1587 he took a quill pen and imagined the head of Mercury – fabled as the inventor of the arts – with lines that are flamboyantly expressive while being subject to the strictest control (fig. 35). So impressive was the resulting drawing that it is thought to have been acquired by one of the greatest collectors of the age and a connoisseur of the bizarre and the fantastic, the Holy Roman Emperor Rudolph II.[5] Even when it was dressing up in borrowed clothes, however, drawing – in Goltzius's exceptionally skilled hands – was rapidly developing its own character as an independent medium.

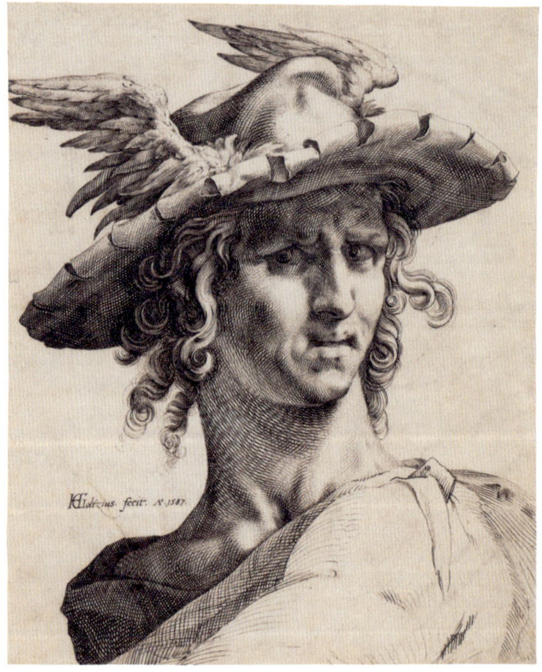

35. Hendrick Goltzius, *Head of Mercury*, 1587. Pen and ink.

Astounding, yes; virtuosic, certainly; but to many all this had begun to feel like the end of something. Towards the end of the sixteenth century some Italian artists began to have misgivings about the cultivation of super-refinement. They rejected the contortions and distortions of Mannerism

                                    THE STORY OF DRAWING

and tried instead to adopt a more naturalistic approach. As for where drawing fitted in to this project, then that all depended on the artist. One of those determined to rethink picture-making was Michelangelo Merisi da Caravaggio (1571–1610), whose fleshy and dramatically lit figures are so apparently three-dimensional they seem to shoulder their way out of their canvases. Not a single drawing by Caravaggio is known. He would have practised drawing as part of his apprenticeship, and later he probably made planning sketches, then discarded them after they had served their purpose. X-rays and infra-red reflectography, techniques that can penetrate paint layers and reach the underlying surface, have shown that he drew with a brush directly onto the canvas in order to establish his composition – a drawing that was obliterated as the paint layers accumulated.[6] But for other artists, drawing was vitally important as a way of reconnecting with the world. The Carracci – brothers Agostino (1557–1602) and Annibale (1560–1609), and cousin Ludovico (1555–1619) – were tireless draughtsmen. It was said by a contemporary historian, writing in 1686, that they 'ate and drew at the same time, bread in one hand and chalk or charcoal in the other'.[7] Sheets

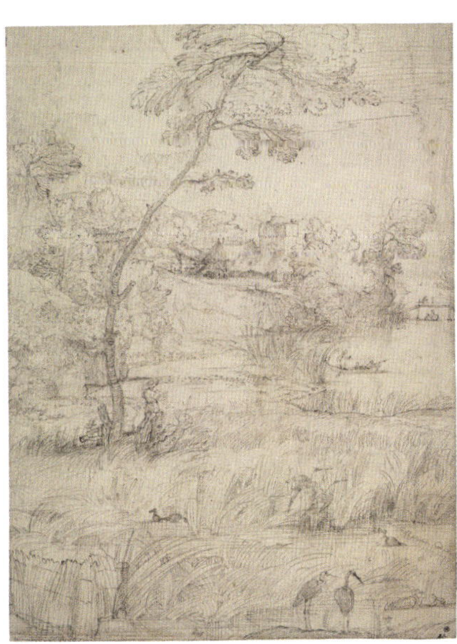
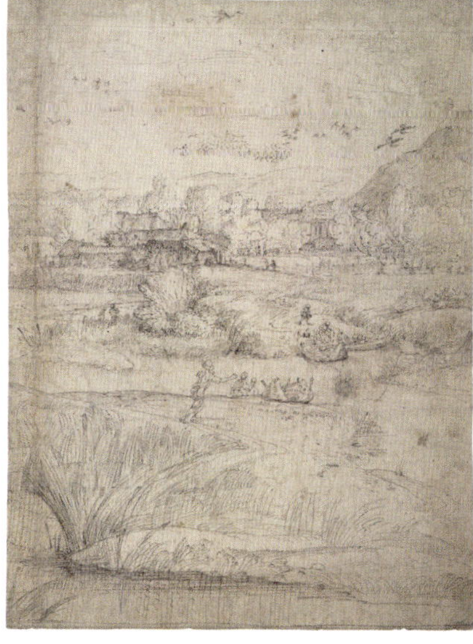

36. Agostino Carracci, *River Landscape with Figures and Boats*, c. 1572–1602. Pen and grey ink.

by Agostino teem with overlapping figures both nude and draped, and whatever else caught his eye. His brother Annibale became fascinated by street traders, making not just three or four drawings of them, but seventy-five. They went out onto Bologna's streets and into the countryside in search of new scenes. It is hard to imagine Titian sitting outside to draw the view; his compositions have a languorous, indoors air. The Carracci, however, wanted to flap away the heavy atmosphere of erotic mystery and to study the actual appearance of the country. The quick, precise penstrokes of a rivery landscape by Agostino with which he depicts reeds, bullrushes, egrets and ducks, alongside human figures busy manoeuvring little boats, are as fresh as the morning breeze (fig. 36).

In the 1580s Agostino and Annibale, along with Ludovico, formed an academy in the latter's studio in Bologna that came to be known as the Accademia degli Incamminati, the Academy of the Progressives. This, among the earliest art academies in Italy, began as an informal group of artists who met to draw from life.[8] The Carracci placed great emphasis on observing the natural world, and even took their

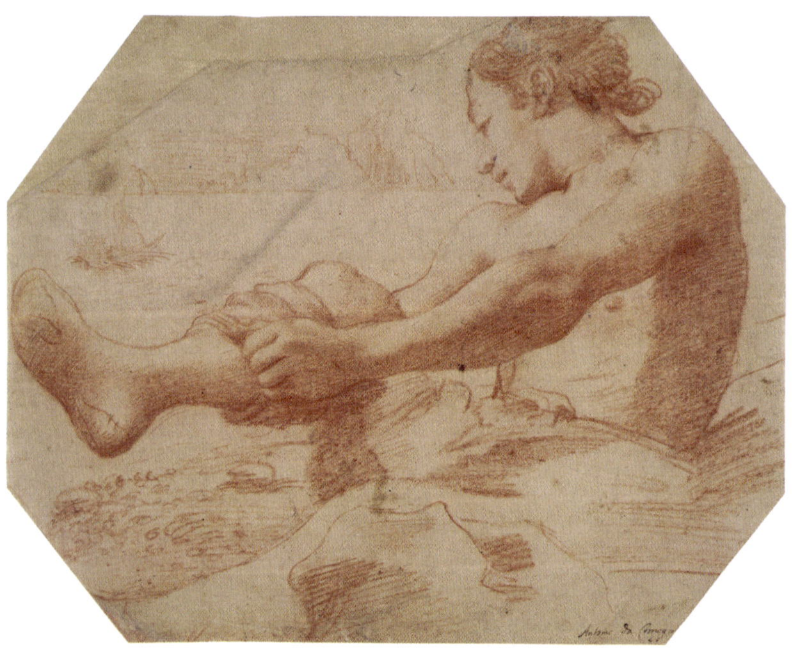

37. Annibale Carracci, *A Young Man Pulling on a Sock*, c. 1585–90. Red chalk.

   THE STORY OF DRAWING

students on field trips into the country in order to sketch plants, trees and landscapes. Most important, however, was the study of the human figure, nude or clothed, sometimes adopting a pose, sometimes in informal attitudes. One chalk drawing by Annibale represents a boy pulling on a sock, presumably in the act of getting dressed after a modelling session (fig. 37); another shows a naked boy who has fallen asleep, the very picture of sunlit contentment. Nothing could be further from the contorted poses beloved of Mannerist artists. Annibale often used large sheets of paper because it allowed him to be expansive, to focus on the bulk and roundedness of the human figure, qualities he then channelled back into his paintings. His masterpiece was the gallery ceiling in the Palazzo Farnese in Rome, which he decorated between 1597 and 1601, which bursts with frescos that joyfully celebrate the power of love with classical gods, youths, stone herms, airborne putti – and a staggering amount of bare flesh.

Annibale's drawings are so evidently the building blocks of his paintings that the connection seems inevitable. Not all artists, however, had the option of making drawing central to their art. When the Carracci were young men, they attended an academy in which they were able to draw both from the antique and from the life model, and when they returned home they would not rest until they had drawn the poses again from memory. In this spirit of cheerful camaraderie they would pose for each other. Artemisia Gentileschi (1593–1654), however, had access to little of this because of her sex. Although she was taught by her artist father in his Roman workshop, where she learned to draw and to paint, she had to forgo opportunities that would have come the way of other Italian artists to study and draw musculature and bone structure from a living model.[9] As a mature artist it is thought that, like Caravaggio, she roughed out the composition directly onto the canvas before beginning to paint. Knowing that she was excluded from the life room of drawing academies, when we look at Gentileschi's mature work her achievements are all the more impressive. What we witness is the successful overcoming of an obstacle that would have prevented most artists from taking another step.

In Bologna, however, where the Carracci had established their academy, things were different. Ever since the time of the popular artist-nun Catherine of Bologna (1413–1463), who became the patron saint of the Bolognese artists' academy, there had been a strong tradition of female artists working in the city, and this overlapped with an equally strong culture of drawing.[10] Like Gentileschi, Lavinia Fontana (1552–1614) was trained in art by her artist father, who had no sons and wished her to take over his studio. She became renowned as a portraitist, and although she seems mostly to have worked in oil, she used coloured chalks for small portrait drawings, their scale and high level of detail suggesting that at least some were intended as works of art in their own right.[11] Fontana drew fashionably dressed men and women; nuns and friars; her fellow artist Federico Barocci; a self-possessed young woman with hypertrichosis universalis, a condition that has covered her face with hair. With a delicate touch of her chalks, Fontana captures in each a subtle quirk of character – a young nun gazes at the artist with an air of gentle amusement (fig. 38); a friar with an unruly shock of hair looks as though he is caught in mid-sentence, earnestly debating a point; an elegantly dressed lady smiles a little archly as though sharing a joke. Each of these informal portraits speaks of the artist's rapport with her sitters and their pleasure in her company. The only drawing in which the sitter's expression gives little away is the one she made of herself.

No female artist of the city, however, was as famous for her drawing as Elisabetta Sirani (1638–1665). Her mentor Carlo Cesare Malvasia, the historian of Bolognese art who also left detailed records of Carracci working practices, paid her the greatest compliment of which he was capable. She was so brilliant, in his opinion, that she had virtually cast off her femininity and 'acquired the virile sex'. No, better than that. She was, he concluded, 'beyond any man'.[12] What Malvasia was responding to so breathlessly was Sirani's bold and dynamic use of graphic media to work out her ideas for compositions, the creative process unfolding on paper in front of his very eyes:

I can truthfully say, having been present many times when some commission for a painting came, she quickly took the chalk, and placing the sketch down swiftly in two marks on white paper (this was the great master's only method of drawing, which was practiced by few, not even by her father), dipped a small brush in ink wash; from this quickly appeared a spirited invention that

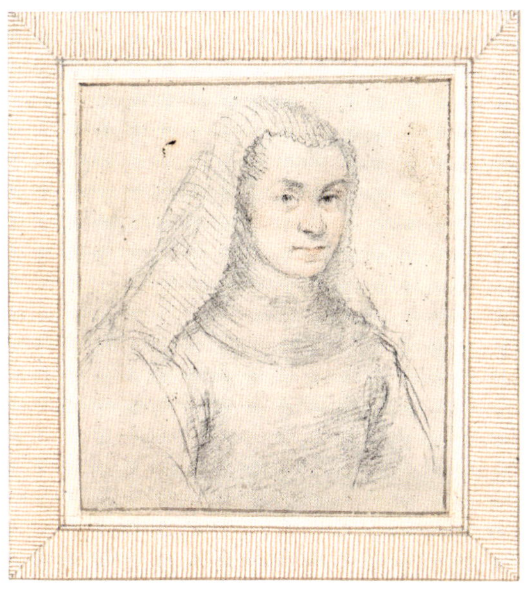

38. Lavinia Fontana, *Nun or Young Woman with a Veil*, *c.* 1577–95. Red and black chalk.

seemed to be without drawn or shaded strokes, and heightened together all at once.[13]

Looking at Sirani's preparatory studies today, it is easy to appreciate the bold decisiveness that so impressed her biographer (fig. 39). As he describes, Sirani often planned her compositions with a brush dipped in ink, a tricky and potentially unruly medium, but one that she mastered because it enabled her rapidly to establish the basic structure of a figure group on paper without getting bogged down in unnecessary detail. Her drawings – powerful but not pretty, practical rather than eye-pleasing – were avidly collected in Bologna, and as a result as many as 150 have survived today.[14]

Sirani's ambitious paintings of allegorical groups, martyrdoms and Madonnas all relied on her thorough knowledge of the human figure. As a young artist, had she found a way of drawing from the living model? No studies of the male nude by her are known, though who can say what arrangements she may have made behind closed doors, of which even Malvasia was unaware.[15]

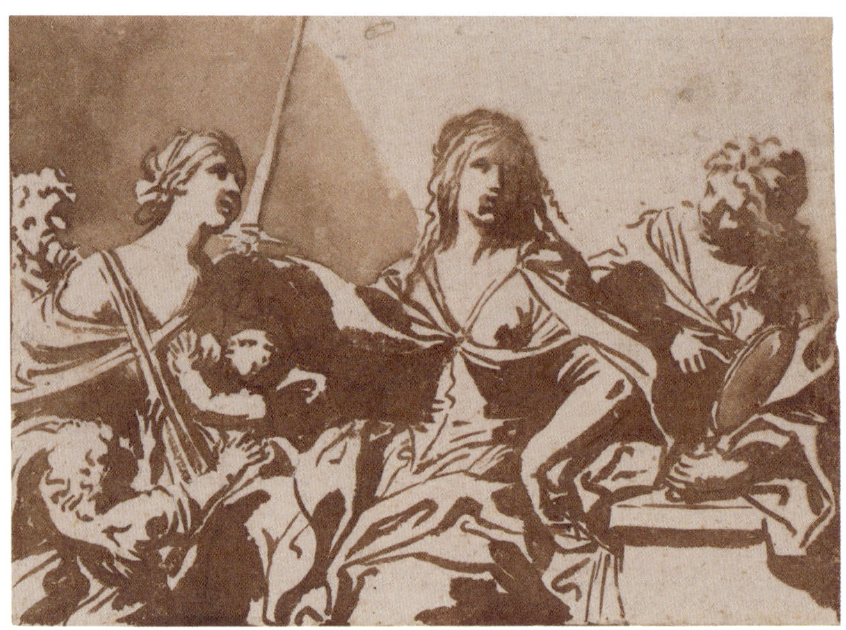

39. Elisabetta Sirani, *Study for Allegory of Justice, Charity and Prudence*, *c.* 1664. Brush and brown wash over traces of red chalk.

Back in the late sixteenth century, the artistic centres of Bologna and Rome may have been bubbling with creativity and innovation but Isfahan, where Shah 'Abbas I had relocated the Safavid government in 1597–8, was becoming world famous not only for the richness and splendour of its palaces and gardens but also as a centre for the production of art and artefacts. 'Abbas, determined to revive the economy and to make the city the most breathtaking in Persia, built mosques, colleges, palaces, gardens, baths, caravanserai and a two-kilometre-long bazaar. By various means, including forceful repatriation into the city of Chinese potters and Armenian silk producers, he made sure that textiles, carpets and ceramics were manufactured there on an industrial scale.

Among the artists to accompany the Safavid court to Isfahan was Riza-yi 'Abbasi (*c.* 1565–1635). At the time Annibale was painting nude figures on the ceiling of the Palazzo Farnese, Riza was thinking about clothed ones; while Annibale's mind was on the expressive capacity of a tensed thigh or a raised arm, for Riza much could be conveyed by the flutter of a scarf or the folds of a turban. He specialised in figure

	THE STORY OF DRAWING

drawings, whether portraits or genre pictures, which would be mounted in albums, the pages of which were usually richly decorated with border designs. Within these pages he created a world of refinement through which the elegant and the richly dressed stroll or lounge. Riza describes these with a calligraphic line that gently but precisely spears character; when looking at his drawings, one often suspects a wry smile on the artist's part. In one, a young man with a round face and slight double chin, clad in a pale pink robe spangled with gold motifs pulls a shawl tightly around his shoulders (fig. 40). It is a cold day:

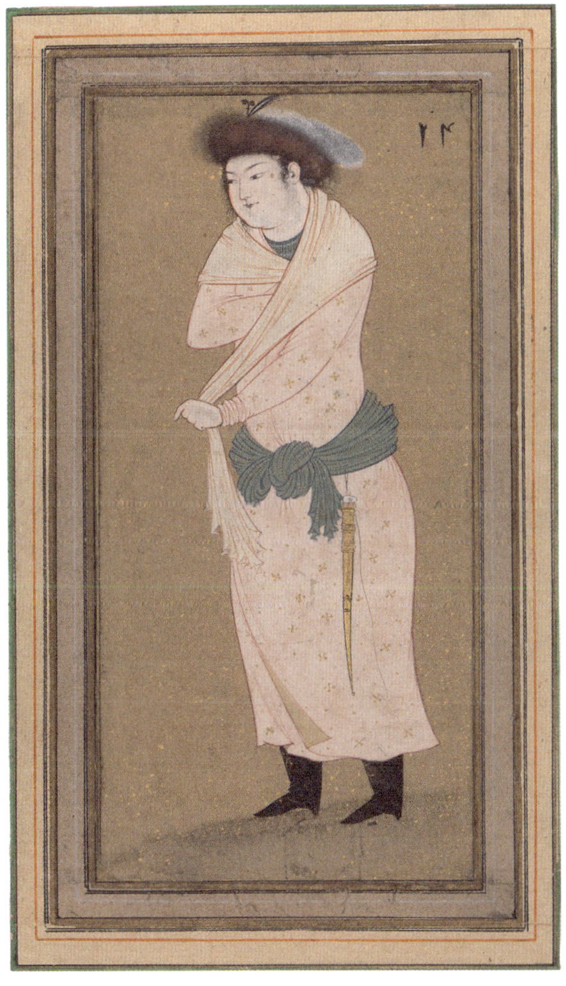

40. Riza-yi 'Abbasi (attrib.), *Portrait of a Man*, *c.* 1600. Ink, bodycolour and gold on paper.

there is no background except for dabs of gold paint, which might be a stylised form of snow, and yet this is no image of winter chill and dire struggle. He is protected from the weather by a fur hat – Riza depicts its fuzzy aureole with the finest of wispy brushstrokes – and a thick sash, tied around his comfortably rounded waist. Only the hem of his robe, which flips back as though caught by a chilly gust of wind, suggests the young man is engaged in a battle against the elements, and then only of the mildest kind.

CHAPTER 9

CULTURE AND COLONISATION

HAD ANYONE EVER seen an Aspidochelone or a Basilisk in the wild? Well, no. But few doubted their existence because there they were, in the pages of medieval bestiaries – and not just in one book, but in countless others. The weight of authority was established through small acts of repetition like snowflakes forming a drift. But times were changing. In the sixteenth and seventeenth centuries individuals were beginning to question time-honoured tales and to wish to see things with their own eyes. Drawing, which could provide clear visual evidence, was one of their most important tools.

Colonial enterprises opened up routes to distant shores. In 1585 an English gentleman called John White (active 1577–93) boarded a ship bound for North America in an expedition promoted by Walter Raleigh with the purpose of founding the first English settlement on American soil. As a 'limner' – an artist who specialised in detailed watercolour drawing – it was White's task to record the human inhabitants of this unfamiliar world, their customs and ways of life, as well as the native flora and fauna. He drew a settlement and a fishing expedition, women carrying infants and a couple sitting down together to eat. Down on his sheets of paper went the unfamiliar creatures and foodstuffs he encountered: a puffer fish and a red-footed booby, a plantain and a pineapple.[1] Most striking of all are the people whose full-length portraits he drew: those who posed for him included a chief in his regalia (fig. 41), and the wife of a Timucuan chief of

Florida, covered with elaborate tattoos and holding corn cobs and a dish of prickly pears. One of White's subjects, a young woman, tucks one foot behind the opposite ankle and places both hands protectively on her shoulders, covering her chest, apparently shy of this strange man's intense scrutiny. Today, many who view these images share her discomfiture. While the impression that emanates from his drawings is of generosity and friendly cooperation on the part of the Native Americans, White was not making such detailed records disinterestedly, but to provide crucial information about subjects from food and crops to building materials and weaponry to aid future colonisers. In spite of their engaging immediacy, his numerous drawings were cogs in a machine that would go on to crush countless indigenous people in its workings.

It was not always necessary, however, to make perilous voyages to see, and draw, extraordinary things. Natural and man-made products were being carried around the globe at this time in unprecedented numbers as colonies were established and trade routes developed,

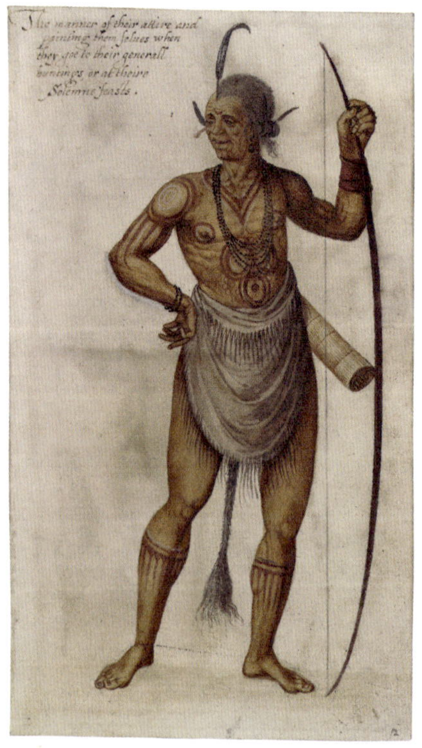

41. John White, *A Native American 'Werowance' or Chief*, *c.* 1585–93. Watercolour and graphite, touched with bodycolour and gold.

transforming how people understood the world. In 1612 the Mughal Emperor Jahangir, who was fascinated by exotic creatures, sent his servant Muqarrab Khan to Goa, on the west coast of India, then under Portuguese rule, to purchase some of the unfamiliar birds and animals he had heard were brought there by Portuguese traders. These creatures often featured as part of larger narrative scenes in Mughal art, but Jahangir decided that they deserved to have their portraits drawn, in the same profile format as an important personage and with a high degree of naturalism. 'As these animals appeared to me to be very strange,' he wrote, 'I both described them and ordered that painters should draw them in the *Jahangirnama* [Jahangir's memoirs], so that the amazement that arose from hearing of them might be increased.'[2] Among those Khan arranged to have carried back to the court at Agra was a chameleon. He chose his court artist Ustad Mansur (active *c.* 1590–1630), to whom he was later to grant the title Nadir al-Asr (Wonder of the Age), for his skill: in his portrait Mansur conveys not only the distinctive character of this little beast, but also the bumpy texture of its scales, by patiently applying hundreds of dots of vivid green bodycolour (opaque watercolour) with the tip of a fine brush.[3]

A few years later, in March 1621, a zebra was brought to the court, a present to Jahangir from the nobleman Mir Ja'far, presented at the beginning of his sixteenth regnal year. Ja'far had acquired it from a party of Turks who had brought it with them from Habesh, a region incorporating present-day Ethiopia, which at the time was an Ottoman colony. Jahangir scrutinised the animal with intense interest. As he recalled:

At this time I saw a wild ass, exceedingly strange in appearance, exactly like a tiger. From the tip of the nose to the end of the tail, and from the point of the ear to the top of the hoof, black markings, large or small, suitable to their position were seen on it. Round the eyes there was an exceedingly fine black line. One might say that the painter of fate, with a strange brush, had left it on the page of the world.[4]

Suspicions were raised that its black stripes might have been inked on by a trickster, but after careful examination its markings were found to be genuine. Again, Jahangir asked Mansur to draw the beast's portrait. With the finest of brushes the artist captured the subtlety of the transitions, blurred by hair, from black stripe to white, and the soft sheen of the animal's coat (fig. 42). Having had it recorded in such naturalistic detail, Jahangir sent the beast as a gift to Shah 'Abbas at Isfahan, with whom he often exchanged exotic gifts. He prized the drawing, which, as a connoisseur, he perhaps valued more highly than the zebra itself, and inscribed it himself in Persian with details of its creation. It was eventually inherited by Jahangir's son Shah Jahan, when, with the addition of decorative borders, this exquisite record of an African animal that had been caught up in the currents of global trade was bound into a royal album.

Mughal miniatures were themselves subject to these currents. Rembrandt Harmensz. van Rijn (1606–1669) was a passionate collector who filled his house in Amsterdam with prints, drawings, paintings, books, classical busts, corals, shells, animal specimens, armour,

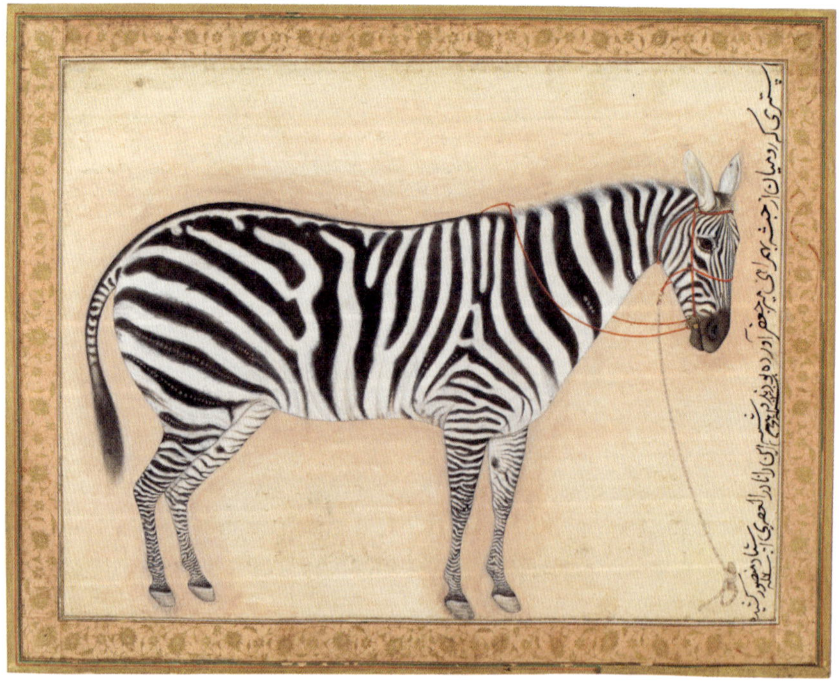

42. Ustad Mansur, *A Zebra*, 1621. Bodycolour and gold.

THE STORY OF DRAWING

weaponry and ethnographic objects of many kinds.[5] A contemporary noted that the artist 'took advantage of whatever came hither from the four parts of the world'.[6] Even after he had been declared bankrupt in 1656 he continued to acquire, amassing prodigious quantities of art, antiques and curiosities. Seventeenth-century Amsterdam, head-quarters of the Dutch East India Company which had a monopoly on trade with Asian countries and imported goods from Chinese porcelain to elephants, was a place in which extraordinary items from remote regions of the globe might turn up in any of the little shops along Warmoesstraat, near the docks. It was a good – or perhaps a bad – place for anyone afflicted by the collecting bug.

Among the imports that caught Rembrandt's attention in the late 1650s, when he was in his early fifties, was a group of Mughal portrait miniatures of emperors, princes and courtiers, probably bound together in an album, that would have been shipped to the Netherlands from the Indian port of Surat, a Dutch trading post. It is tempting to imagine a shop owner, familiar with Rembrandt's tastes, waiting for him to call in one day to browse, then producing the precious album from behind the counter, confident that the artist would be astonished by the images it contained and perhaps willing to pay a high price. However Rembrandt came by the drawings, for someone with as profound an interest in portraiture as him and so beguiled by foreign luxury goods, these drawings, which created a splendid effect with such graceful economy of line, could hardly fail to appeal.

But there was more to it than that: these Mughal portraits intrigued and inspired Rembrandt to the extent that he made no fewer than twenty-three copies of them in pen and brown ink, sometimes adding wash to emulate the pistachio-green backgrounds that often occur in such portraits (fig. 43). It was as though by taking a pen in his hand and drawing faces, hands, turbans, sashes, jewellery and swords, he was getting as close as he could to the original artists, inhabiting their ways of working and matching them to his own. Copy, however, hardly seems the right word: they were instead versions, or creative adaptations; Rembrandt felt free to simplify costume details and to alter poses, while at the same time paying close attention to the fea-tures and psychology of each sitter. With a few strokes of the pen he causes individuals to spring from the page.[7] Copies can be flat and disappointing; these drawings are lively and characterful. In them,

Rembrandt conducts a conversation with a contemporary, if very different, culture.[8] The value he placed on these works can be inferred by his choice of expensive Asian paper, probably Japanese *torinoko*, another product brought to Amsterdam by Dutch overseas trade. With a faint yellowish colour and a smoother, more lustrous surface than European paper – its name, meaning 'hen's egg', aptly describes its appearance – it gave these drawings an air of luxury, helping them to speak the same refined language as the Mughal portraits.

With careful handling, an album of Mughal miniatures could arrive in Amsterdam with the pigments as fresh as the day they were applied. Specimens of birds, animals, reptiles and plants, however, were rarely unchanged by their journeys. They shrank and faded, or suffered from their methods of preservation. Occasionally, artists

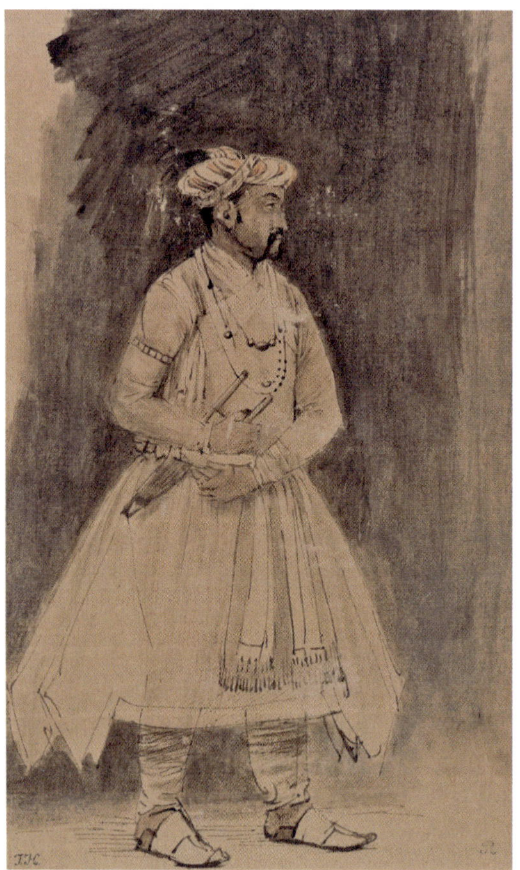

43. Rembrandt van Rijn, *A Mughal Nobleman (Prince Daniyal) after a Mughal Miniature, c.* 1656–61. Pen and brown ink with grey and brown wash, touched with red chalk and white heightening.

 THE STORY OF DRAWING

became so tantalised by these husks that they took drastic measures in order to witness the brilliance and variety of living things in their natural habitats.

1699: the Dutch colony of Suriname, on the northeast coast of South America. The heat is stifling and the jungle a forbidding tangle of thorn bushes; it would be madness to try to penetrate it. But Maria Sibylla Merian (1647–1717) has not come all this way only to turn back now. Back in Holland and Germany she had made a name for herself with her meticulous flower paintings, but her imagination had always been captured by insects and their apparently miraculous life cycles: from her own careful observations and drawings she produced an illustrated book with fifty plates describing the 'wonderful' metamorphosis of caterpillars, moths, butterflies, grubs and flies, *Der Raupen wunderbare Verwandlung und sonderbare Blumennahrung* – the wonderful metamorphosis of caterpillars and their strange flower-food. From 1690 she lived in Amsterdam, to which some of the most extraordinary and wide-ranging specimens of natural history had been brought. 'In Holland,' she later recalled, 'I saw with wonderment the beautiful creatures brought back from the East and West Indies.'[9] She realised, however, that she could only learn so much from stuffed birds, lizards preserved in jars and frames crammed with specimens of butterflies and beetles, and passionately wanted to study these creatures in the wild – so much, in fact, that at the age of fifty-two she secured funding from the Dutch government, packed her drawing materials along with wooden specimen boxes, bell jars and butterfly nets and arranged a berth on a ship bound for Suriname.

Merian and her younger daughter Dorothea Maria, who accompanied her, seemed an odd pair to the Dutch colonists overseeing their sugar plantations. They 'mocked me for seeking anything other than sugar in the country', she recalled.[10] But she persevered, questioning indigenous people about the properties of native plants and relying on enslaved plantation workers to clear paths for her when she made expeditions into the wilderness.[11] On these trips she collected unfamiliar insects and caterpillars and fed them on leaves in her garden, where she observed and drew them, making painstaking studies of their appearance, behaviour and vivid colours. She had taken watercolour paints out to Suriname, along with brushes and sketchbooks with vellum leaves – which was not only more durable but also provided a smoother surface than ordinary paper, thus allowing her to capture the maximum amount of detail. She drew giant silk moths the size of dinner plates and lantern flies that – apparently – astonished her when she opened their box and found them blazing with light from their proboscises.[12] And she imagined dramatic, deadly encounters: a tarantula preying on a hummingbird and a caiman fighting with a snake. When she returned to Amsterdam it was with reptiles preserved in brandy, pressed plants and many boxes of butterflies and beetles, and – perhaps most valuable of all – her sketchbooks in which she had captured things that could only be recorded on the spot: insects on what she considered to be their food plants and the sequential

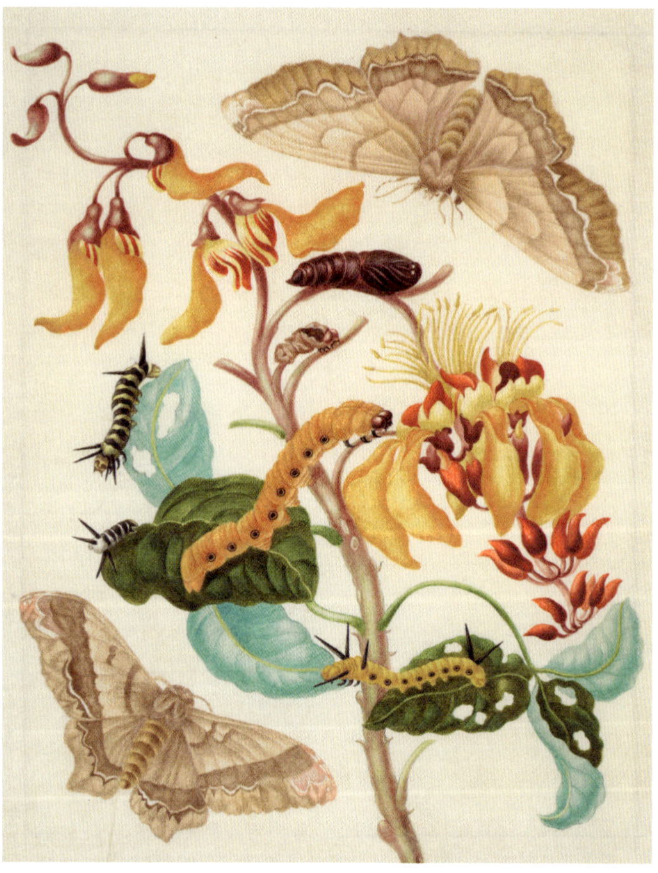

44. Maria Sibylla Merian, *Swamp Immortelle with Giant Silk Moth*, 1702–3. Watercolour and bodycolour with gum arabic on vellum.

   THE STORY OF DRAWING

stages of their metamorphoses. Back at home, with the studies she had made in the heat of Suriname in front of her, she set about making large-scale watercolour drawings in preparation for one of the most magnificent illustrated books of the era, the *Metamorphosis Insectorum Surinamensium* (1705; fig. 44). She told a friend that its pages, full of brilliant colour, contained 'many amazing rare things which have never been seen before'.[13] One hundred and twenty years after John White's voyage to the coast of North America as part of the colonisation project, Merian took advantage of Dutch incursions into Suriname to present drawings of foreign plants and creatures for their intrinsic interest and intellectual value.

CHAPTER 10

PECULIAR GROUND

AFTER HE BOUGHT the manor of Het Steen near Mechelen in 1635, the great Flemish painter Sir Peter Paul Rubens (1577–1640) painted landscapes that are so operatic they look as though they might burst into song. There are sweeping vistas over rivers, bridges and mountains towards distant hills; there are tall, elegant trees; and there are dramatic skies, often spanned by brilliant rainbows. The Flemish countryside did not actually look like that, of course. Rubens was working within a sophisticated artistic tradition, and these painterly performances were orchestrated to impress and charm the eye as it wandered from one pleasing feature to another. Suppose the 'landscape' of that time and place was a recipe: it would be a quantity of unprocessed trees, hills, fields and valleys whisked together with an equal measure of Arcadia until emulsification was achieved, poured into a mould the shape of Greek myth or a biblical story, and baked until flecked with golden light.

In Rubens's landscape drawings, on the other hand, we can see him responding more directly to the natural world. We do not know how many such sketches he made, but only a small number survive, mostly thought to have been made late in life and to depict the kind of country that surrounded Het Steen.[1] There is nothing grand about the landscapes in these drawings, and no elevated platform from which to imagine we are lords of all we survey, as we find in the paintings – instead they offer a walker's-eye view of low-lying fields, streams, bridges, pollarded willows and woodland. It is as though Rubens has temporarily put aside the noble titles he has been granted by Philip III and Philip IV of Spain and Charles I of England and become plain Squire Rubens, walking his estate in country coat and stout boots, taking an interest in wattle fences and casting a critical eye over footbridges. Most surviving drawings have the realistic, outdoors air of having at least been begun on the spot, even if some may have been worked up later. One, however, among his most tender and personal landscapes, has an inscription that seems to send the viewer tumbling through a trapdoor to the 1630s and the bank of a Flemish lake. It is an atmospheric sketch of a line of trees reflected in water that Rubens has drawn with light scribbles of black chalk, adding a little white to suggest the play of light on foliage and water (fig. 45). The sun is setting, so he has subtly blended touches of red and umber chalk near the horizon to convey its brilliant glow.[2] On the sheet he has recorded the curious phenomenon that prompted him to make the drawing: 'The reflection of the trees in the water,' he writes, 'is browner and more perfect in the water than the trees themselves.'[3] One can picture him waiting on the bank, watching

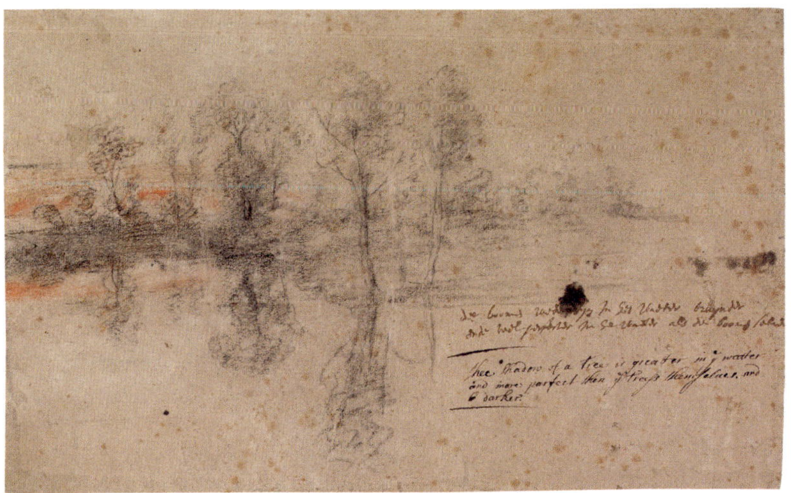

45. Peter Paul Rubens, *Trees Reflected in Water at Sunset*, c. 1635–8. Black, red and orange chalks, heightened with white, on buff paper.

for those few seconds when the sun was aligned behind the trees so that their reflection fell in perfect symmetry, and making haste to record the fleeting visual effect on paper so as to fix it in his mind before it was gone, dusk fell, and it was time to go indoors.

As a subject, landscape could offer freedom. Sometimes artists sketched out in the country in order to study nature with a view to incorporating a particular element into a painting – the gnarled and split trunk of a tree, or the transition from pastureland to woodland – but often it was for its own sake. An oil painting was a significant investment of time, money and resources: it needed careful consideration. Would a patron buy it? Would it be a worthy addition to an artist's body of work? There were many constraints. Drawing, on the other hand, was quick and cheap: it presented the opportunity to record the apparently insignificant and the easily overlooked; to spend time looking at a scene that might at first sight appear unprepossessing. In the 1640s and early 1650s Rembrandt made many drawings of the Dutch landscape for pleasure, walking the farmland outside Amsterdam in search of subjects, sketchbook in pocket, often with students in tow.[4] He might choose to draw a windmill on a bulwark – a common enough sight in the polders, but by paying close attention to it he found the grace in its turning sails and a quiet strength in its solidity and the deep shadow it cast (fig. 46). He drew farmsteads with dung heaps, dovecotes and haystacks, rutted lanes, a bend in a river and a view of boats from a bridge. He usually used simple, unshowy pen or brush with brown ink for these drawings, sometimes adding wash for emphasis and atmosphere. He sketched the countryside in the same way he sketched men, women and children: because he was passionately interested in the ordinary and its subtle variations and unexpected moments of beauty – and with lines of great economy, he channelled what he saw onto paper.

Other artists were no less passionate about drawing the landscape and yet they took a radically different approach. Six hundred miles south of Amsterdam, at his home near Bologna, the leading Baroque painter Giovanni Francesco Barbieri (1591–1666) – known since childhood as il Guercino, 'the squinter' – drew imaginary landscapes in his spare time. He did this apparently for no other reason than to amuse himself and his friends. None of his many landscape

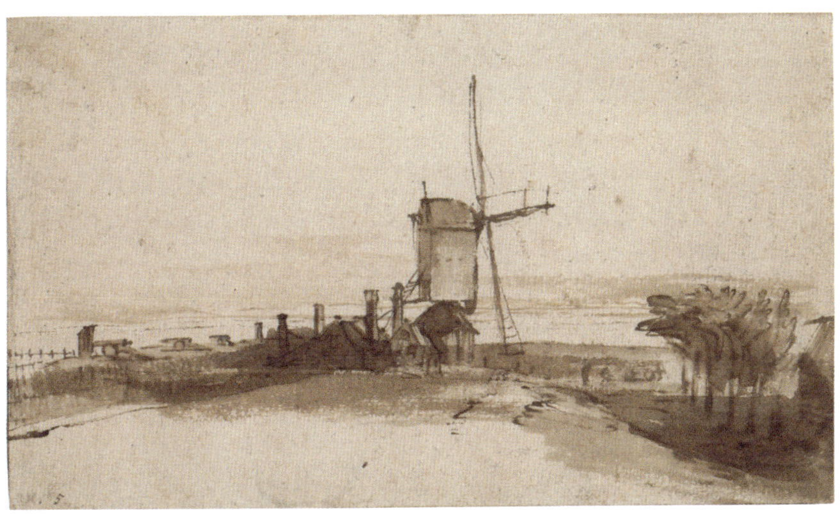

46. Rembrandt van Rijn, *The Grain Mill 'De Bok' on the Bulwark 'Het Blauwhoofd'*, *c.* 1645. Pen and brown ink and wash.

drawings was made as a preparatory study for an oil painting.[5] Guercino loved to imagine wide stretches of sunny landscape, emphasising breadth and space with long horizontal strokes of the pen that encourage the eye to range over hillsides, cliffs and bridges, church towers and castles, and to wonder about the business of the horsemen and foot travellers on the road. He created the illusion of great distance by easing the pressure so that his pen left finer lines, as though the detail were dissipated in the space.[6] He drew in the way that some people invent stories, allowing a fanciful landscape to unfold, full of wind-blown trees and busy individuals, and to tell whatever tales it had up its sleeve.

Further south still, from the 1620s to the mid-1640s Claude Gellée (1604/5–1682), known as Claude Lorrain – a French-born painter who lived in Rome all his adult life – made frequent sketching expeditions into the Roman Campagna. A favourite walk was along the left bank of the Tiber as far as Acqua Acetosa, about two miles upstream of Rome.[7] During these trips he made many hundreds of drawings in sketchbooks recording his surroundings: woods, meadows, trees, distant hills, farm buildings, ruins, the towns of Tivoli or Nemi, the Tiber valley, the meanderings of the river itself.

He valued them highly and kept them at his elbow when he was painting subjects drawn from history or myth, which he imagined taking place within recognisable landscapes outside Rome. And yet he referred to his drawings not for specific details, but rather to stimulate his imagination: they rarely give the impression that Claude was particularly interested in topography. For him, a sense of place was both simpler and more complex. What interested him, and what he captured on paper, was the luminous intensity of the sunlight, and the ways it fell on foliage and on water. Shape mattered more than detail. He drew with brown ink and used a brush for liquid washes, creating richly evocative atmospheres. In his oil paintings he interleaved past and present, and a similar layering can be found in his drawings. One made around 1640 focuses on the edge of a wood; at first glance it is a closely observed study of tightly grouped trees with ivy snaking up their trunks (fig. 47). Look again: both the contrast between the dark wood and the airy open space, and the figure emerging from the trees who strikes a poetic pose, lend it a mysterious, dreamlike mood – a feeling enhanced by the tone of the blue paper.[8] This is evidently a specific place, but at the same time Claude suggests that it is one haunted by the past and charged with poetic feeling.

Drawing also came to serve a distinctly practical function for Claude. In the mid-1630s, by which time he was a highly successful artist, he discovered to his horror that his paintings were being forged and so devised a way of authenticating his work. Around 1635 he began what he called his *libro di verità*, or book of truth (also known as the *Liber veritatis*), a pictorial record, in his usual pen, ink and wash, of each painting before it left his studio. This remarkable catalogue became a major work of art in itself.

Artists could turn to the subject of landscape in response to distressing political situations. While Claude was enriching the Roman Campagna with layers of poetry and myth in a way that appealed to aristocratic patrons, in China artists were facing the traumatic rupture of long-established tradition. In 1644 the Ming dynasty collapsed, and in the chaos that followed as the Manchu army took control, many artists, loyal to the old regime, withdrew from the capital and sought both refuge and inspiration in the natural

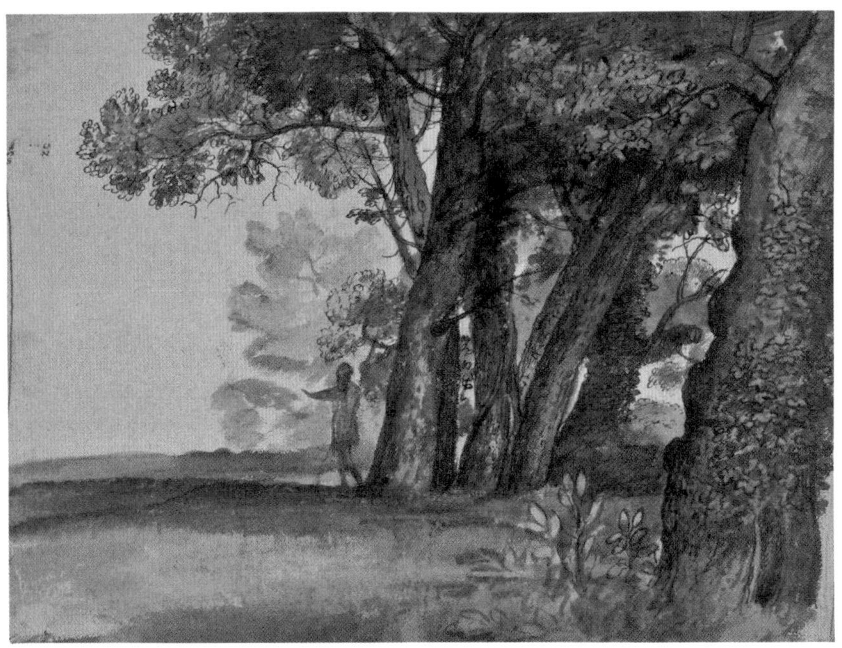

47. Claude Lorrain, *Landscape with a Figure by a Group of Trees*, c. 1640.
Pen and brown ink and wash on blue paper.

world. Emulating revered masters had for centuries been central to artistic practice in China. Now, with collections less accessible than before, some artists began to develop individual styles. These *yimin* – 'leftover subjects' – looked at their surroundings afresh, and with a new psychological intensity: for those who settled in Anhui province in eastern China, the dramatic peaks of Huangshan, the Yellow Mountain, became significant as a place that seemed impervious to Manchu occupation. Those in Nanjing, the second capital of the Ming dynasty, were exposed to engravings and perhaps also oil paintings by Western landscape artists, imported by Jesuits who had established a centre there in the sixteenth century. Artists such as Gong Xian (1618–1689) and Fan Qi (1616–1694) began to incorporate elements of the shading and perspective they found there into their own works.

Among the most eccentric of these individualists was Zhu Da (1626–1705), a scion of the Ming royal family. Just a young man at the time of the dynasty's collapse, he fled his hometown Nanchang and became a Buddhist monk. During these years he painted and wrote poetry, often highly critical of Qing officials, and took the artistic name Bada Shanren. This literally meant 'Mountain Man of the Eight Greats', but given that he loved wordplay, it is assumed he chose it because the Chinese characters from which it is formed resemble the words for both 'laugh' and 'cry' – perhaps, in his opinion, the only logical reactions to the new order of things. He suffered periods of apparent insanity during which he behaved with extravagant oddity, although it is possible that he feigned mental unbalance in order that the Qing authorities would conclude that he was harmless and leave him alone. Although Zhu Da was steeped in artistic tradition – among his works is an album of drawings dating from around 1692 in which he copied compositions both by the tenth-century master Dong Yuan and by his thirteenth- and fourteenth-century followers – he had great independence of mind and struck out into new territory, creating enigmatic images for which there was little precedent.[9] A hanging scroll he drew late in life of ornamental rocks and fish apparently swimming in a pond is audaciously abstract (fig. 48). Calligraphic brushstrokes loop and dash, leaving frayed edges where the artist chose to draw with dryish bristles. The rocky forms seem solid enough, but it is impossible to tell whether we are looking downwards into a pool, or across – there is no horizon line by which to navigate. The fish – characterful creatures evoked with economical strokes of the pen – seem not to know either; most appear as though seen from the side, but a rogue one is seen from above. The viewer is left disoriented, with

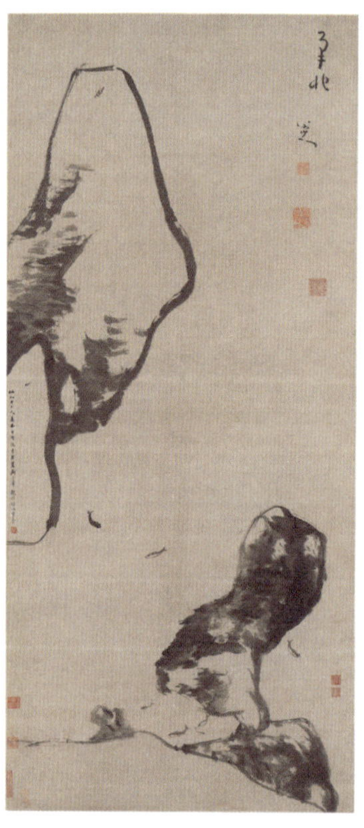

48. Bada Shanren (Zhu Da), *Fish and Rocks*, 1699. Hanging scroll; ink on paper.

THE STORY OF DRAWING

only Zhu Da's artful brushstrokes for guidance, and the suspicion that on this occasion he may have been laughing.

Perhaps the most dramatic and psychologically charged artistic response to the transition from the Ming to the Qing dynasty was an album drawn on silk by Huang Xiangjian (1609–1673). His father had been appointed county magistrate in Yunnan, a mountainous province in southwestern China, in 1643, and for several years Huang heard nothing from his parents and had no way of knowing whether they had suffered in or even survived the armed conflicts that followed the upheavals of 1644. So in 1652 he took drastic action, setting out from his home in Suzhou, just west of Shanghai, to travel the 1,400-mile journey to rural Yunnan to find them; the family was eventually reunited and Huang escorted his parents back home. Three years after his return, still traumatised by his ordeal, he sat down to commemorate the most perilous stage of his route, from northwest Guangdong through west Hunan to east Guizhou. His visual story unfolds not only the precipitous paths zigzagging over mountain ranges and the broad, swift-flowing rivers that he had to negotiate, but also the hostile garrisons at which, injured and poor, he had to plead with soldiers to let him pass (fig. 49). Huang draws himself at various points along the path, a lonely, determined figure, trudging along with a staff over his shoulder. He added an inscription expressing the hope that the act of making the handscroll – casting

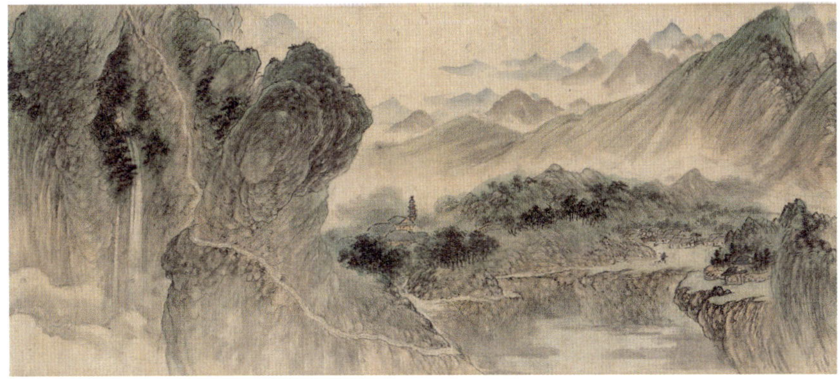

49. Huang Xiangjian, *Searching for my Parents*, 1656.
Handscroll; ink and colour on silk.

his mind back, and giving shape to the peaks, gorges, waters and mists of the landscape through which he passed during those anxious days – would serve to exorcise the trauma he suffered. He gave the landscape such an acutely psychological dimension that the entire scroll becomes a kind of self-portrait.

CHAPTER 11

Searching for the Self

WHAT WERE PORTRAITS for? In London, Jonathan Richardson (1667–1745), who ran a successful portrait business, thought deeply about this question. He came to the conclusion that the role of a painted portrait was to present its subject in the dignified pose they might adopt at a 'Publick Assembly', and to act as 'a sort of General History' of their lives.[1] This focus on the outer person at the expense of their inner self, however, came to nag at him. Later in life, when Richardson had more time on his hands, he began to ponder how drawing could be used as a divining rod in a search for the private self.

In 1728, when he was in his early sixties and in semi-retirement from the face-painting business, Richardson began what would become one of the most profound projects of self-examination ever undertaken. One day, in early May, he took a large sheet of blue paper and sticks of black and white chalk and sat down in front of a mirror to draw his own face. In the resulting work, his expression is guarded – curious and a little uncertain – as though he has pushed open a door but hesitates at the threshold. Over the next ten years he continued to go back through that door, drawing himself again – and again – and again. No one knows how many portraits he created in this way, but it could be as many as 300. Using chalk on blue paper, graphite on slips of vellum and occasionally pen and ink, he explored aspects of his character and his changing moods in drawings that were never meant to be seen by anyone but himself, his beloved son Jonathan Richardson Junior (himself the subject of many drawn portraits) and his closest friends.[2]

In some drawings Richardson met his reflection with a direct and uncompromising gaze as if to assess his state of mind, while in others he presented himself as suave and self-possessed. Sometimes, pencil in hand, he looked back into the past; consulting painted self-portraits dating from earlier in his career, he drew himself as he looked when he was a young man, just starting out as a professional artist. At other times he playfully tried out alternative selves; drawing gave him a freedom he never found in oil paint. He imagined himself crowned with bay leaves, like a celebrated poet; or in profile, as if commemorated on the face of a coin. One day he dressed up in a fur hat, just as Rembrandt had done in one of the numerous self-portrait etchings that Richardson revered. Another time he was inspired by a portrait drawing he owned by the celebrated sculptor Gian Lorenzo Bernini (1598–1680) to pick up a piece of red chalk and draw his own face in the same style.[3]

Richardson also used drawing to confront his own mortality: among his most poignant self-portraits is one he made on a late November's day in 1735, when he laid aside props and playfulness, sat bareheaded in front of his glass and scrutinised what he saw there with unflinching honesty (fig. 50). He set down on paper his ageing features and sagging skin, not with the bold lines he had often used before but with hesitant, almost tentative strokes. That day he drew himself with apparent acceptance and not without sympathy – a state of mind he had perhaps reached through rigorous self-investigation.

In other contexts, portrait drawing could be flamboyant, theatrical and decidedly public. Early eighteenth-century Venice, the birthplace of the portraitist Rosalba Carriera (1673–1757), was an international city, busy with British, French and German travellers. Many of these were passing through because it was an essential part of what became known as the Grand Tour, a leisurely journey through France and Italy with stays at Paris, Florence, Rome and Naples. The well-to-do young men who took the tour benefited – if they were so inclined – from the valuable opportunities it offered to learn on the spot about the history, politics, art, architecture and languages

 THE STORY OF DRAWING

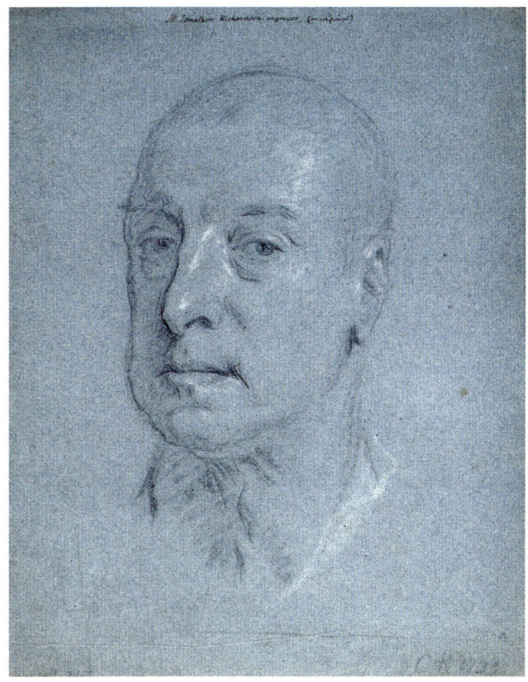

50. Jonathan Richardson, *Self-Portrait*, 1735. Black chalk heightened with white on blue paper.

of European countries and to enter into debates about the political and cultural issues of the day. But serious study was tempered by exciting social opportunities. If aristocratic youths on the Grand Tour travelled to Rome in order to walk reflectively among the remnants of the classical past, they pitched up in Venice to have fun, often timing their visits to coincide with the famous *Carnevale* that preceded the period of Lent each year.

Although they may not have realised it, many Grand Tourists were on a journey of self-discovery and self-definition, and this shines out from the portraits they commissioned while abroad. Imagine you were one of them: you would naturally choose the artist best suited to create the image you wanted to project to the world. While in Rome you might commission an impressive oil painting, perhaps full-length, from an artist such as Pompeo Batoni (1708–1787), that reverberated with allusions to your wealth and status and set the scene by including a recognisable ruin or work of art in the background. In Venice, however, you might be inclined to choose a softer, more intimate kind of portrait, in which case you would visit the studio of the famous Carriera, who became so sought after she declared herself 'attacked by the English'.[4] Her innovative portraits zoomed in on her sitter's faces to produce images that focused intensely on the individual, and largely jettisoned the usual props signalling wealth and status. She achieved this through the medium of pastel: Carriera drew, rather than painted, portraits and raised the status of the medium by demonstrating how it could convey the psychological states of her sitters and the sensuous lustre of skin, hair and eyes. Although this dry, powdery medium had the disadvantage of being fragile and easily spoiled by touch – portraits had to be framed and glazed to protect their surfaces – it needed no drying time like oil paint. The portrait could be collected from the artist's studio as soon as it was complete and packed up to be shipped back home.

Among the visitors to knock on Carriera's door in the early 1730s was the young Irish aristocrat Gustavus Hamilton, 2nd Viscount Boyne (fig. 51). In her portrait, Carriera includes no props to convey his identity. Quite the opposite, in fact: at any moment, it seems, the sitter could disguise himself with the *bauta*, or traditional Venetian carnival mask, that he wears casually pushed to the side of his head. Pastel itself was a medium capable of both revealing and concealing; free of the formality of oil painting, it is one in which the mask and the intimate self can be hard to untangle. Here Carriera, a master of the medium, mimics the various textures in front of her, from the soft, powdery skin of her sitter's slightly androgynous face to the sheen of his coat and the luminosity of his eyes. And yet alongside this virtuosic treatment of surface, Carriera also conveys a subtle guardedness she has perceived in Hamilton's expression – a youthful vulnerability faintly perceptible behind the mask.

The year 1720 had been a milestone in Carriera's career. Not only had she been admitted in January to Bologna's Accademia Clementina, an art academy founded in 1706, but she also had the opportunity to travel to Paris. She and her brother-in-law, the painter Antonio Pellegrini (1675–1741), had been introduced to Pierre Crozat, a wealthy banker and art collector with a particular passion for drawings. 'Crozat *le pauvre*', as he was ironically called to distinguish him from his yet wealthier brother, invited the Venetians to stay at his grand house on the Rue de Richelieu. With a purpose-built gallery

　THE STORY OF DRAWING

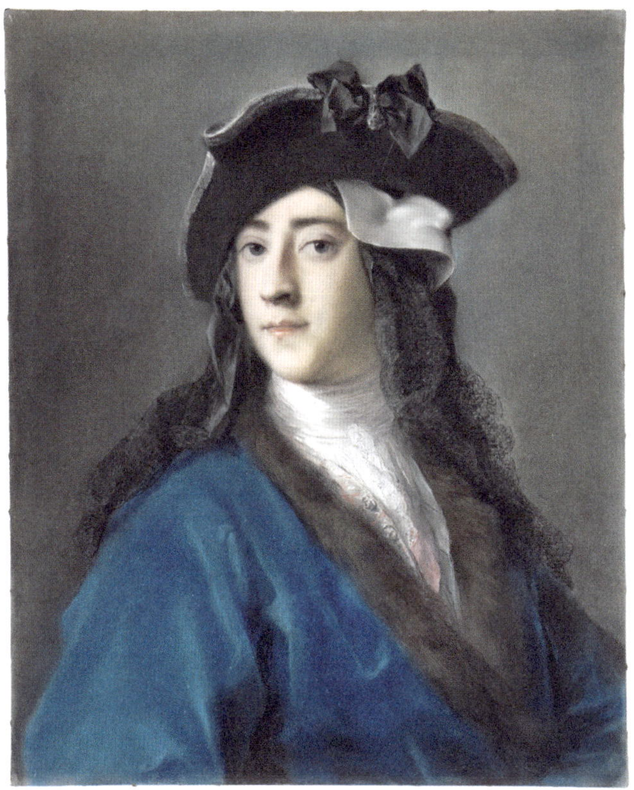

51. Rosalba Carriera, *Gustavus Hamilton (1710–1746),
Second Viscount Boyne, in Masquerade Costume, c.* 1730–1.
Pastel on paper, laid down on canvas.

to house his collection, the Hôtel de Crozat offered what amounted
to a highly concentrated Grand Tour. The year that Carriera spent
in France was a resounding success: she was commissioned to draw
a pastel portrait and a miniature of Louis XV, then a boy of ten,
and the following year was received into the prestigious Académie
Royale de Peinture et de Sculpture. But perhaps her most profound
experiences came through the friends she made among Parisian artists, chiefly another some-time resident of Crozat's house, Antoine
Watteau (1684–1721).[5] Watteau, employed by Crozat to paint
a decorative scheme representing the four seasons in his dining
room, perfected a genre in French painting that became known
as the *fête galante*, in which groups of elegantly dressed young
people disport themselves in a parkland setting. Carriera's sensitive,

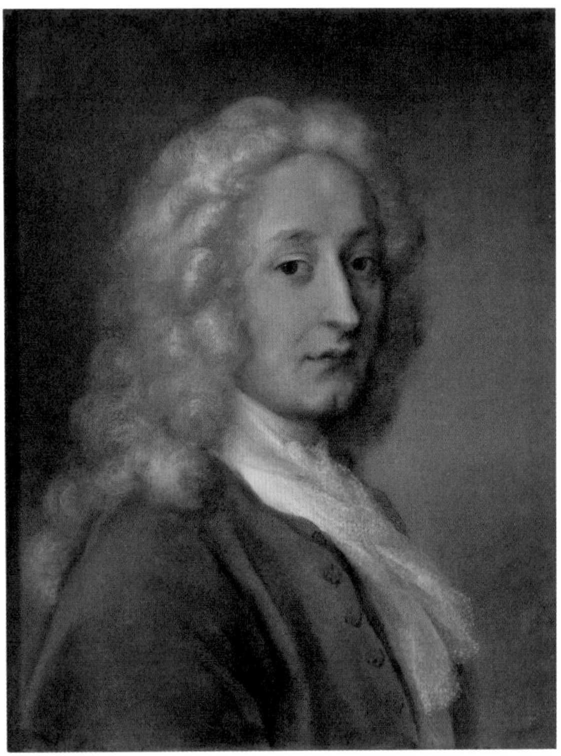

52. Rosalba Carriera,
Antoine Watteau, 1721.
Pastel.

psychologically penetrating pastel portrait of Watteau, drawn just months before his death from tuberculosis at the age of thirty-six, captures the same mood of wistful melancholy that hangs over his paintings (fig. 52). His eyes do not quite meet the viewer's, his gaze instead seeming to be turned reflectively inwards.

But Watteau did look at the world, and drew it fluently, incisively and with an apparently boundless interest in humanity and subtle variations of pose and expression. Workers, dancers, soldiers, actors, performers and musicians; the fashionably dressed, the semi-dressed and the nude; heads of men, women, children and animals from numerous angles – all went down on paper. While other artists made drawings as part of the process of planning a composition, Watteau did the opposite. He drew for its own sake on the pages of bound volumes, so that when he came to devise a painting he could turn the pages and choose a particular head or figure that would suit the composition he had in mind. He even made counterproofs – prints made by pressing a slightly dampened sheet of paper against the surface of a

                          THE STORY OF DRAWING

freshly made chalk drawing to take an impression – in order to create a useful mirror image of a pose he particularly liked. He made huge numbers of studies from models, and according to his first biographer, the Comte de Caylus, 'owned some fashionable costumes, and some theatrical ones, in which he used to dress his models of both sexes, until he found someone prepared to stay still, who he drew in whatever pose they adopted, much preferring those that were simpler'.[6]

Watteau drew with black, white and red chalks, often combining the three in a technique known as *trois crayons*. He chose fibrous buff paper because its mid-tone and slight texture acted as a foil for the rich chalky pigments. Despite the sheer number of sketches he produced, he did not fall back on a formula, but instead combined his materials as required by each individual subject.[7] One day he studied the head and shoulders of a young black boy, drawing him once, twice, three times on the same sheet, asking him to adopt three different poses in order to explore his features and expressions (fig. 53). Watteau

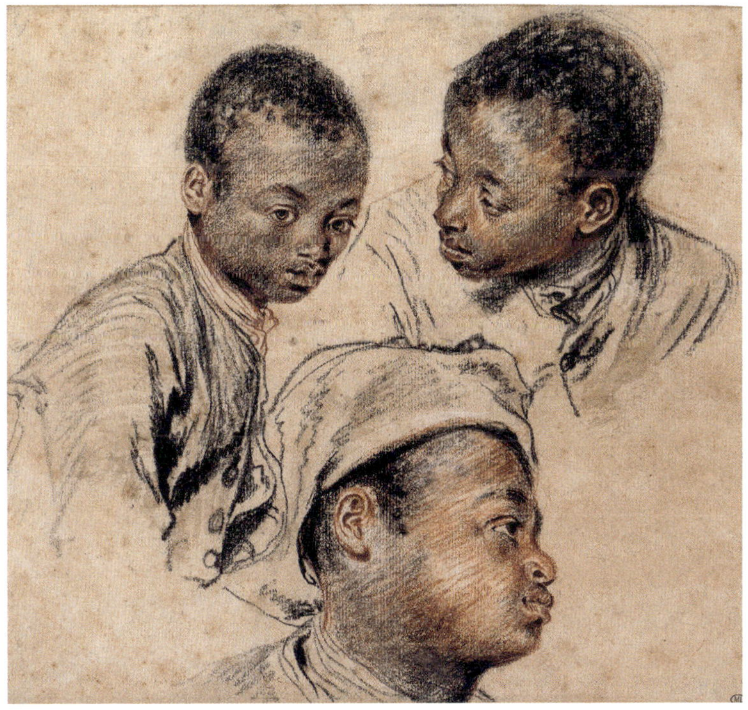

53. Antoine Watteau, *Three Studies of a Young Man*, c. 1718. Black, red and white chalks with grey wash.

blended red and black chalks to convey the colour of the boy's skin, and added touches of white to suggest the fall of light on his cheek and forehead.[8] Watteau returned to this lively sheet of studies twice, using the head at top right for figures in two separate paintings. At one time the drawing was owned by Pierre-Jean Mariette (1694–1774), one of the greatest connoisseurs and collectors of drawings of the era, who considered such works by Watteau to be *'d'une vérité frappante'* – of a striking truthfulness.[9]

CHAPTER 12

PLACES OF THE MIND

DRAWING WAS EXCELLENTLY suited to describing the visible world, whether the stripes of a zebra or the turn of an ankle. What, though, about the realm of the imagination?

Tourists to Venice not only wished to mark their visit with portraits of themselves: they wanted representations of the city, too. If they went to Rome to see classical antiquities and Florence for its magnificent works of art, they visited Venice because it was a spectacle in itself, not only during *Carnevale* – which coincided with the opera season – but at all times of year, whether May sent reflections dancing over the old stones or November veiled the palazzi in mist. One had only to stroll or drift through its streets and canals to see hundreds of exquisite vistas composing themselves for a few seconds at a time before one's eyes. Naturally many artists set themselves up to create *vedute*, or views of the city, to sell to tourists, and among the artists who made a living doing this was Giovanni Antonio Canal (1697–1768), known as Canaletto – little Canal – to distinguish him from his father Bernardo Canal (1664–1744), a painter of theatrical scenery.

But even Venice could be improved. Canaletto began his working life with his father, painting scenery for operas by Antonio Vivaldi in his native city and Alessandro Scarlatti in Rome, and he brought the skills he had learned from theatrical perspective and illusionism to his city views. Although later he 'solemnly excommunicated the theatre', as he put it, when he came to concentrate on producing realistic views he had few scruples about moving buildings around or eliminating them entirely, changing proportions and altering perspectives to suit his compositions.[1] In the early 1740s, probably because the outbreak of the War of the Austrian Succession in 1740 interrupted tourism and made it difficult to send paintings abroad, he more or less stopped painting *vedute* and focused instead on drawing. Many of the pen and ink drawings he produced at this time were *capricci* – a word derived from the Italian for the capering of a goat, indicating fanciful or fantastical content. Existing buildings might find striking new settings in these drawings: San Marco, for instance, could be rolled to the edge of the lagoon, and one of the lions from the Piazzetta dei Leoni removed from its setting and perched on a shore amid fragments of broken architecture. Others were entirely imaginary, the familiar Venetian architectural vocabulary mixed up to create new sentences. Canaletto imagined grand courtyards lined with towering facades, monumental staircases topped with great urns and ruined arches overgrown with plants (fig. 54). His *capricci* are evocative poetry to the crisp prose of his *vedute*. Rather than the fine, regular strokes of the pen he used to depict many Venetian buildings and squares, which he usually made over carefully ruled graphite lines, in these drawings he allowed his quill to waver inkily, to meander and hesitate. He took up a brush and painted atmospheric grey watercolour washes to darken the skies and shadow the crumbling masonry. These drawings seem intended to provoke reflections on the passing of time – although it is a pleasurable sort of melancholy. His Venice is a stage, and his drawings amusing, scene-setting backdrops to the unfolding theatre of Venetian life.

Giovanni Battista Piranesi (1720–1778), an artist of a younger generation, also drew serial city views and architectural fantasies; but that is largely where the similarity ends. In the mid-eighteenth century the cultural climate was changing fast. Enlightenment thinking was pushing people to look at the world in new ways and ask fundamental questions: how do we know things? Can we trust our senses? What is our relationship with the past? History was a constant presence for Piranesi. He spent his early years in Venice, but it was the architecture of Rome, where in 1740 he went to work as a draughtsman, that came to haunt his imagination.[2] For him, the relationship between ancient and modern buildings was dynamic and by no means clear cut; he responded both intellectually and

    THE STORY OF DRAWING

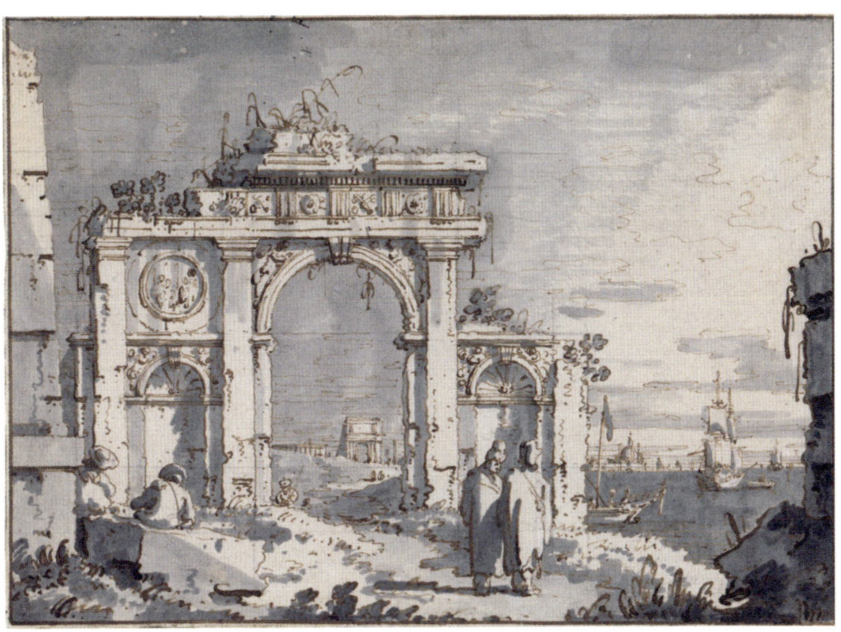

54. Canaletto, *A Capriccio of a Ruined Arch on the Shores of a Lagoon*, *c*. 1740–60. Pen and ink, with bluish-grey wash, over graphite.

emotionally to the monumental architecture that surrounded him. While still in his early twenties and producing topographical drawings of the city to be etched and used to illustrate guidebooks, he found an outlet for his passion by drawing architectural fantasies in which he reimagined triumphal arches and colossal palace facades. They were not *capricci* so much as dystopian dreams of totalitarian rule. His original, visionary approach supercharged his *Vedute di Roma*, a series he had begun by 1747 and on which he was still working at the time of his death. Overwhelming and unsettling, these large-scale etchings were so dramatic that when the German writer Johann Wolfgang von Goethe, who had come to know Rome through the *Vedute*, first visited the city, he confessed that at first sight the real thing did not quite measure up.[3]

Piranesi's drawings and etchings, whether of ancient buildings in Rome or Paestum or structures from his imagination, drag the past into the present where it bristles with unspent energy. In his series of *Carceri*, or prisons, he goes further, explicitly exploring architecture as a metaphor for physical and psychological oppression. First issued as a set of etchings between 1749 and 1750 and reissued in reworked form in 1761, Piranesi's *Carceri* images dwell obsessively on dark and complex prison interiors that stretch out of sight, seemingly into infinity. One drawing reveals his process of designing each space: having lightly sketched some broad structural details with a pen, he added watery areas of wash with a brush to suggest mysterious and occluded areas of the vast echoing spaces, to blur definite lines and thwart the eye as it searches in vain for logical linear structure, even just a safe place to rest (fig. 55).[4]

Towards the end of the eighteenth century and the beginning of the nineteenth, the nightmarish *Carceri* images struck a chord with a generation of Romantic writers who were interested in exploring the darkest corners of the mind. Samuel Taylor Coleridge described them to his friend Thomas De Quincey as:

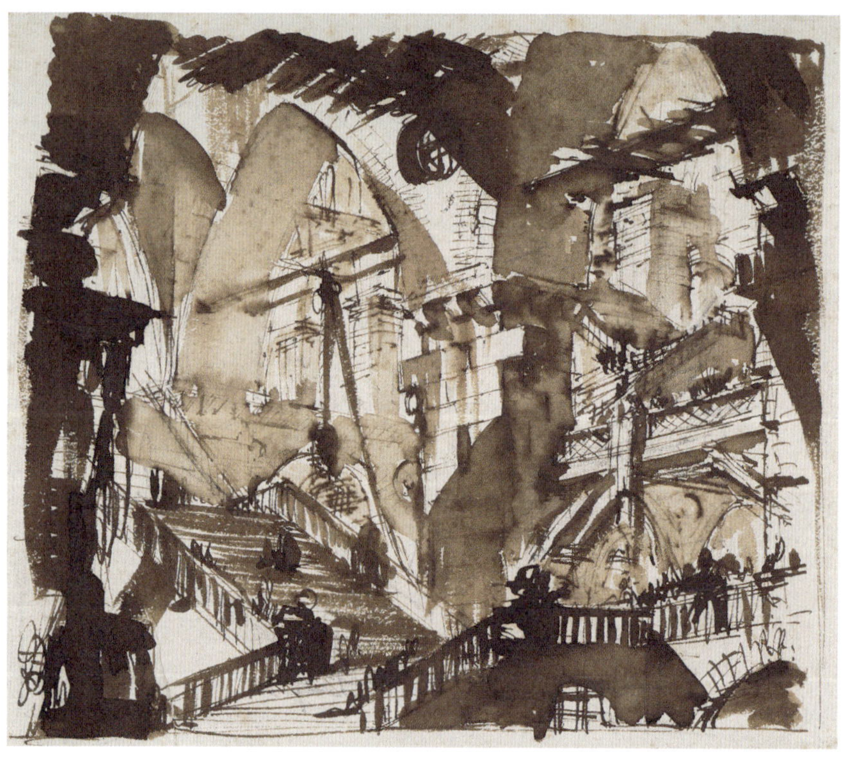

55. Giovanni Battista Piranesi, *An Imaginary Prison*, c. 1755–61.
Pen, brown ink and wash over black chalk.

                                    THE STORY OF DRAWING

vast Gothic halls: on the floor of which stood all sorts of engines and machinery, wheels, cables, pulleys, levers, catapults, &c. &c. expressive of enormous power put forth and resistance overcome. Creeping along the sides of the walls, you perceived a staircase; and upon it, groping his way upwards, was Piranesi himself: follow the stairs a little further, and you perceive it come to a sudden abrupt termination, without any balustrade, and allowing no step onwards to him who had reached the extremity, except into the depths below.[5]

One should perhaps, however, be wary of imposing a Romantic interpretation on to these images. Prison scenes in early eighteenth-century theatre and opera were common, and Piranesi's *Carceri* owe much to designs by decorative and architectural artists such as Francesco Galli Bibiena (1659–1739), Marco Ricci (1676–1730) and Luigi Vanvitelli (1700–1773).[6] And yet the fractured, vertiginous staircases and windowless vaults that Piranesi conjured up with his pen, brush and etching needle resonate long in the mind and express an aspect of the human condition with piercing accuracy.

Elsewhere it was recognised that the very act of drawing could liberate the imagination. One day, the English artist and drawing master Alexander Cozens (1717–1786) was giving a lesson during which he was reflecting on landscape composition when his eye fell upon a scrap of paper spoiled with an inky blot.[7] The form of this mark seemed to him to suggest a landscape, so he took a brush and doodled on the sheet, which he then pushed over to his student, who 'improved' the composition with a few lines of his own. Discovering that Leonardo da Vinci himself, in his *Treatise on Painting*, had recommended a similar 'method of assisting the invention' that involved paying attention to accidental marks on dirty walls that might evoke some figure or subject in the artist's mind, Cozens developed his idea into a method for creating ideal landscapes (fig. 56). The artist should begin by forming a 'blot', which, he explained in a drawing manual, 'is an assemblage of dark shapes or masses made with ink upon a piece of paper ... All the shapes are rude and unmeaning, as they are formed with the swiftest hand.'[8] At the next stage, the artist should take a piece of semi-transparent paper, lay it over the

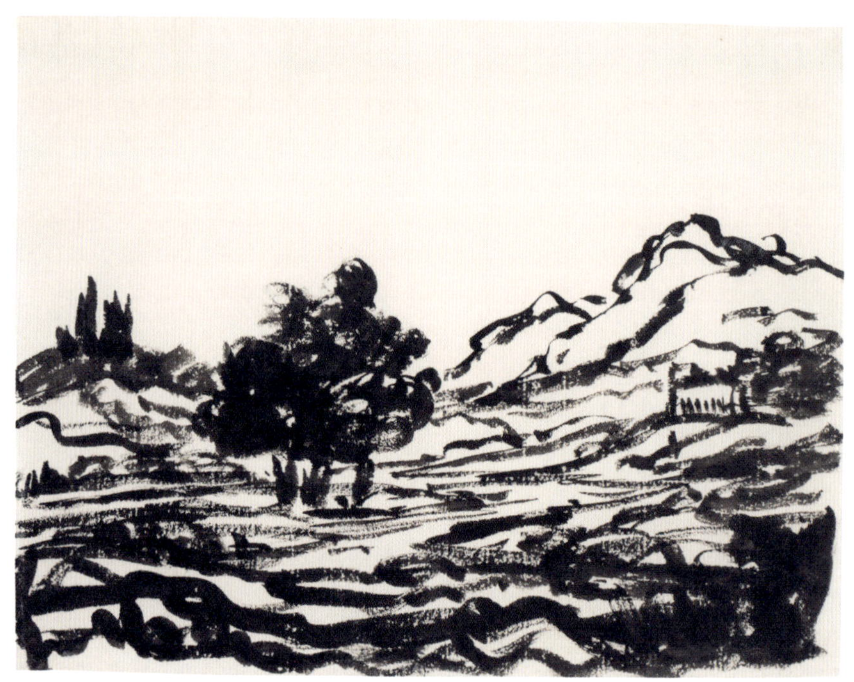

56. Alexander Cozens, *'Blot' Landscape, c.* 1750–86.
Brush and black ink.

top of the blot and begin a drawing of whatever landscape form it suggested, whether mountains, forests or valleys – thus coming up with an entirely original composition. This artistic Rorschach experiment was designed to tap directly into an inner reservoir of creativity that could, in Cozens's theory, be sealed by too much conscious thought.

If the imaginations of Cozens's students could be tickled into life with an inky brush, that of Thomas Gainsborough (1727–1788) was set in motion by prosaic household objects. His highly successful portrait business – 'phizmongering', as he disparagingly called it – in the fashionable spa town of Bath kept him away from the landscapes he loved and which, as a young man in Suffolk, he had drawn compulsively.[9] So, when relaxing in the evenings, he gathered his drawing materials and imagined them instead. Calling for a little folding table kept under the kitchen dresser, he would assemble a few props with which to create model landscapes: he found that lumps of coal served as rocks, sand or clay could be formed into banks,

                    THE STORY OF DRAWING

and stems of broccoli, artfully arranged, made convincing groves of trees, while if bushes or ponds were needed, moss and mirror-glass would do very well. Once he was satisfied, he would take inspiration from the tabletop scene and draw a landscape with rich, dense strokes of black and white chalk, rubbing it here and there when he wanted a smoky effect and sometimes adding watercolour with a small sponge that he held with sugar tongs (fig. 57). The coal, broccoli and mirror-glass, however, were only catalysts. The drawings Gainsborough made from them were shaped by his vast mental database both of the Dutch and Flemish landscape art he loved and of the countryside scenes he had by heart. As his first biographer recorded, there was 'not a Picturesque clump of Trees . . . nor hedgerow, stone, or post . . . for some miles round about the place of his nativity, that he had not so perfectly in his *mind's eye*, that had he known he *could use* a pencil, he could have perfectly delineated'.[10]

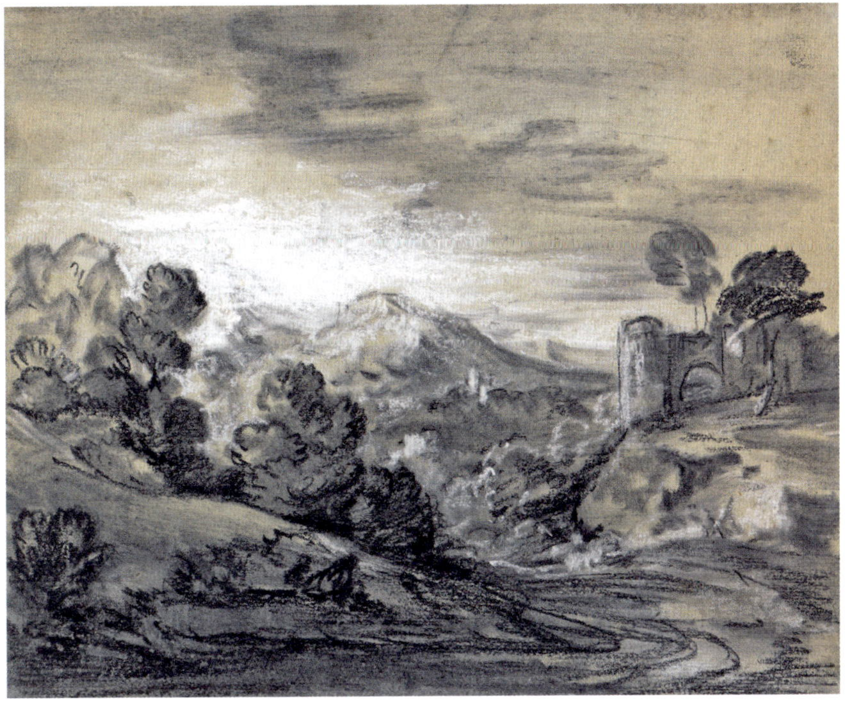

57. Thomas Gainsborough, *Wooded Landscape with Castle*, c. 1785–8. Black chalk and stumping with white chalk on light blue paper, faded to buff.

Throughout history men and women have gazed up at the night skies and wondered about the moon. Philosophers, writers, artists and dreamers have all projected fantasies onto its face; some have imagined this alternative world to be a place of divine presence, or as home to the man in the moon, while others have imagined voyaging there. Imagination was first tempered by fact in 1609, when the Italian scientist Galileo Galilei trained a telescope at it and made a series of drawings documenting its phases. By the late eighteenth century, advances in telescopy allowed the moon's surface to be studied in greater detail than ever before. Among those entranced by the astonishing new world that appeared through the telescope's lens was the artist John Russell (1745–1806), a technically brilliant pastellist who modelled his style on that of Rosalba Carriera and specialised in portraits and sentimental 'fancy pictures'.

Russell had been fascinated by the moon since he was a young man, when one evening a sculptor friend had invited him to look through the telescope in his garden. Over the years Russell made many sketches of the moon's surface, but in 1795 his interest became intense when, with the help of the astronomer William Herschel, he gained access to the most up-to-date telescope available, a Dollond achromatic refractor. The same year he created a vast pastel drawing of the moon's surface, over five feet square. Russell's process was painstaking and systematic. When the weather allowed, and the moon was at a suitable phase, he trained the telescope on a small part of it at a time and made a careful drawing. Eventually he pieced these together – 137 in total – in order to create his great pastel (fig. 58).[11] A scientist would probably have chosen to draw the full moon, yet Russell – who was, after all, a portraitist – preferred to wait for it to be gibbous so that the shadow emphasised its rounded form and raking light threw craters and ridges into high relief. The resulting pastel, which today hangs on the staircase of Oxford's History of Science Museum, is astonishing and captivating. When completed, it was the most accurate representation of the moon's surface to date, and Russell used it as a model when he produced engravings for a groundbreaking lunar globe that he called

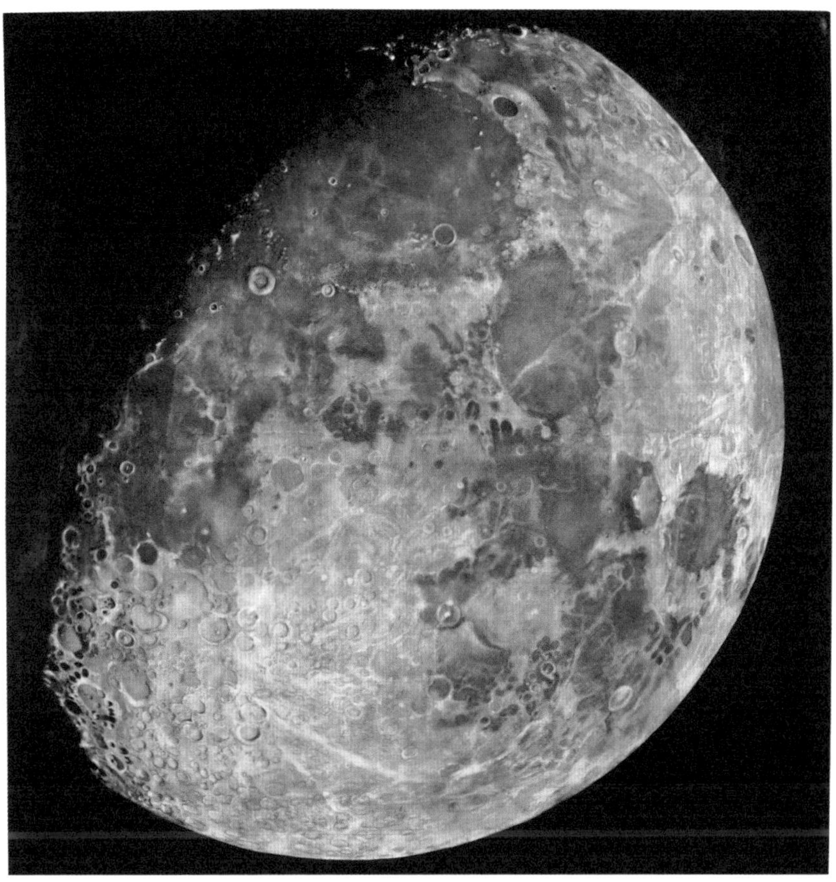

58. John Russell, *Moon*, 1795. Pastel.

the 'selenographia' after Selene, the Greek goddess of the moon. But the sense of wonder the moon has always evoked is not reduced but magnified by this searching portrait. With the sensuous medium of pastel, Russell brought this place of dreams and legends so close one can almost reach out and touch it.

CHAPTER 13

MARBLES AND MODELS

A SKETCHBOOK CAN act as a visual diary. As we turn the pages we can often pinpoint where an artist was, and whom they met. Ideas flare on the sheet which might – or might not – grow exponentially. Sometimes, in the pages of a young artist's sketchbook, we can watch them as they find their way, define themselves and come into focus.

Angelica Kauffman (1741–1807), a young Swiss artist, took a new sketchbook with her when she set out for Italy with her father, a portrait painter and muralist, and made drawings in it over the next three or four years. Recognised as a prodigy, Kauffman had undertaken several portrait commissions herself before she was fifteen, so when she arrived in Florence in 1762 at the age of twenty-one it was with distinct ambitions. She wanted to be more than a portraitist and to paint the grand scenes from history, literature and myth that were, at the time, regarded as the highest form of art. But as a woman, she faced a familiar problem: pictures like these, which told their stories through poses and gestures, naturally required a thorough training in human anatomy. Although within months of her arrival in the city she was elected as a member of Florence's prestigious Accademia del Disegno (founded in 1563), the doors of the spaces in which aspiring male artists learned by drawing the nude model were still closed to her. The same was true of the Accademia di San Luca in Rome, where father and daughter settled the following

year, as well as its associated Accademia del Nudo.[1] By following a
curriculum of drawing and being instructed on subjects from anatomy
to perspective, male students acquired the grounding they needed to
practise as artists. No less important was the social environment, and
the atmosphere of talk and debate through which they made lasting
friendships and connections.

So how did Kauffman, on the outside of this, make her way? If
you turn the pages of her sketchbook, you can trace her industrious
campaign.[2] She engaged female models to pose for her; she made
studies of drapery; she travelled widely and copied paintings, sculptures,
prints and drawings; she drew portraits, particularly of the British
community in Rome – a clever strategy, as many became her friends;
she took lessons in perspective, possibly from Piranesi, whose portrait
appears in these pages; and she studied the antique sculpture that
made the entire city a potential art academy for those who wished
to learn.[3] There were the Capitoline Museums, which had opened
in 1734, and which housed celebrated ancient statues such as the

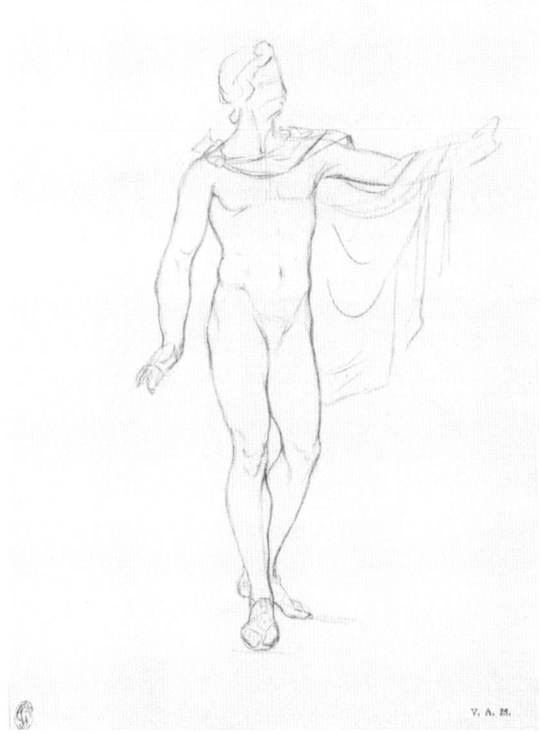

59. Angelica Kauffman,
page from a sketchbook
used in Rome: *Apollo
Belvedere*, c. 1762–6.
Graphite and black chalk.

Dying Gladiator (a wounded Celt) and the Spinario (a boy pulling a thorn from his foot); there were aristocratic private collections, such as those in the Farnese and Borghese palaces; and there was the Belvedere Courtyard in the Vatican, which was purpose-built to display antique sculpture including the Belvedere Torso and the Apollo Belvedere. A drawing in Kauffman's sketchbook of the latter, deft and economical strokes of black chalk establishing its outlines and musculature, gives a vivid sense of her presence in the space (fig. 59). It is, however, noticeably more summary than the drawings on other pages.[4] Did she attract unwelcome attention, this young woman with her sketchbook, staring intently at a strikingly beautiful nude male body? Did she cut her sketching session short as a result? There can have been little privacy for her in the courtyard. At the Uffizi in Florence, she obtained permission to copy pictures in a private room.

As well as drawing marble sculptures and plaster casts of male figures, Kauffman copied life drawings by other artists.[5] But it was an inadequate, second-hand way of acquiring knowledge of musculature and bone structure; lack of access to the nude model was an obstacle that would hamper female artists until the end of the nineteenth century. A sense of how improper it would have seemed for a female artist to appear in the life room is underlined by an oil painting of 1771–2 by Johan Zoffany (1733–1810), which represents founder members of the Royal Academy of Arts (founded in 1768), one of whom was Kauffman, who had settled in London two years previously and quickly risen in the male-dominated art world. The new academicians gather together in the life room in the presence of a nude male model, so Kauffman and the only other female member, Mary Moser (1744–1819), are represented by their portraits hanging on the wall.[6]

But Kauffman was nothing if not enterprising. Frustrated by her exclusion, she took matters into her own hands and arranged private life-drawing classes by asking a model regularly employed at the Academy to sit for her at home at nearby Golden Square. Many years later, a member of London's art establishment heard an old rumour of this and took it upon himself to investigate. He tracked down and interviewed the model, by then an old man, and was told that although he 'did frequently sit before Angelica Kauffman at her

                              THE STORY OF DRAWING

house . . . he only exposed his arms, shoulders, and legs, and that her father, who was also an artist and likewise an exhibitor at the Royal Academy, was always present'.[7]

'The antique will not seduce me,' announced Jacques-Louis David (1748–1825) before leaving Paris for Rome in 1775.[8] He had, in fact, been longing for the chance to go, presumably for the opportunities it offered to study Italian Renaissance and Baroque paintings. Three times already he had tried and failed to win the coveted Prix de Rome, which enabled prizewinners to study at the Académie de France, established in the city since 1666. When success arrived at the fourth attempt, David found his certainties eroding. François Boucher (1703–1770) was a distant cousin, and although the older artist had declined to take him as a student, his style exerted a distinct influence. There could hardly have been a greater contrast between the softness and frivolity of Boucher's paintings and the heroic works of art and fragmented grandeur that David found in Rome. Seduced in spite of himself by the antique, over the next five years he abandoned himself to the art and architecture of the city, eventually making around 2,000 drawings that he pasted into albums. As his friend the archaeologist Alexandre Lenoir put it, 'like a schoolboy he set about drawing, for a whole year, eyes, ears, mouths, feet and hands and was content to execute complete figures after the most beautiful statues' (fig. 60).[9] It was as though he were learning a new language in which individual body parts were words, to be assembled together with the grammar of compositional groups. The drawings in his albums formed a glossary to which he would go for inspiration for the rest of his career – the art of ancient Rome had become central to his way of thinking.[10]

As a prominent member of the radical Jacobin party, David went on to apply this visual language to the paintings he created in the service of the French Revolution, drawing on its directness and strong outlines to underline the republic's fundamental difference from the *ancien régime*. This new art would meet the latter's Rococo flourishes with discipline, and counter its licentiousness with moral seriousness. It was to play an active part in politics and society, even recording events as they occurred. On 16 October 1793, from his place among the crowds who gathered to watch Marie Antoinette being carted towards the guillotine, David made a rapid pen sketch

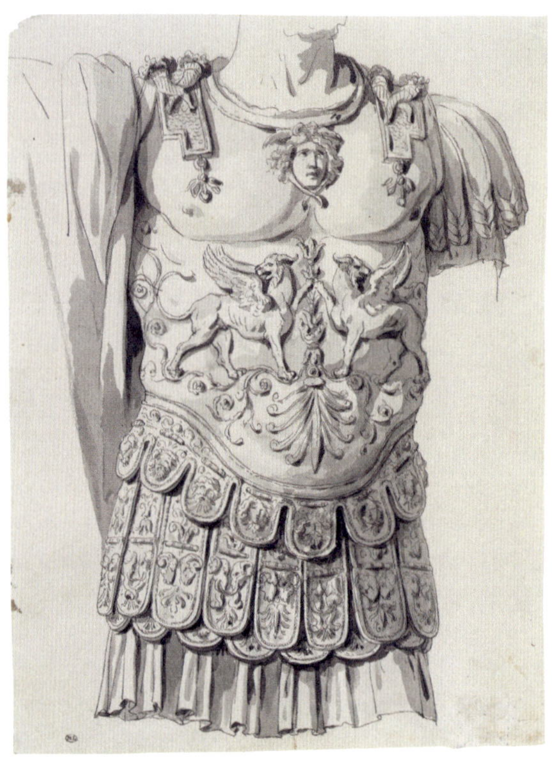

60. Jacques-Louis David, *A Roman Cuirass, Copied from a Colossal Statue of Mars in the Capitoline Museum, Rome,* c. 1775–80. Black ink and grey wash.

of the former queen in profile, noting her crudely scissored hair poking out in tufts from beneath a simple mob cap, her downcast eyes and the rigid set of her mouth (fig. 61). With an uncompromising linearity in opposition to the flattering Rococo shading that had formerly been applied to the queen, David reframed her in revolutionary terms. This dispatch from the front line is as direct and shocking as a shout.

David may have become the most influential artist of what became known as Neo-classicism – a style that took inspiration from the art of ancient Greece and Rome – but it spread beyond painting to colour just about every aspect of life in the late eighteenth and early nineteenth century. The 'neo', or new, in its name was important: its appearance was strikingly modern. The style's ubiquity in design was partly due to its pared-down linearity; it lent itself to the decoration of domestic objects of all kinds, from teacups and vases to chairs and tables. After a period spent as a designer for the firm of Josiah Wedgwood, in 1787 the aspiring English sculptor

  THE STORY OF DRAWING

John Flaxman (1755–1826) travelled to Rome in order to draw from the antique. Not long afterwards he was commissioned to illustrate the Homeric epics the *Iliad* and the *Odyssey*, which on being engraved and published in 1793 became outstandingly popular; reprints and piracies spread the images far and wide. Flaxman had looked hard at Greek vases, and engravings reproducing them, and from these models he developed an innovative drawing style. Cutting out all superfluous lines and shading, the spare outline drawings with which he gave visual form to the poems were startlingly simple, leaving broad areas of untouched blank page.[11] Nonetheless, they packed a psychological punch: Flaxman had discovered a way of boiling down the drama to form a rich emotional concentrate.

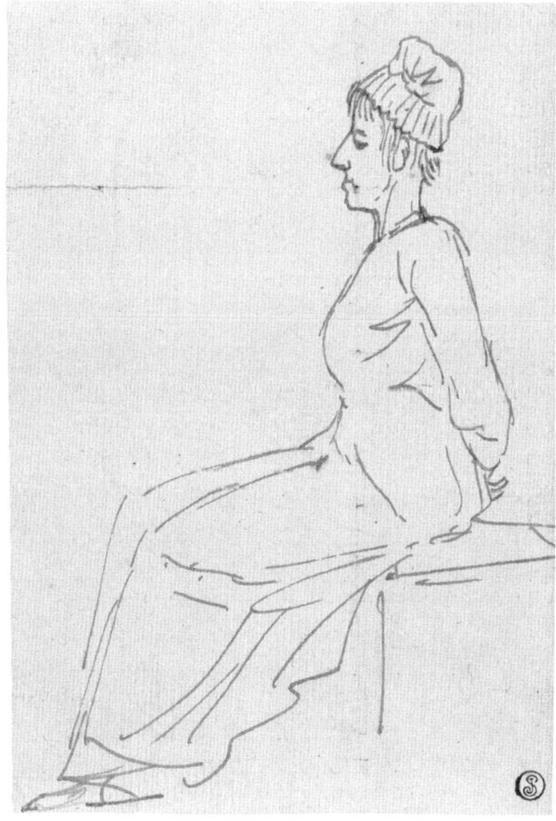

61. Jacques-Louis David, *Marie-Antoinette, Queen of France, Led to Execution*, 1793. Pen and brown ink.

A figure sits hunched in an attitude of despair, one hand covering his face (fig. 62). Perched on a stone block at the base of two gigantic

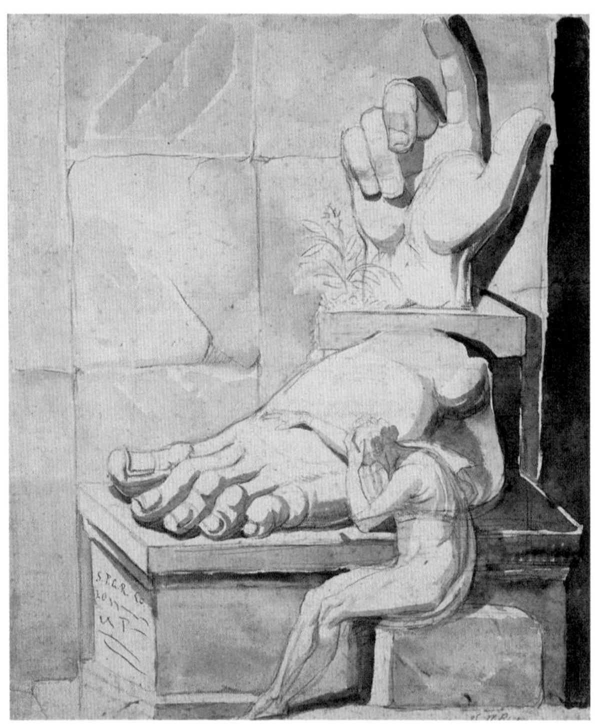

62. Henry Fuseli, *The Artist Moved by the Grandeur of Antique Fragments*, *c.* 1778–9. Pen and sepia ink, wash and red chalk.

pieces of marble sculpture, he reaches out to touch the foot of the Colossus of Constantine (displayed then, as now, in the courtyard of the Palazzo dei Conservatori in Rome), his hand as feeble as a small bird against its muscular bulk. Above his head, as if in mockery, Constantine's massive right hand points a finger up towards the sky. It is a challenge the figure looks unlikely to meet.

The Swiss artist Henry Fuseli (1741–1825) drew this scene around 1778–9, after eight years spent in Rome. If many European and British artists regarded the city as an extension of the art academy, with antique sculptures as exemplars of supreme artistic achievement, Fuseli and the international circle he gathered around him were more concerned with the emotional intensity they sensed smouldering beneath the surfaces of these works of art. 'Expression animates, convulses, or absorbs form,' he wrote a few years later. 'The Apollo is animated; the warrior of Agasias is agitated; the Laocoon is con-vulsed; the Niobe is absorbed.'[12] To him, these admired sculptures were not passive but alive with their makers' feelings and capable

THE STORY OF DRAWING

of evoking passionate responses in those who contemplated them. Fuseli's choice of fluid inky wash and vivid red chalk for the drawing that came to be called *The Artist Moved by the Grandeur of Antique Fragments* makes these sculptures feel alive: the marble toes seem about to twitch, the hand to straighten its other fingers. For Fuseli, these awe-inspiring fragments posed questions that went to the heart of what it was to be human: how could one measure oneself against the ancients? Comprehend the passage of time that eventually saw even this once-colossal statue tumbled down and broken up, and come to terms with its implications for one's own mortality? Reach deeply into one's soul and find the courage to create in the face of such magnificence?

This highly charged drawing dates from the year of Piranesi's death, and it has been suggested that Fuseli made it to commemorate this artist who shared his intense emotional response to the evocative contrasts between ancient and modern that were built into the fabric of the city.[13] But if it looks back, it also looks forward to new ways of looking at the world in which drawing played a major role.

CHAPTER 14

OBSERVATION AND IMAGINATION

THE CLEAN, MODERN lines of neo-classicism seemed proof against superstition, designed to harbour no dark corners in which the disturbing or the monstrous could gather. Yet as the eighteenth century progressed, many artists began to look inwards, increasingly enthralled by the fantastic and the supernatural. Private and experimental, drawing was the arena in which these ideas were explored.

In 1770s Rome, Fuseli and his circle of artists from Denmark, Sweden, France, Scotland and England absorbed lessons from the antique sculpture and Old Masters that surrounded them, but rejected academic restraint in favour of expressive exaggeration.[1] If the confident lines of David and Flaxman spoke of intellectual clarity and control, the billowing, swelling inky washes now dashed and leaked onto paper by these artists murmured of inchoate, unruly emotions and ideas. Ghosts and witches were represented with contorted poses and vehement gestures; states of horror and madness were conveyed with dramatic chiaroscuro contrasts between light and dark. When these artists looked into the liquid depths of the ink, it was as though they found the darkest corners of their minds reflected there. Fuseli looked the hardest and reached the furthest. In England, where he settled after Rome, he explored erotic and pornographic fantasies with ink and watercolour on paper, obsessively drawing courtesans engaged in sexual role play and his wife Sophia with a fetishistic focus on her intricate and gravity-defying coiffures.[2] The result is a series of enigmatic drawings whose exceptional finesse is matched only by their outstanding strangeness; they can only have remained clandestine in his lifetime.

But if Fuseli plunged deeply into his imagination and into plays and poems for his material, Francisco Goya (1746–1828), who had left Spain to study in Rome himself between 1769 and 1771, turned his eyes on the world around him. He saw enough there of horror, cruelty and perversity in human behaviour to fuel a lifetime of picture-making. The career he pursued as a painter took him to the heart of the Spanish court and brought him an international reputation, yet it is his prints and drawings that most people know today. After an illness in 1792–3 that deprived him of his hearing, he began to record his thoughts and observations through drawings in sketchbooks or 'journal albums'.[3] On these pages Goya focused with fierce intensity on human nature: he began with drawings of women dancing, cleaning or sleeping, but then went on to create more ambitious groups of figures interacting with each other: arguing, inflicting pain or getting drunk. With these situations he held up a mirror to humanity, exposing cruelty, self-deception and ignorance.

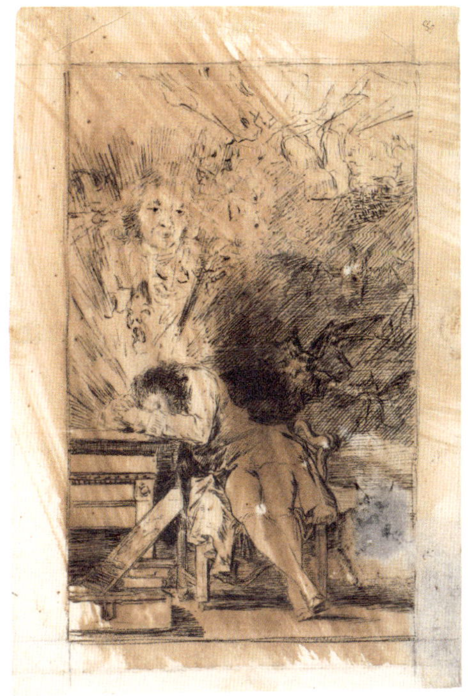

63. Francisco Goya, *The Sleep of Reason Produces Monsters*, *c.* 1796–7. Pen and iron-gall ink.

He gave many of his drawings pithy captions. 'The sleep of reason produces monsters', says one, which he adapted for a series of etchings he called *Los caprichos – Fantasies –* published in 1799 (fig. 63). Goya's initial drawing for the plate is a self-portrait: an artist lays his head on his desk, and his room fills with sinister bat-like creatures and faces that shout and grimace as if in pain, materialising amid radiating lines scratched furiously onto the sheet as though the man's mind is generating these ghostly visions. The message is a moral one: clear thinking is essential if one is to keep horrors at bay. But the horrors came anyway. 'It's no use crying out', announces a red chalk drawing which he etched for a series called *Los desastres de la guerra* (*Disasters of War*); 'There is no one to help them', remarks another with equal bleakness. Both depict the injured and the dying, lying helpless on the ground. Not published until 1863, long after Goya's death, this series was provoked by the violence he witnessed during the Peninsular War, when in 1808 he was summoned to Zaragoza to record acts of Spanish resistance against French forces. In further groups of drawings Goya focused on the oppression suffered by the Spanish people under the Inquisition, and on themes of witchcraft and superstition. Whether Goya observed or imagined the subjects, all dwell on conflict, pain, stupidity, torture or oppression – on the absence of reason and tolerance governing human affairs and the irrational instincts that rush in to fill the void. Never had humanity's failings been drawn so relentlessly or from so many angles.

William Blake (1757–1827) was as fiercely critical of injustice as Goya, yet he expressed his outrage in terms of dreams and visions, parables and allegories. It was how his mind had always worked; as a small boy, Blake had witnessed angels singing in the branches of a tree on Peckham Rye common and spotted the biblical prophet Ezekiel in the fields. Later in life he summoned the spirits of Socrates, Charlemagne, Merlin, Boudicca and Robin Hood to appear before him in a London room so that he could draw their portraits. For Blake, the visionary world was every bit as real as the external one and could be reached by means of the imagination, and through drawing: at one point he claimed to be 'really drunk with intellectual vision whenever I take a pencil or graver into my hand'.[4] A political radical, he set out his vision for humanity's redemption – not with

                                THE STORY OF DRAWING

earthy sketches like Goya, but in hand-printed prophetic works of cosmic scope and boundless ambition.

A commission to produce illustrations for John Milton's epic poem *Paradise Lost* in the early 1800s gave Blake the opportunity to visualise a spiritual universe in which great forces not only of good and evil but also the more human impulses of ambition and control, subversion and authority were at play. In his watercolour drawing of a beautiful, heroic Satan calling the other rebel angels to conference, he drew on what he knew of the work of Michelangelo, in particular his mastery of the human body as an instrument for expressing shades of emotion (fig. 64). It is significant that Blake knew Michelangelo's work through reproductive engravings that gave it a powerful linearity: even when he was using watercolour washes to suggest three-dimensional form and space, Blake, who had himself trained as an engraver, employed a distinctive, supple ink contour. As much as his lines swirl, swoop and flame, they capture and express character with the incisiveness of those drawn by his

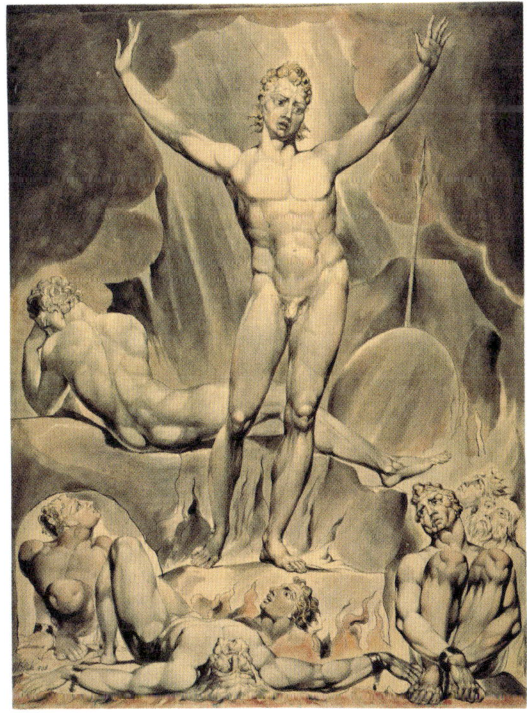

64. William Blake, *Satan Arousing the Rebel Angels*, 1808. Pen and ink and watercolour.

friend John Flaxman. For Blake, line was a moral issue. 'The great and golden rule of art . . . is this,' he wrote: 'that the more distinct and sharp and wiry the bounding line, the more perfect the work of art; and the less keen and sharp this external line, the greater is the evidence of weak imitative plagiarism and bungling . . . Leave out this line and you leave out life itself: all is chaos again.'[5] The lines Blake drew around his visions tether his gods, angels, devils and prophets to the human world and make them matter.

One day Blake was looking through a sketchbook belonging to John Constable (1776–1837), when he came across a drawing of fir trees on Hampstead Heath. 'Why, this is not drawing, but inspiration!' exclaimed Blake. 'I meant it for drawing,' was Constable's sarcastic reply.[6] In his own work, Blake had little interest in the landscape except as a symbolic setting for human or divine interaction. But for Constable everything in the natural environment, from the clouds drifting across the sky to the weeds growing at the side of a country lane, was worthy of the closest and most sustained attention.

The son of a gentleman farmer who owned land and mills on the Suffolk–Essex border, the young Constable spent a lot of time walking the fields and towpaths around his family home. Before his marriage in 1816, he returned there during the summer months and filled pocket-sized sketchbooks with drawings made outdoors. 'I live almost wholly in the fields and see nobody but the harvest men,' he wrote to his fiancée one August day in 1815.[7] Looking through these sketchbooks now is to walk alongside him on the paths and field margins and to see the scenes that caught his eye and where he stopped to draw them. Page after page, sometimes several fitted neatly onto the same tiny sheet, there are cornfields, hillsides, green lanes, ploughing teams, cottages, cows, mill ponds and labourers with scythes slung over bowed shoulders (fig. 65). Constable would take these sketchbooks back to London with him for the winter months when, working on a painting in his studio, he would turn the pages to be reminded of precious details that would reconnect him to the Suffolk landscape. Many years later, a drawing of a tumbledown fence on an old sketchbook page might suddenly be needed. Most landscape painters of the period generalised, as though it were improper to look too closely at the country, but not

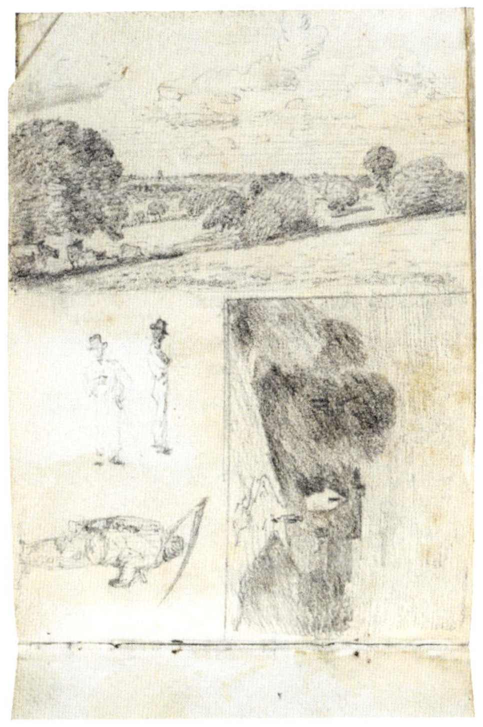

65. John Constable, page from a sketchbook, *c.* 1813–15. Graphite.

Constable. His particular kind of art, he once wryly observed, was 'to be found under every hedge and in every lane, and therefore nobody thinks it worth picking up'.[8]

Constable put graphite pencils in his pocket when he went out to sketch. He chose them because graphite was a versatile medium: good for both fine lines and thicker strokes, but also capable of producing deep shadows, and less liable to smudge or spill than either chalk or ink. They are so ubiquitous today that it can come as a surprise to remember that the high-quality processed graphite Constable was using had first became available as late as 1795, when he was already nineteen years old – though the pure mineral had been used as a drawing material since the second half of the sixteenth century (see Glossary). Constable used graphite pencils not only for sketchbooks but also for large and impressive drawings that are fully works of art in their own right (fig. 66). He had got to know the material so thoroughly he could exploit its range to the full, using it to make marks from the hard and linear to the soft and tonal, and plumbing its colours from silver to deep pewter

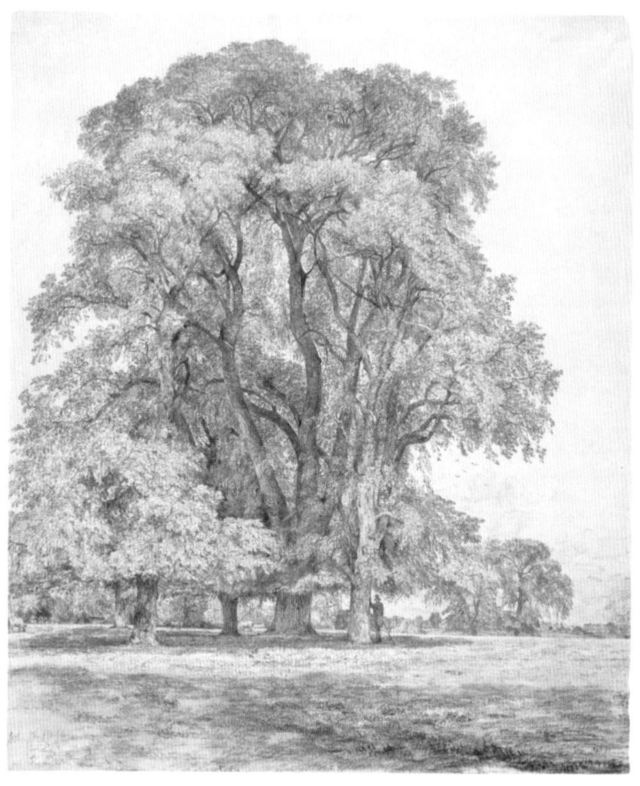

66. John Constable, *Elm Trees in Old Hall Park, East Bergholt*, 1817. Graphite, with slight grey and white washes.

grey. When he was drawing the trees he loved so much, he pushed its capabilities to attain a level of detail and complexity that had never before been achieved in nature studies.

Human sitters were to Jean-Auguste-Dominique Ingres (1780–1867) what trees were to Constable, and precise graphite was just as well suited to the subject. In fact his pencil portraits became so famous they threatened to overshadow what he considered to be his more serious work. 'Is this where the man who draws the little portraits lives?' asked tourists in Rome when they reached Ingres's door, eager to commission a likeness during their stay. 'No,' came the exasperated reply. 'The man who lives here is a painter!' Even so, after Napoleon's fall in 1814 and the withdrawal of Napoleonic forces from Italy, 'little portraits' were a reliable source of income for Ingres, now left in a precarious financial position as other avenues were cut off. The British, isolated for many years from the continent by the French Revolutionary and the Napoleonic Wars, were exhilarated by the prospect of foreign travel and were particularly keen to take advantage of the kind of elegant yet informal portraiture of which Ingres was a master.[9] Ingres lavished as much care and attention on the faces and clothes of many of his sitters as Constable did on his favourite trees, using the finest of detail for faces on smooth wove paper – itself a relatively recent invention – and fluid, bravura lines for clothes to make his portraits sparkle with vivacity and humour (fig. 67).

And though Ingres may have wished to be known primarily as a painter, drawing was fundamental to his vision and practice, the scaffolding that supported everything else. It was, he said, 'not just reproducing contours, it is not just the line; drawing is also the expression, the inner form, the composition, the modelling. See what is left after that. Drawing,' he concluded, 'is seven-eighths of what makes up a painting.'[10]

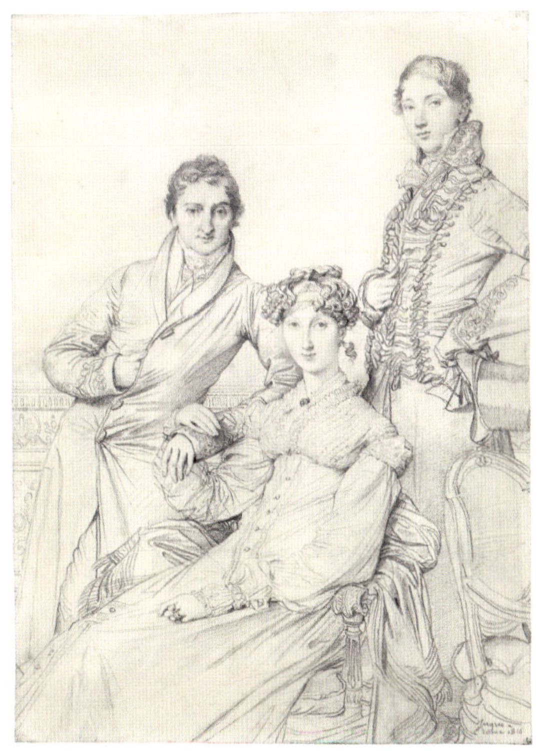

67. Jean-Auguste-Dominique Ingres, *Mr and Mrs Joseph Woodhead and Mr Henry Comber in Rome*, 1816. Graphite.

As Constable grew older, the emotional temperature of his work rose. He still painted men driving ploughs and operating locks under bright, showery English skies, but there was an increasingly spiritual dimension to his bursts of rain and sunshine.[11] It was a quality that was explored further by his German contemporary Caspar David Friedrich (1774–1840). But while Constable focused on the working, industrial landscape, Friedrich sought out remote, barren places and made them resonate with emotion and spirituality. 'Extremely simple, barren, serious and melancholy', was the verdict of Wilhelm von Kügelgen (1802–1867), a fellow painter in Dresden. 'An ocean of fog from which a single rock reaches up for the sun, a desolate beach by moonlight, a shipwreck in a sea of ice, these and similar things Friedrich painted and breathed into them a strange life.'[12] He could have been describing a group of drawings that Friedrich made in the mid- to late 1830s, towards the end of his life, which were inspired by the lonely, rocky beaches of the German island of Rügen on the Baltic Sea, a remote place rich in prehistoric sites (fig. 68). Oil paint would have been too strong for the subtle mood Friedrich sought to capture; he was fascinated by the light effects of dusk and dawn and he conveyed the atmosphere of twilight with a cool, pale wash of sepia ink, the colour of sadness and memories. Combined, Friedrich's highly controlled outlines describing boulders, pebbles and tufty grass, his subtle and delicate wash and the rising moon that casts a subdued path of light over sea and beach create the effect of a landscape seen in a dream; specifics of place are subsumed by a feeling of infinity. Using the simplest of means with great skill and delicacy, Friedrich orchestrates a tranquil elegy for human life.

Drawing offered a vital way of plugging into the world, whether natural or supernatural. For Eugène Delacroix (1798–1863), it was a near-constant activity, and offered a visceral way of expressing the teeming sensations that pressed upon him. He drew swiftly, with lines that were often unruly, explosive, agitated and emphatic. Their purpose was to capture the essence of the subject, in the heat of the moment, as it appeared either to his eye, or to his mind's eye. The cool, refined finish that was so important to Friedrich was of little significance to Delacroix.[13]

　　　　　　　　　　　　　　　　THE STORY OF DRAWING

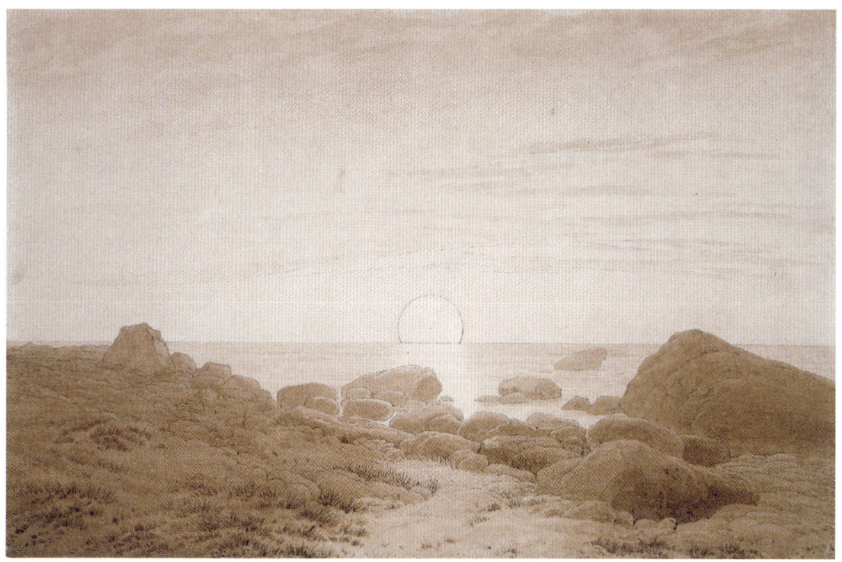

68. Caspar David Friedrich, *Rocky Beach with Moonrise*, c. 1835–7.
Brush and brown ink over graphite.

Delacroix was not known as a draughtsman in his lifetime, but on his death more than 8,000 works on paper were found in his Paris studio.[14] They ranged from academic drawings and careful copies of Old Masters to urgent sketches from nature, from scribbled and barely coherent first thoughts to finished, independent works of art. They included numerous notes and drawings, often vividly coloured, from his 1832 visit to Spain, Morocco and Algeria, which, when he had had the chance to mentally process them, provided him with reference material for the rest of his life. And they recorded his many visits to the zoo at the Jardin des Plantes in Paris, where he would sit down by the cages of lions and tigers, panthers and jaguars to watch the animals, pitching the speed of his drawing hand against their lithe and unpredictable movements. One sheet he covered with graphite drawings of the head and skull of a lion; on another he took a brush loaded with deep black ink and with a few economical strokes sketched the stripes of a crouching tiger (fig. 69).

For Delacroix, drawing was a way not just of connecting with the strange and the exotic in nature, but also of expanding one's own experience, one's very being, through the process. 'Why is it

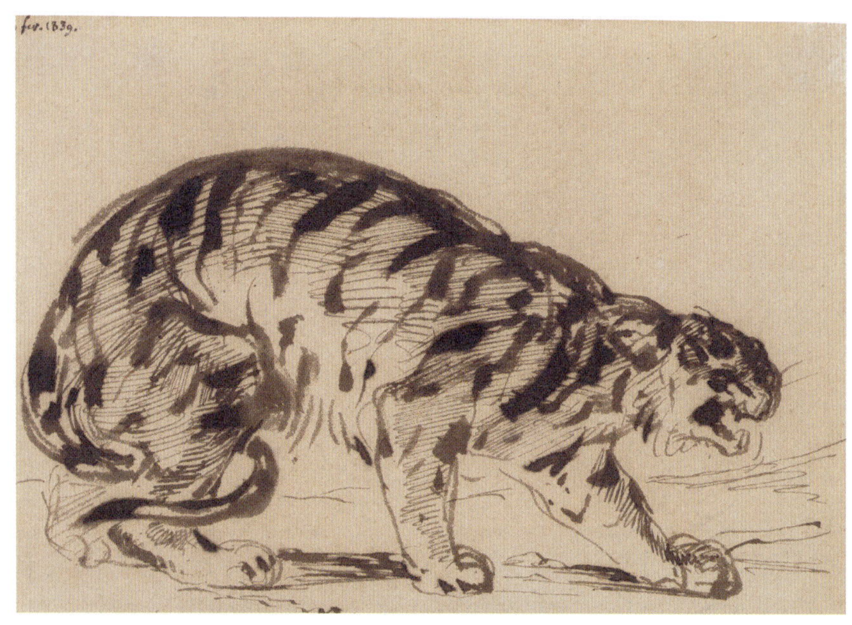

69. Eugène Delacroix, *Crouching Tiger*, 1839.
Pen and brush and iron-gall ink.

that these things have stirred me so much?' he asked himself in his journal in 1847 after a visit to the animals.

> Can it be because I have gone outside the everyday thoughts that are my world; away from the street that is my entire universe? How necessary it is to give oneself a shake from time to time; to stick one's head out of doors and try to read from the book of life that has nothing in common with cities and the works of man.[15]

CHAPTER 15

NEW SUBJECTS, NEW METHODS

K ATSUSHIKA HOKUSAI (1760–1849) was an artist of prodigious
energy. By the end of his life this 'Old Man Mad about Drawing',
as he signed himself, had produced nearly a thousand paintings and
many hundreds of drawings and illustrated books. At festivals he
had given performances in which he delighted audiences by creating
giant drawings, dashing around huge sheets of paper with a broom
that he dipped into a bucket of ink – thus anticipating performance
art by around a century and a half.[1] So when he was asked to
produce a visual encyclopaedia of the kind that were often used in
East Asia as teaching aids for children, naturally the project mush-
roomed, leaving its conventional boundaries far behind to become
The Great Picture Book of Everything. This compendium of the
entire world was all the more extraordinary because, in reality,
Hokusai was only allowed to experience a small part of it. During
his lifetime the Tokugawa shoguns who governed Japan imposed
strict limitations on contact with the outside world and forbade its
people from travelling abroad; the country only opened its borders
in 1859, a decade after Hokusai's death. So instead he used his
imagination to travel to India and ancient China, where he examined
the origins of Buddhism and the development of human civilisation.
He was equally happy drawing mythical beings, historical figures
doing impossible things and people from different countries that he
probably never saw. Likewise, his drawings of the natural world

cross fluidly into the supernatural one, combining acutely observed birds and animals with imaginary ones: a bear sits in a waterfall, patiently waiting for a fish to catch, and a rather crumpled elephant is fussed over by diminutive attendants, while elsewhere a nine-tailed spirit fox is vanquished by a Buddhist sutra and a peacock shares a drawing with a phoenix. Whether real or invented, contemporary or historical, each scene is animated by the artist's warmth, wit and imaginative sympathy.

Hokusai's original drawings for *The Great Picture Book of Everything* are in themselves a remarkable survival. In Edo-period Japan, an artist making drawings for an illustrated book would prepare so-called 'block-ready' designs for the specialist woodblock cutter. These drawings were pasted onto the surface of the blocks, and so destroyed in the process of cutting. For some reason Hokusai's 103 postcard-sized drawings for his encyclopaedia never got this far – could he have fallen out with his publisher? – so the sheets survive, and preserve the subtlety of his pen and brush strokes. In a drawing of the Daoist master Zhou Sheng climbing a cloud-ladder to reach the moon (fig. 70), Hokusai differentiates the earth-realm from that of the sky by making atmospheric dashes that fade higher up the sheet and are replaced by a graded wash; and the choppy, nail-shaped lines that suggest the rugged texture of the mountain peak contrast with the serpentine lines of the figure as he appears to flow smoothly upwards towards his goal. Depicting a subject simultaneously absurd and richly human, the drawing could be seen to epitomise Hokusai's entire project.

Had they been able to meet, Hokusai and Honoré Daumier (1808–1879) would have had a lot to say to one another. At the time the Japanese artist was constructing his visual encyclopaedia, in France Daumier was contemplating the panorama of Parisian life. Rather than a book, his framework was the satirical press: the availability of cheap wood-pulp paper had led to a boom in daily illustrated newspapers such as *Le Charivari* (founded in 1832) that published cartoons and caricatures. This in turn led to a huge opening up of subject matter for graphic art, especially after 1835 when the government prohibited political caricature and the paper had to fall back on images of everyday life. In the middle decades of the century the French economy was growing rapidly, and Daumier was poised to cast a keen eye on how everyone – from lawyers

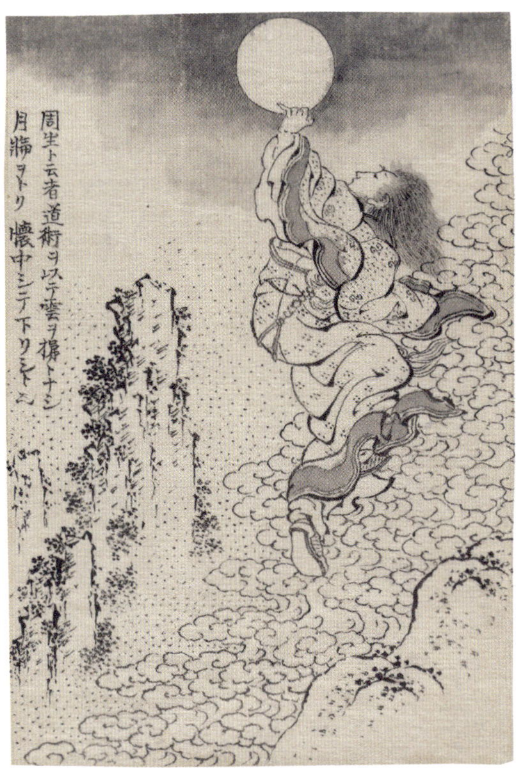

70. Katsushika Hokusai, *Daoist Master Zhou Sheng Ascends a Cloud-Ladder to the Moon*, 1820s–40s. Pen, brush and ink.

and the *haute* and *petite bourgeoisie* to street traders and clowns – was dealing with the challenges and opportunities brought by this new world. He made nearly 4,000 drawings for *Le Charivari*; no 'original' works survive of these because they were reproduced by lithography, a commercial printmaking process popularised in 1820. Daumier worked directly onto the lithographic stone, and once his drawing was inked and printed, the stone was wiped clean, ready for the next. It was a fast process; it had to be, if it were to keep pace with urban life. Daumier also made numerous drawings on paper that were reproduced as wood engravings in other publications.[2] He may have been prevented from making overtly political satires, but the varied strokes of his chalk or quill, whether they were fluent curves, wobbly scribbles or angry zigzags, were enough to convey his opinion on any subject.

Daumier's subjects were predominantly urban, but in the mid-nineteenth century, as towns and cities became increasingly populous and industrialised, many artists focused intensely on rural life. The artist's close friend Jean-François Millet (1814–1875), who grew up in Normandy and later settled in the village of Barbizon, south-east of Paris, thought peasant life and labour worthy of close and sustained attention. If Daumier's unruly, restless lines seemed to embody the bustle and hustle of the city, Millet drew in a way that expressed stillness and monumentality, even when he was representing rural labourers at work, striding through a field to sow seeds, arms swinging; raising a mallet high before whacking it down on a hatchet to split wood; or shouldering colossal bundles of firewood (fig. 71). As well as making preparatory sketches for oil paintings, Millet made a great many large-scale drawings as independent works of art. He drew men and women with black chalk, charcoal, Conté crayon or pastel, all media that produce slightly blurred outlines. As a result his figures exist in a dreamlike haze, and often seem on the point of dissolving into their landscape backgrounds like ghosts. The opposite of Daumier's restless individuals, Millet's calm rural

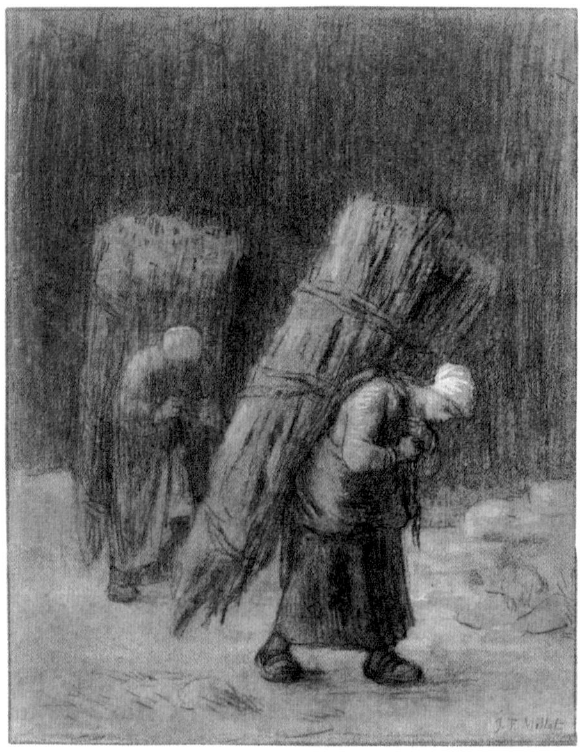

71. Jean-François Millet, *Women Carrying Faggots*, *c.* 1858. Charcoal heightened with white gouache on grey-blue paper.

   THE STORY OF DRAWING

labourers have a universal air; with few specific details to tie them to the modern world, they could be from any era. It has always been like this, they seem to say, as the year turns and the familiar seasonal work comes round again, and it always will be.

Millet honoured the past, and so did Hokusai. Both used drawing to hook onto history, whether they were imagining scenes from antiquity or making the past visibly shadow the present. Elsewhere, artists were thinking hard about the past and how it related to contemporary art. As the effects of the Industrial Revolution were felt ever more pressingly, they tried to work out where things went wrong – and how far they had to reach back in order to put them right.

During the first half of the nineteenth century, an idea arose in Europe and Britain that art urgently needed to be reformed, and that artists, if they were to create authentic and spiritually uplifting paintings and sculptures, must turn away from factory chimneys and crowded cities and look instead to the bright, clear days of the early Renaissance.

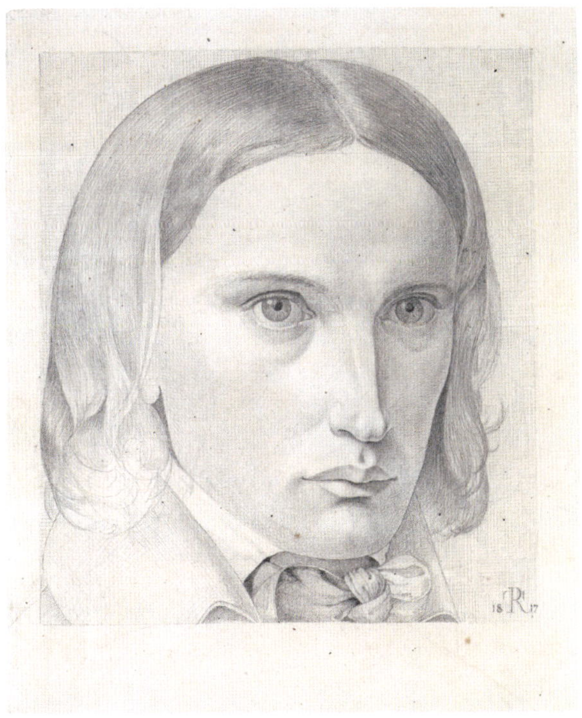

72. Theodor Rehbenitz, *Self-Portrait*, 1817. Graphite.

In Rome in the 1810s, the art of Dürer and early Raphael inspired an idealistic group of German, Swiss and Austrian artists. They got called the Nazarenes after Christ's childhood home, partly because of their passion for biblical subjects but also for their appearance; seeking to disassociate themselves from the modern, industrialised world, they grew their hair and wore long cloaks of an archaic style. A portrait drawing in graphite by the German artist Theodor Rehbenitz (1791–1861) captures something of the group's intensity and commitment to linear clarity – something of its austere spirituality, too (fig. 72). In rural southeast England in the 1820s, the 'Ancients', a group led by the London-raised Samuel Palmer (1805–1881), also rejected contemporary art, and viewed the agricultural landscape through the transformative lens of the early German engravers, adopting their repertoire of delicate dashes and fine, wiry lines. Both these groups felt that something valuable had drained away from art, but that it could be regained through an intense engagement with the past. At the century's midpoint the idea erupted again, and with such force that it would shape British art for the rest of the century.

In September 1848 a group of young artists gathered in a room on London's Gower Street, just north of the British Museum. They had all studied at the prestigious Royal Academy Schools, which effectively meant painstakingly drawing plaster casts of antique sculpture for as long as it took to gain enough expertise to enter the Life Room where, at last, they would be permitted to draw from the living model. In many cases, this took years. If discipline and conformity were meant to be instilled by this practice, though, it could not be called a success. The central figures of the group, Dante Gabriel Rossetti (1828–1882), William Holman Hunt (1827–1910) and John Everett Millais (1829–1896), rebelled against what they saw as the meretricious rubbish that was displayed at the Royal Academy's annual exhibitions. Art had been going downhill for 300 years, they argued, becoming mannered and derivative. It urgently needed a reset: in order to create work that was true to nature, these young men felt they had to push the vastly influential figure of Raphael out of the way and find alternative inspiration in the art of the early Renaissance. The name they invented for themselves, the Pre-Raphaelite Brotherhood, signalled their allegiance to artists such as Jan van Eyck (*c.* 1390–1441), whose Arnolfini portrait had recently

arrived at the National Gallery in London, Dürer and Italians of the
fourteenth and fifteenth centuries including Taddeo Gaddi (active
c. mid 1320s–1366) and Benozzo Gozzoli (*c.* 1420–1497), whose
frescos in the Campo Santo in Pisa they knew through line engravings.
Along with their frequent choice of historical or literary subjects,
which included an especial interest in Arthurian legend, this might
suggest that they were dustily antiquarian, but no: this radical group
was looking back in order to take British art forward.

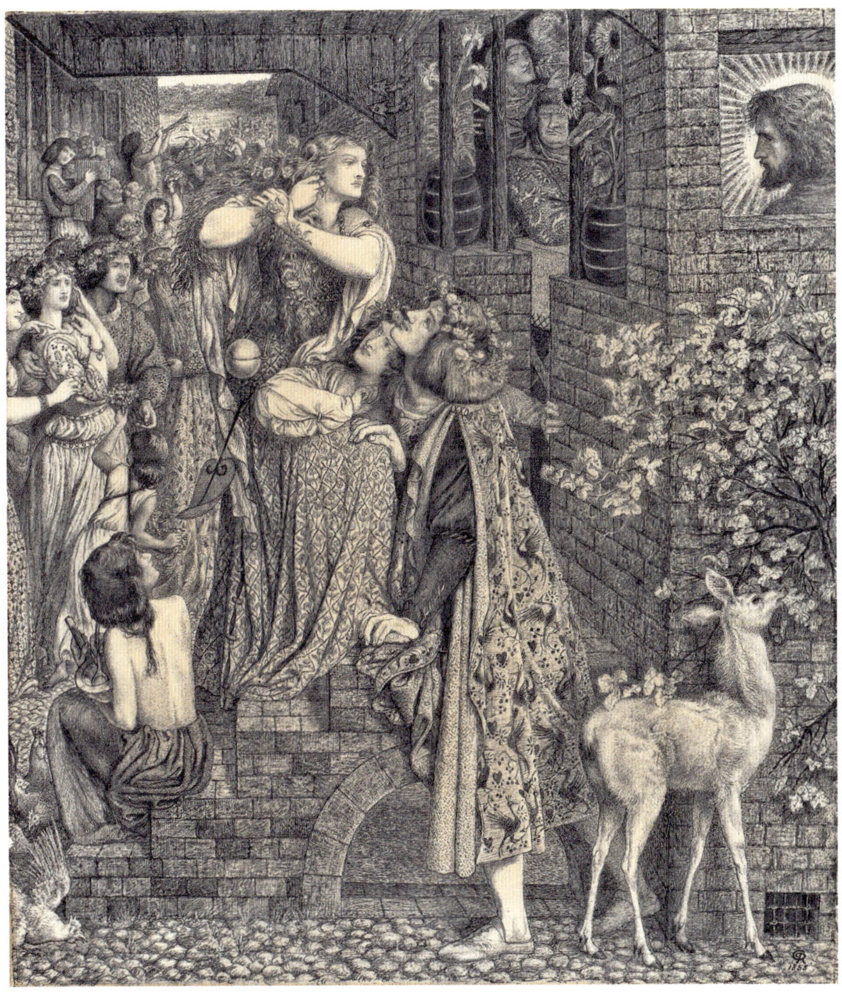

73. Dante Gabriel Rossetti, *Mary Magdalene at the
Door of Simon the Pharisee*, 1858. Pen and ink.

Drawing was at the heart of the Pre-Raphaelites' mission to rethink art, and they treated it as a fully independent medium.[3] It was on paper that they made many of their experiments – inspired by the Campo Santo engravings as well as by Flaxman's illustrations, Holman Hunt and Millais both drew in crisp, meticulous outline, paring their images down to essential elements. Rossetti made densely patterned compositions in response to engravings by Dürer, using a narrow steel nib – the first properly flexible one of which had been patented in 1831 – to build his images with minute dots and dashes. All were transfixed by fine, linear detail, as though it provided an antidote to the 'slosh' they hated.[4] Rossetti's pen and ink drawing *Mary Magdalene at the Door of Simon the Pharisee* (fig. 73), a biblical subject, is so richly detailed it is hard to take in at a glance; rather, it asks the eye to crawl over it like an insect, exploring this and then that part.[5] Rossetti must have imaginatively inhabited the composition for weeks as he painstakingly constructed it on paper.

Rossetti used drawing materials unconventionally. He was impatient with tuition, preferring to forge ahead experimentally than to take instruction. This lack of formal training sometimes resulted in disaster, as with a commission for murals inside the new Oxford Union building in 1857. Painted directly onto a thin skim of whitewashed plaster, they soon lost their brilliant colours as pigments sank back into the brickwork.[6] But it could also lead to innovations. One such was Rossetti's use of watercolour, a medium that had long been employed in Britain for landscape views. Conventionally, watercolour was applied to paper in dilute form, to take advantage of its translucency. When in the 1850s Rossetti began to use it for detailed compositions on medieval themes, he worked tiny dabs of colour into the paper with a brush moistened with the minimum of water in order to achieve the jewel-like optical effect of a medieval manuscript illumination. Like his disciple Edward Burne-Jones (1833–1898), however, who drew on sheets of vellum (prepared calfskin) for its medieval associations but used a modern steel nib, Rossetti was not austerely historicist, but took advantage of new artificial pigments that had recently come onto the market. These included emerald green, cobalt and purple carmine, colours that shimmer with a beetly iridescence, adding to the drawings' otherworldly atmospheres.[7] The Pre-Raphaelites might have gone forward by way of the past, but they allowed the industrial present to light their way.

     THE STORY OF DRAWING

CHAPTER 16

MEDIUMS OF MODERN LIFE

WATERCOLOUR – PIGMENT SUSPENDED in water, quick-drying and mercurial – was the ideal medium for catching nature on the move: a breeze bending the summer grasses, an evanescent shimmer in the air. When Berthe Morisot (1841–1895) worked in oil paints and pastels she allowed the sketchy strokes of the medium to remain visible – but fluid watercolour enabled her to take this further, and to create works that looked radically unfinished. 'Never does Mademoiselle Morisot finish a painting, a pastel or a watercolour,' remarked a reviewer of the third Impressionist exhibition in 1877 (Morisot exhibited in seven of the eight exhibitions organised by the Impressionists between 1874 and 1886, only missing one because of the birth of her daughter in 1878). 'It is as if she were composing prefaces to books she will never write.'[1] He was, however, missing the point: Morisot's intention was not to labour over three-volume novels on canvas and paper, but to describe the experience of being in the landscape under changing French skies, there and then, *en plein air*. Whether her subject was a woman sitting on a bench holding a parasol or a carriage trotting through the Bois de Boulogne, with flickering translucent watercolour Morisot could capture sunlight itself on paper.

Watercolour had the advantage of being highly portable. Since the late eighteenth century firms had been producing convenient little cakes of pigment bound with gum arabic that fitted neatly into paintboxes. One bright day in 1875 Morisot sat down on the grass on a hillside outside Cambrai, near the Belgian border, where she was visiting her younger sister Yves and her small daughter. While Yves was getting comfortable, Berthe opened her paintbox and laid out her brushes, a jar of water and a saucer for mixing. First she began to draw, quickly sketching her sister's and niece's position with a graphite pencil (fig. 74). She then mixed her colours, fresh and fluid, slipping them onto the paper before they could dry: a yellowish green pooling around her sister's shoulders, and a bluish one to indicate the lush grass around them with vigorous upright strokes for the stalks. She created highlights in the sitters' dresses simply by leaving areas of the white paper there untouched. Behind them the girl's hat lies on the grass, an afterthought of hatband and brim briefly dashed in over the green; on the right a woman walks away towards a group of houses, her transparency revealing that she too was a late addition, this incidental figure who happened to arrive on the scene. And all the time Morisot worked, her eyes

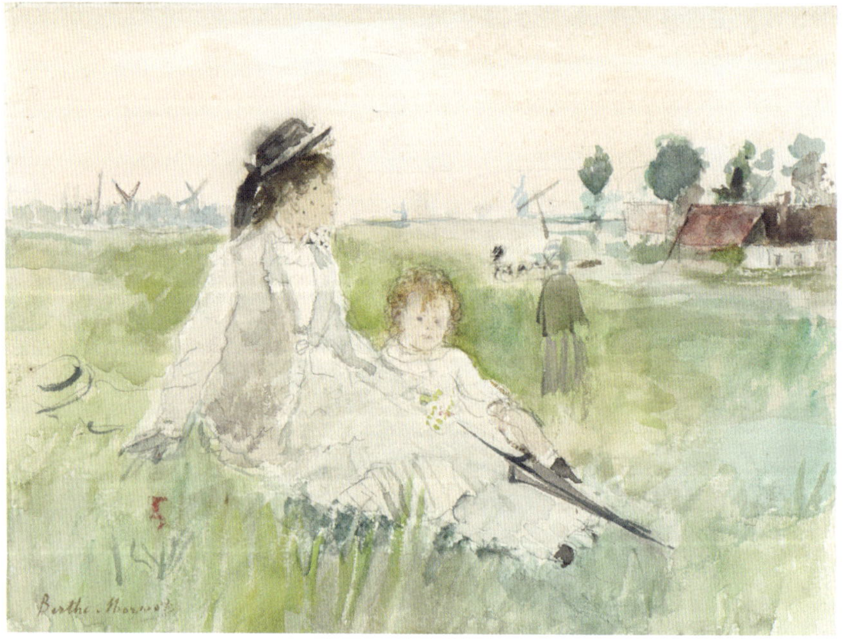

74. Berthe Morisot, *A Woman and Child Seated on the Grass*, 1875. Watercolour over graphite.

 THE STORY OF DRAWING

flicking between her paper and the scene in front of her as the light changed, the wind moved the grass and people came and went, her little niece watched her intently. Her solemn face, pink in the summer warmth, is the still centre of her aunt's sketch.

Although he was a founder member of the Impressionists, Edgar Degas (1834–1917) was in some ways the odd one out. He was bored by the country and had little patience with rural scenes, choosing urban subjects instead. Rather than painting or drawing *en plein air* and attempting to capture the effects of bright sunlight bouncing off foliage, he preferred to work indoors from sketches and memory and loved the harsh or atmospheric effects of artificial light. And while he was lauded as the quintessential 'Painter of Modern Life', as the Irish novelist George Moore put it in an article about him, he also set great store by learning from the Old Masters.[2] During a tour of Italy he made when in his early twenties he filled not just sketchbooks but his visual memory, too, with a store of images upon which he drew for the rest of his life. It was only after copying and recopying the masters, Degas once remarked with a conviction only thinly veiled by flippancy, that one could 'reasonably be permitted to paint a radish from the life'.[3]

Drawing was always central to Degas's creativity. If he was to capture events in the fleeting and fragmented ways they unfolded, whether in a ballet class or on the racecourse, it was the only way his hand could keep pace with his eye. It was these sketches, sometimes several to the sheet capturing different angles and poses as though in freeze-frame, that he laid out in his studio when he was working on a painting at the easel. But Degas also came to regard drawing as a fully independent art form, with the same status as oil painting. And it is characteristic of this artist who combined respect for tradition with a ruthless dedication to modernity that the medium that facilitated this was pastel, with its strong associations with French artists of the eighteenth century such as Watteau, Boucher and Jean Siméon Chardin (1699–1779). Except for Delacroix, few artists of the early nineteenth century had used it, so it was, for Degas, unclaimed territory. Although held lightly in place by the paperweights of the past, it rippled with potential to be used in novel ways.

Pastel allowed Degas to draw in colour: he dragged dazzling hues across the paper, layering, juxtaposing strokes and experimenting with wet and dry pigments. When he was drawing dancers, he tried to replicate the spectator's visual experience, keeping contours of limbs precisely linear, rubbing other areas to create ethereal effects, and relishing the dramatic impressions the medium could create of faces and bodies spotlit from below (fig. 75). When he drew racehorses, he used wormy lines for the restless animals' sweating flanks and straight hatched strokes for waving grass. Painting in oil could be cumbersome – certainly Degas found it so later in life. Pastel, however, combined the strength of paint with the fluency of drawing. Partial and contingent, vivid and swift: pastel drawing was, for Degas, the Medium of Modern Life.

Degas's subjects were often dramatic and arresting. But what about a bowl of fruit, an armchair or a familiar view: could they be as eye-catching as jockeys and ballet dancers? Paul Cézanne (1839–1906)

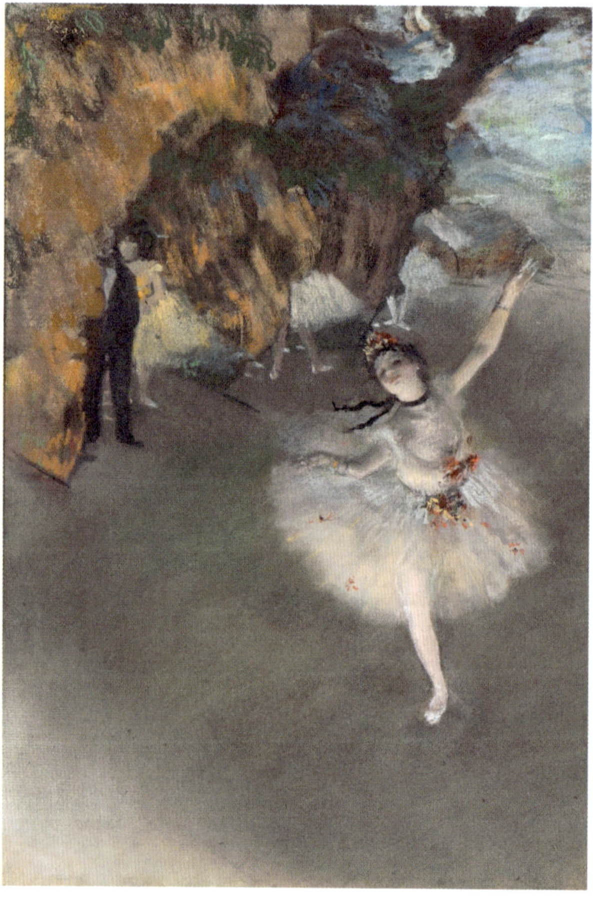

75. Edgar Degas,
Ballet, c. 1876–7.
Pastel on monotype.

THE STORY OF DRAWING

thought so. He once said he would 'astonish Paris with an apple', and succeeded.[4] Although he associated with the Impressionists and participated in their exhibitions of 1874 and 1877, Cézanne felt that they placed too much emphasis on superficial appearances; he wanted to plunge more deeply into the world, to discover how to express the solidity of objects and their essential truths. He wondered about perspective, too: did things really appear to the eye as Western artists had been representing them for all those years? Or was it just a convention – could an alternative be found? Pencil or brush in hand, Cézanne grappled daily with these mysteries of surface and form. As a result, his drawings are not always easy to look at: they can be messy, fractured and full of broken contours – rebarbative rather than inviting. It is as though he were inventing a new visual language with which to express what he felt needed to be said about the world. We, the viewers, have to get to grips with it too – but are rewarded by getting to play our part in Cézanne's thought process.

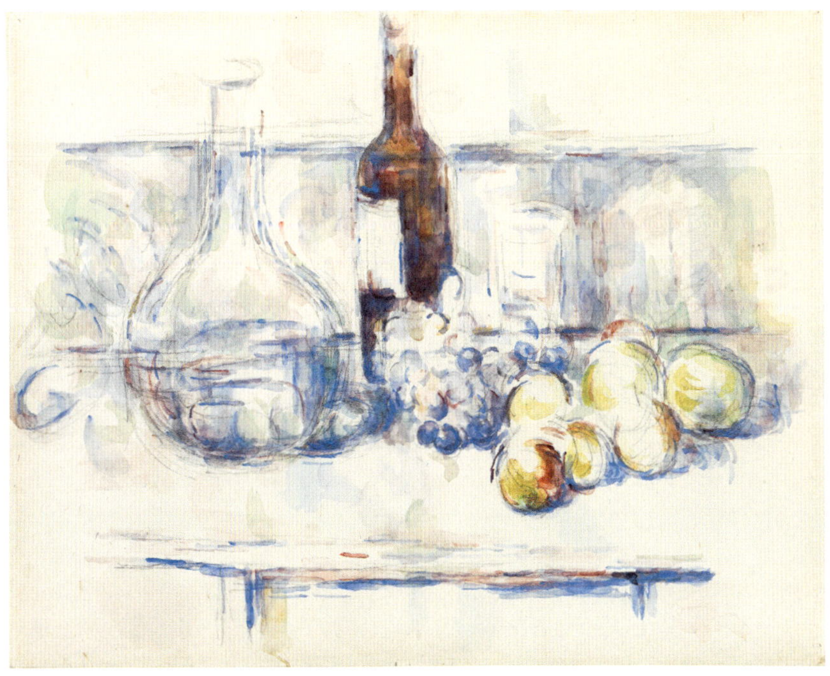

76. Paul Cézanne, *Still Life with Carafe, Bottle and Fruit*, 1906.
Watercolour and graphite on pale buff paper.

In the last years of Cézanne's life, these visual experiments culminated with a magnificent sequence of watercolours of still-life subjects – nothing ostentatious, just objects to be found in the cupboards and sideboards of most bourgeois households of the time: carafes, jugs, bottles, fruit, dishes, pots and pans (fig. 76). Drawing with the tip of the paintbrush, with carefully placed dashes, dabs and curving lines – and leaving some areas of paper untouched to contribute their brightness – he explored translucency and reflectiveness, solidity and presence. He tested the material presence of things. Cézanne's pencil marks are visible, sometimes underneath the luminous patches of watercolour, sometimes scrawled and looped over the top, the hard-won grammar that supports his kaleidoscopic poetry.[5]

In February 1888 Vincent van Gogh (1853–1890) got on a train in Paris bound for Arles in the South of France. He was nearly thirty-five, and it was eight years since he had made the life-changing decision to become an artist. He had lived in Paris with his brother Theo for the past two because, of all European cities, it was the place that most pulsed with artistic energy, and he needed to be at the heart of it. But now he was ill and overwrought; he wanted to find peace in the country and to pursue his idiosyncratic dream of becoming a peasant painter. As the train rattled south, he gazed out of the window at the unfolding landscape and thought about the Japanese prints that had arrived in Europe since Japan opened its borders, and that had so powerfully captured his imagination in Paris. He had collected and studied them avidly, finding a model for his own work in their clarity and bright colours. Now, escaping from the muddle and dirt of the city, in his mind his destination itself began to take on those qualities; later, in a letter to his friend Paul Gauguin, he admitted to looking at the countryside from the train to see ' "if it was like Japan yet!" Childish, isn't it?'[6]

Southern France may not, in reality, have been much like Japan, but it *was* an exciting new beginning. The agricultural landscape surrounding Arles, which changed its appearance with the seasons, offered a multitude of subjects that Van Gogh set about exploring. He often used the vantage point of the hill of Montmajour for the panoramic views it offered over the country, and made large, detailed drawings of fields, hedges, crops, haystacks, carts and scattered

    THE STORY OF DRAWING

farmhouses, but he also sketched urban subjects from numerous angles: the town from the wheat fields, a tile factory, rooftops, street scenes and smoking chimneys. But as beguiled as he was with the characteristics of his new environment, when he climbed Montmajour to survey the scene he was also seeing the landscape 'with a more Japanese eye', as he put it in a letter to his brother that June. Paradoxically, looking through this artistically constructed lens helped him to see his surroundings more clearly. Japanese artists, he surmised, drew 'quickly, very quickly, like a flash of lightning', and he attempted to bring some of the same spontaneity and linear precision to his own drawings.[7]

Van Gogh also wanted to stoke his art with a primitive energy, and he achieved this by exploiting a drawing material that was rooted in the landscape itself. He was not always able to afford oil paint and canvases, but paper and ink were cheaply available in the shops and he was able to make his own pens for free. He cut

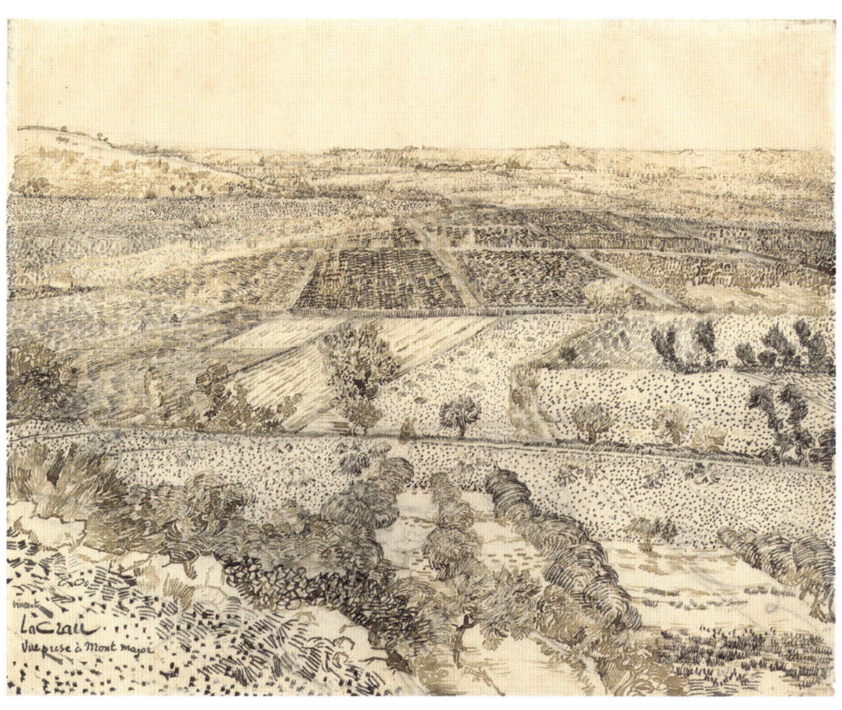

77. Vincent van Gogh, *La Crau Seen from Montmajour*, 1888.
Graphite, pen and reed pen with light brown and dark brown ink.

locally growing reeds, dried them and, with a penknife, removed pith from the shafts to form them into barrels and shaped the ends into broad nibs. Rembrandt, an artist he revered, had drawn with a reed pen – an ancient writing instrument, used by the Egyptians and later the Romans – but in modern times, few other artists had. The marks reed pens make are distinct from those produced by quills or steel nibs: because the shafts are stiff and have little capacity for holding liquid, they do not glide over the paper but make blunt lines that quickly become fainter as the ink runs out.[8] Van Gogh embraced this earthy graphic dialect, relishing its limited but powerful repertoire of bold, short strokes and characterful dots and dashes. A drawing he made in July 1888 from Montmajour of the distant hill village of La Crau swarms with detail (fig. 77). Here he swaps between a conventional nib for flowing lines and a reed pen for short, stubby lines and dashes, and uses two shades of ink to create the illusion of depth, sometimes deftly crossing one set of lines over the other, as with the crops in the central fields. All the way to the horizon, the drawing bristles with closely observed textures and hums with the liveliness of harvest time. A drawing material that to many artists would have been restrictive was, to Van Gogh, a liberation.

As the century wore on, for some artists the Impressionist project of depicting the light and colour of the natural world as they struck the senses began to seem restrictive. There were many who still rushed outdoors to capture the essence of everyday life, but there were others who retreated from it; *plein air* was all very well, but daylight blotted out other kinds of vision. Indoors, what came to the fore were the strange and fantastical beings that appeared in the mind's eye. Two French artists, Odilon Redon (1840–1916) and Georges Seurat (1859–1891), were turning their eyes inwards, attentive to the images that were taking shape in the dark rooms of their imaginations.

Can eyeballs rise like hot-air balloons? Giant spiders caper and grin? A man's head grow like a cactus in a plant pot? While Morisot, Degas and their Impressionist associates were re-drawing the modern world in fresh and vivid ways, Redon was doing the opposite: exploring his nightmarish fantasies in smoky, nebulous drawings he called his *noirs* – his black drawings. 'All my originality,' he recorded in his memoir, 'consists in bringing to life, in a human way, improbable beings and making them live according to the laws of probability, by putting – as far as possible – the logic of the visible at the service of the invisible.'[9]

Redon's 'logic of the visible' – the means, in other words, by which he could give form to evanescent ideas and subtle or terrible emotions – was largely provided by charcoal. With its propensity to smudge and be effaced, in the way the most absorbing dreams usually evaporate from our memories on waking, it was a medium that ideally embodied his subjects. His drawing *Eye-Balloon* represents an enormous eye pointing heavenwards like that of a saint beseeching heaven, harnessed to a severed head that it carries on a dish on an inexplicable journey over a desolate and marshy landscape (fig. 78). In creating it, Redon exploited the ease with which charcoal may be erased from the paper, rubbing out areas from the

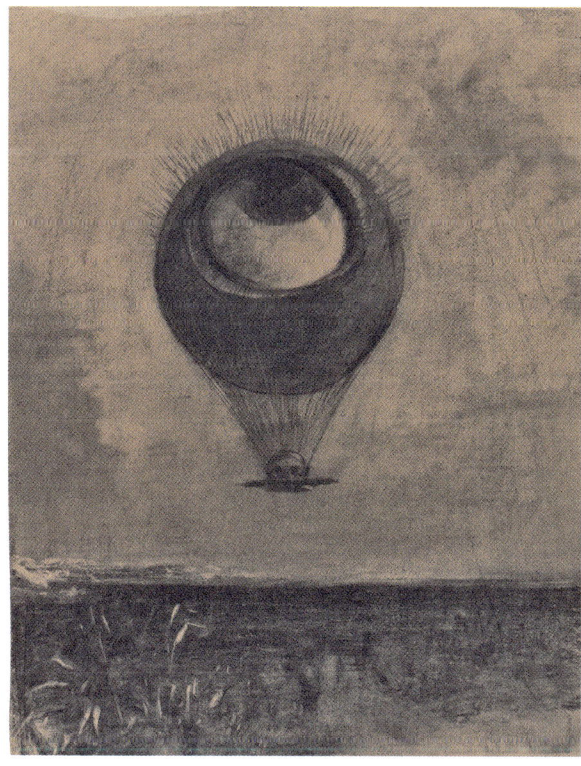

78. Odilon Redon, *Eye-Balloon*, 1878. Charcoal and chalk.

eye and the dark clouds of the surrounding sky for highlights and also removing pigment with a few precise strokes of a stump (a roll of paper or leather) to indicate reeds growing from the indeterminate ground. When in 1882 he made a version of the image as a lithograph – another medium with a grainy, fuzzy appearance – he gave it the title *The Eye, Like a Strange Balloon, Mounts toward Infinity*. What did it mean? According to Redon, a title 'is justified only when it is vague [...] and even equivocal. My drawings *inspire* and cannot be defined,' he continued. 'They place us, as music does, in the world of the ambiguous and the indeterminate.'[10]

Seurat's drawings – many of which he made as independent works of art, to be exhibited as such – are twilight to the sunshine of his paintings. His celebrated pictures *Bathers at Asnières* (1883) and *A Sunday on La Grande Jatte – 1884* (1884–5) teem with life and vibrate with colour; yet when he took up crayon and paper he gravitated towards lonelier, darker subjects. He walked to the edges of Paris where he lingered in search of deserted, in-between places at the edges of the city, sketching the suburban houses and factories there. Even when he was making drawings as part of the process of planning a painting, the isolated figures that appear in them have a different, more sombre air. The fascination with the science of optics that drove him to pioneer precise methods of juxtaposing dots and dabs of colour on canvas to optimise their visual impact also led him to explore the mysterious effects of shadows gathering on paper.

Seurat was inspired not by an ancient drawing material, like Van Gogh, but a modern one. The consistency of the Conté crayon, patented by Nicolas-Jacques Conté (1755–1805) in 1795, had been altered in 1840 by the addition of spermaceti, the waxy substance found in the head of the sperm whale. As well as a more fluid line, this new crayon was capable of producing rich areas of black pigment. Every bit as important to the finished drawing was the surface Seurat habitually chose: a hand-made paper manufactured by a French firm called Michallet with a distinct 'tooth', as bumpy as an orange skin. Seurat built up his drawings on this surface using tone rather than line. Where he wanted a deep, impenetrable area of shadow he pressed firmly with the crayon so that the pigment filled the hollows between the ridges; and where he needed lighter passages he

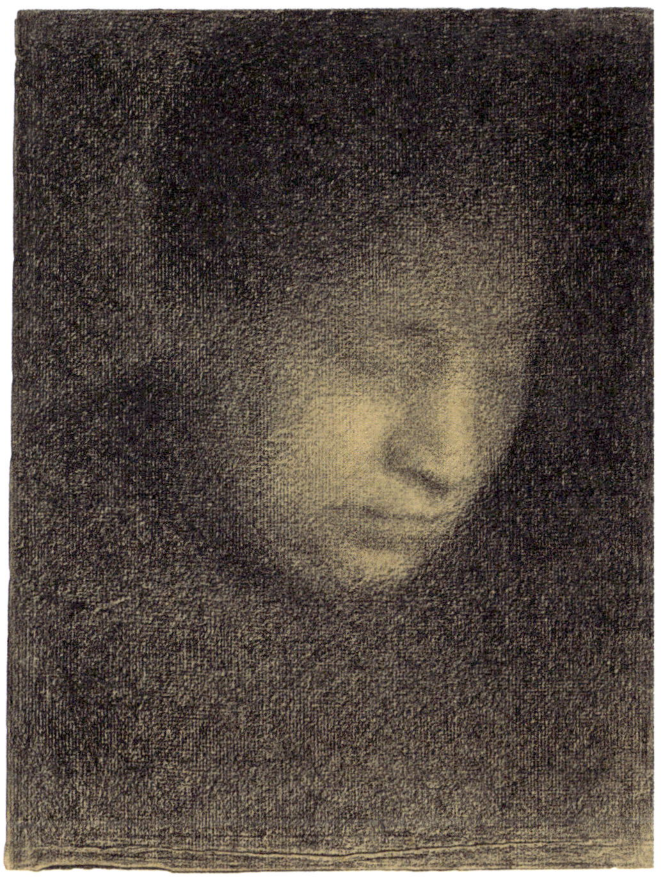

79. Georges Seurat, *Madame Seurat, the Artist's Mother*, *c.* 1882–3. Conté crayon on Michallet paper.

applied it with a gentler hand, stroking the surface of the ridges but leaving the pits untouched so that the black was tempered by dots of the creamy white paper showing through, producing a smoky, luminous effect that Seurat himself called *irradiation*.[11] The effect is almost as though he were drawing in reverse, conjuring ghostly light from patches of dense fog. In a simple, emotionally charged drawing he made in the early 1880s of his beloved mother, her pale face seems to loom out of deep shadow, glowing in the candlelight under her son's gaze (fig. 79).

CHAPTER 17

RETHINKING THE BODY

In the last decade of the nineteenth century, the young artist Aubrey Beardsley (1872–1898) had a vision of the city made beautiful by modern graphic commercials and the bold imagery of posters. 'London will soon be resplendent with advertisements,' he declared, 'and, against a leaden sky, sky-signs will trace their formal arabesque. Beauty has laid siege to the city, and telegraph wires shall no longer be the sole joy of our aesthetic perceptions.'[1] It was a draughtsman's answer to Claude Monet's appreciation of the beauty inherent in another by-product of the industrial age, urban fog.

Beardsley may have been an artist with one foot in the past, whose imagination fed upon ancient Greek vase painting, Japanese woodcuts and eighteenth-century engravings of *fêtes galantes*, but no one embraced the possibilities offered by the present with more verve or acuity.[2] He drew almost entirely for illustrated books and magazines, which only a few years earlier would have meant handing his drawings over to a professional firm of wood engravers to prepare them for reproduction – a stage that inevitably introduced a degree of interpretation. By the late nineteenth century, however, new photographic methods of reproduction eliminated this intermediate process. Moreover, replacing a printing block made from wood, a material liable to break and that therefore demanded relatively short lines, with a stronger zinc plate allowed an artist's own lines to be reproduced with an unprecedented degree of fidelity.

Beardsley was the first artist to realise what this meant for drawing. He no longer had to tailor his lines to the limitations of a commercial printing process, but could allow his fine, flexible nib to trace unbroken contours without breaking them up into shorter strokes, knowing that the zinc block was equal to the task. He took advantage of his new freedom, balancing areas of solid black tone with bounding, super-fine lines, executed with an audacious assurance. The images he created were so unconventional that some outraged critics thought it was a kind of trick; and indeed his drawings were a high-wire performance of superb technical skill. What was perhaps most disturbing to the critics was how he used those lines to describe the human figure. Whether it was the biblical Salome hovering over a pool of black blood clutching the head of John the Baptist, the smartly dressed modern woman commanding urban spaces in periodicals such as the *Yellow Book* and the *Savoy* or a character of his own invention, the Abbé Fanfreluche, all but engulfed by the rich stuffs of his own costume (fig. 80): with his virtuosic line Beardsley seemed to update the human body itself to fit the modern era.

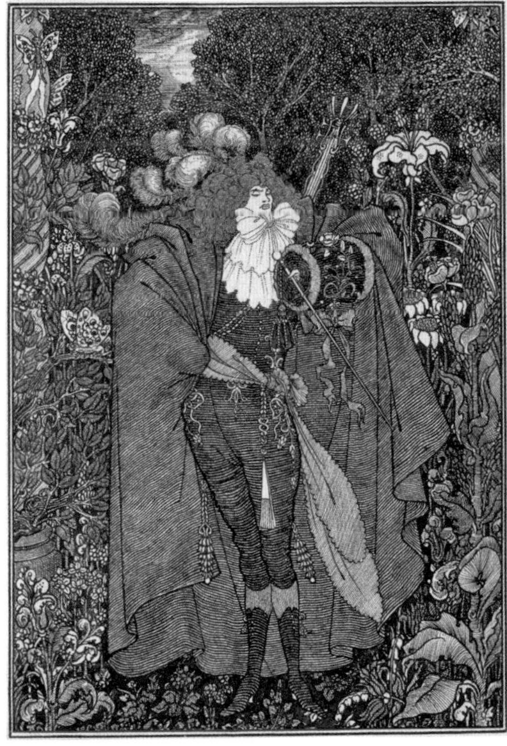

80. Aubrey Beardsley, *The Abbé*, 1895. Pen, ink and wash.

In Vienna at the beginning of the twentieth century Gustav Klimt (1862–1918) looked intently at illustrations by Beardsley, and works by the Dutch artist Jan Toorop (1858–1928) and the Belgian Fernand Khnopff (1858–1921), as well as studying the graphic styles of Japanese prints and ancient Greek art.[3] He too was in search of a new way of representing the world. Alongside a group of young Austrian artists and architects who called themselves the Secession to signal their rejection of a stale and self-satisfied academic art establishment, he devised a new graphic vocabulary. And his focus, like Beardsley's, was almost exclusively on the human figure. How could it be rethought to fit the times? How could its contours express human life as it was shaped by the powerful moral, psychological and sexual forces of an industrial age?

In 1901 Klimt set out his visual manifesto on a large scale when he began work on the Beethoven Frieze, a decorative cycle displayed in the Secession's own building in Vienna, and a visual response to the musical imagery of the final choral movement of Ludwig van Beethoven's Ninth Symphony (1824). The numerous preparatory drawings Klimt made reveal how he drew from models as he worked towards the depiction of individual figures, elongating and distorting as he got closer to his allegorical vision, from the attenuated diagonal forms of the female bodies representing the 'Yearning for Happiness' to the full stop of the naked embracing couple for the conclusion, 'This Kiss to the Entire World'. At this stage Klimt sketched in black chalk on cheap brown packing paper, but as he refined his process he swapped the chalk for silvery graphite and rough utilitarian paper for fine Japanese – a combination he would use for the rest of his life.[4] Using these slightest of materials and with a rapid and flickering line, he became ever more fascinated by female sexuality, repeatedly drawing his models absorbed in masturbatory reveries. His drawings oscillate between silvery precision and abstraction, his figures appearing to float weightlessly in a medium of dreamy eroticism that hardly anchors them to the page (fig. 81).

The younger artist Egon Schiele (1890–1918) boasted so often of the fact that Klimt approved of his work that his adviser told him to stop.[5] In fact the two artists had a great deal in common – central to the work of both was the human figure and the sustained exploration of sexuality. But while Klimt's eroticism hid in plain

     THE STORY OF DRAWING

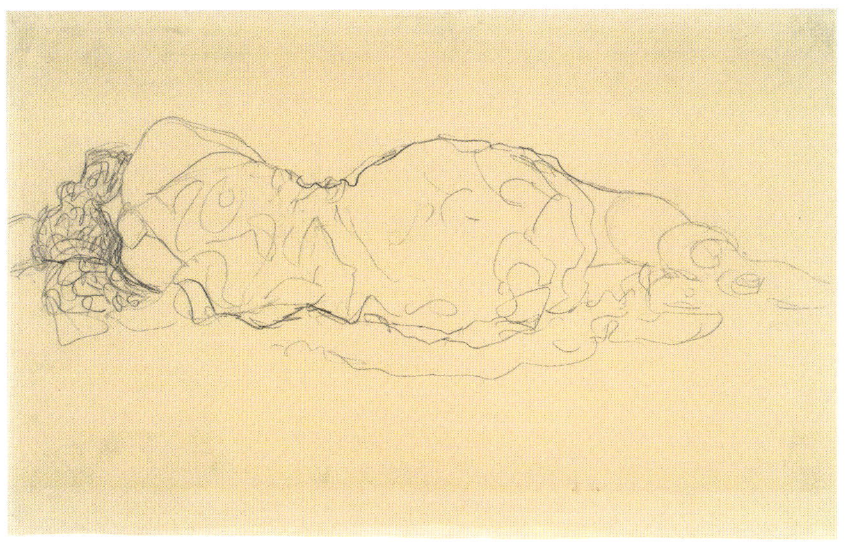

81. Gustav Klimt, *Reclining Woman, c.* 1916–17. Graphite.

sight – some of his most overtly sexual drawings were even published, albeit as illustrations to a small edition of a work by the classical author Lucian – Schiele's was so raw and provocative that he was imprisoned for allowing young people access to his work, and one drawing was publicly burnt in court.[6] When the bodies of Klimt's models are half concealed by drapery, the mood evoked is one of languor and luxury; when Schiele's are half-dressed, the remaining clothes make the exposure of pubic hair, nipples and vulvas intensely disturbing. Klimt's models are so absorbed in their dreams and fantasies they rarely catch our eye, while Schiele's stare insolently back at us: *Warum zum Teufel glotzt du so?* – why the hell are you gawping like that?

Beardsley's career had been cut tragically short with his death from tuberculosis at twenty-five; Schiele died of the Spanish flu in 1918, at twenty-eight, just three days after his wife and unborn child. His work had been developing quickly. A nude self-portrait of 1916 retains the burning core of adolescent angst that had driven his unflinching expressiveness from the outset, but combines it with a sophisticated use not only of line but of colour too (fig. 82). He drew with a virtuosic Beardsley-esque contour but mottled the flesh with stains of rash pink and bruise blue, bringing into being a new

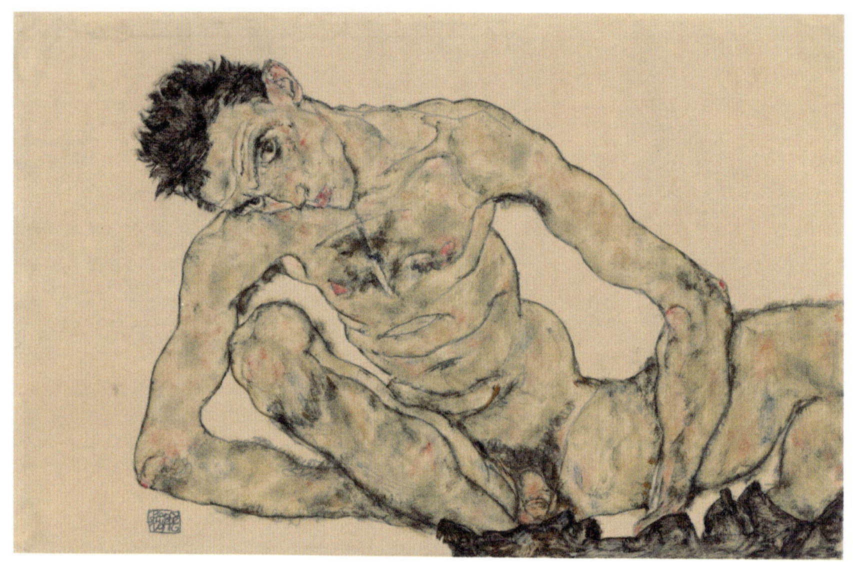

82. Egon Schiele, *Self-Portrait*, 1916.
Graphite and bodycolour.

kind of human figure to suit the dangerous new century: damaged, isolated, quizzical and vulnerable.

Käthe Kollwitz (1867–1945) died shortly before the end of the Second World War, having been forced out of the prestigious Preußische Akademie der Künste in Berlin at the time of Hitler's rise to power in 1933. It was her son's death in action during the First World War, however, that had reaffirmed the course of a career in which she was to focus intensively on conflict, loss and social injustice. As a young woman she had trained as a painter in Berlin and Munich, but turned to drawing and printmaking because as media they were more immediate and accessible to the dispossessed and the working people she championed. Oil paints were too refined to tackle the urgency of human need and misery. Her work was driven, she said, by 'the responsibility of being an advocate. It is my duty to voice the sufferings of men, the never-ending sufferings heaped mountain-high.'[7] Through woodcut and lithography, this successor to Millet developed harsh and uncompromising visual vocabularies of black, white and grey, stark and jagged, the better to express the raw experiences of exhausted workers and grieving mothers – those who rarely found themselves the subjects of art. Her many

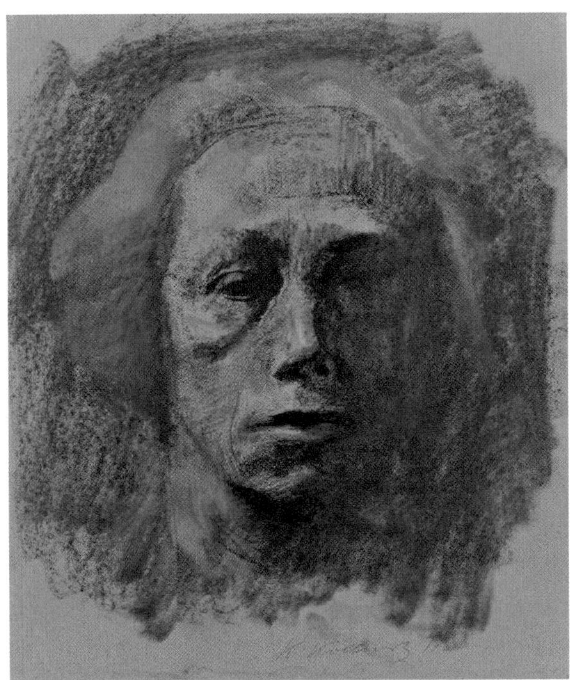

83. Käthe Kollwitz,
Self-Portrait, 1911.
Black chalk, heightened
with violet and
grey chalk, on grey-
brown paper.

self-portraits are poised between the individually penetrating and
the universal: whether inscribed with chalks on paper, an etching
needle on a copper plate or a crayon on a lithographic stone, the
harsh lines and deep shadows with which she inscribes features are
both her own and everywoman's (fig. 83).

In France, the experiments carried out in the second half of the
nineteenth century by Degas, Cézanne and others, and the increased
exposure given to works on paper in exhibitions, had begun to collapse distinctions between drawing and painting and prepared the
way for boundaries to be blurred further in the twentieth. No single
artist, however, reimagined the territory of art – and drawing – with
more iconoclastic energy than Pablo Picasso (1881–1973).

According to family legend, the very first words of the infant
Pablo were to demand a pencil with which to draw.[8] From childhood
onwards Picasso drew compulsively: on paper, in sketchbooks, on
scraps pasted onto Cubist collages, on canvases, cardboard, wood
and ceramic; on tablecloths, menus, napkins and newspapers; on

stones and sand. Over his lifetime it is estimated that he made a total of around 19,000 drawings, without counting the more ephemeral doodles.[9] Picasso drew with such facility and conviction that an air of the uncanny attached itself to his apparent ability to conjure images from thin air.[10] In 1955 the film director Henri-Georges Clouzot approached him with the idea of filming his creative process; the result, *Le Mystère Picasso*, was shown at Cannes the following year (fig. 84). The English artist and collector Roland Penrose, Picasso's future biographer, was there as it was being made. 'Their idea is to make the drawings appear on the screen by absorption onto the back of their paper,' he recorded in his notebook.

> The artist will be hidden but each stroke of the brush will appear like magic as it is made. . . . Each drawing grows from his brush with unexpected lines and patches. As though in a trance he makes an image hitherto invisible become real. Starting with a few rapid structural lines the subject appears in spontaneous realisation, the

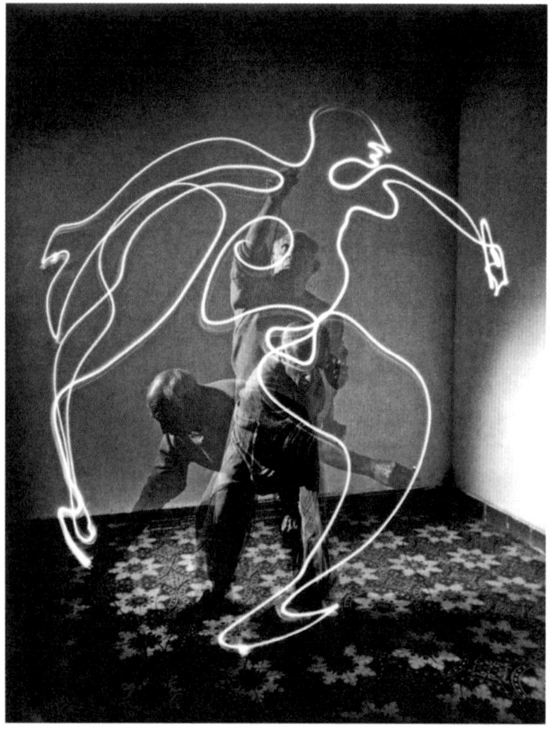

84. Pablo Picasso drawing, film still from Henri-Georges Clouzot's *Le Mystère Picasso*, 1956.

　　　　　　　THE STORY OF DRAWING

authors being himself and his material. Braque, he says, once said that to see him drawing was like a hand removing the dust from a hidden image. But there are moments when dramatic changes take place. The position of an eye already placed in a head which is taking shape fails to satisfy him and is blacked out, whereupon without hesitation it reappears in the only place left, a patch of white that remains, and there with the aid of this luminous highlight it takes its final inevitable position, as though it had always meant to be there, and triumphantly looks out from the drawing, the solution perfect and final. These drawings start from a stark white sheet and, in the space of five minutes, this arid reflector of light which blinds has been transformed into a face, a landscape, a jug holding flowers, in which the light emanates from the objects and lives within them.[11]

Picasso himself made little distinction between drawing and painting, executing many finished works of art in graphic media and creating hybrid compositions that were both, sometimes incorporating an element of sculpture, too. Drawn lines form a prominent factor in many of his major works, from the scored lines of the women's mask-faces in the groundbreaking *Les Demoiselles d'Avignon* (1907), through pencilled and charcoaled elements on the collaged surfaces of numerous cubist pictures in the years leading up to the First World War, to the expressive contours of the vast *Guernica*, made for the Spanish Pavilion of the Exposition Internationale that was held in Paris in 1937.

In Picasso's hands drawing materials themselves were ripe for rethinking. He mixed conventional media freely to achieve specific effects, sometimes adding sand or sawdust for texture, and used materials counterintuitively – sometimes drawing, for instance, with a thick brush loaded with viscous oil paint. He experimented with materials normally thought suitable only for children, such as coloured wax crayons and felt-tip pens. He made marks by scratching, incising, cutting, folding, tearing or drawing a comb through wet pigment.[12] Working across a huge range of styles, his drawings could be exquisitely sensitive, like studies of the face of his lover Marie-Thérèse Walter so gentle they suggest the delicate translucency of her skin, or they could bristle with the crude energy of his crowing charcoal *Rooster* of 1938. Picasso became a master of printmaking processes, whether creating images with white lines on a black background by drawing with a needle on an inked lithographic stone, or using drypoint for its fine, feathery lines, relishing both its extreme delicacy and its capacity to form rich velvety masses.

Picasso's drawings are charged with energy, not recording ideas so much as enacting them, or bringing them into being. He had this creative potential in mind when he observed that 'when you start drawing a line you don't know where it's going to go – it starts and goes on until something stops it or makes it turn'.[13] It was this faith in the creative process as something that could not entirely be rationalised that drove his art through many transformations. He never ceased to recognise the magic inherent in the simplest drawn line.

'I've mastered drawing and am looking for colour,' Picasso once remarked to his friend Henri Matisse (1869–1954). 'You've mastered colour and are looking for drawing.' Late in life, recovering from an intestinal operation he had undergone in 1941 and confined to his bed or a wheelchair, Matisse searched for, and found, new ways of drawing.[14] A lifelong draughtsman, he now focused on the practice with renewed intensity; it was less physically strenuous than painting in oils, while demanding a similar seriousness of purpose. That same year he began a self-searching project that was published two years later as *Dessins: Thèmes et variations*, into which he channelled his long-term preoccupations with the female figure and still life. For each of the book's seventeen themes Matisse began by drawing a subject – a woman sitting in a chair, or a tabletop arrangement of vegetables and leaves – and made repeated versions of the same composition, introducing variations to pose, viewpoint or treatment, observing how a single theme can develop over time and in different circumstances. The effect resembles stop-motion animation. Drawing in this disciplined and serial manner was Matisse's way of exploring the mystery of the creative process that Picasso had identified, in which drawn lines seem almost to develop a life of their own. Matisse reflected on the nature of inspiration to the French poet Louis Aragon, remarking: 'Isn't a drawing a synthesis, the culmination of a series of sensations retained and reassembled by the brain and let loose by one last feeling, so that I execute the drawing almost with the irresponsibility of a medium.'[15]

As though in a practical riposte to Picasso, in the late 1930s Matisse developed a technique that enabled him to combine colour and drawing in a single process – he was, he said, 'drawing directly in colour'.[16] Taking a pair of scissors, he began to create images by cutting into sheets of paper that had been painted with gouache, and arranging the resulting shapes as collages. A commission for a book eventually published as *Jazz* (1947) prompted him to explore the narrative and decorative possibilities of cut-outs with joyful compositions of dancers and acrobats. Before long, Matisse began to make cut-outs on a more ambitious scale, large enough to fill an entire room. There was also, he felt, a sculptural aspect to cutting into paper – something he explored towards the end of his life in his 1952 sequence of four cut-out *Blue Nudes* (fig. 85). With his meticulous and painstaking exploration into the interface between drawing and the human figure, Matisse had not only united line with colour, but also raised the possibility of a third dimension.

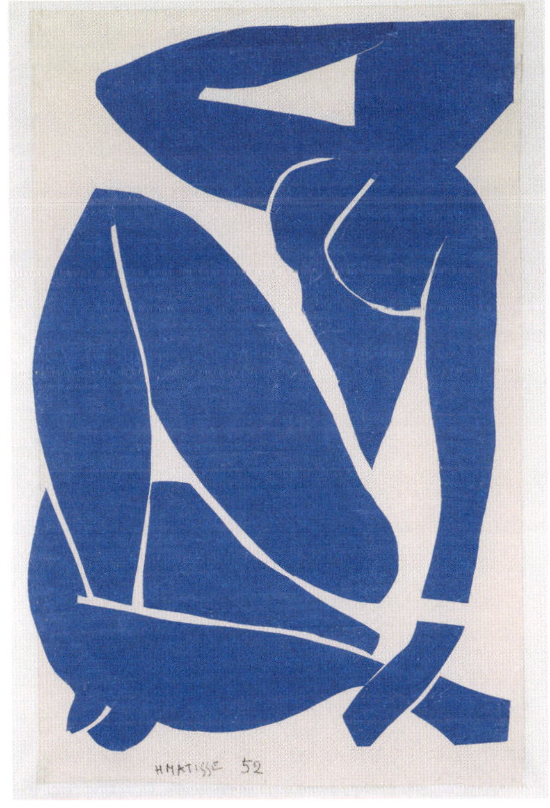

85. Henri Matisse, *Blue Nude (III)*, 1952. Gouache on paper, cut and pasted.

CHAPTER 18

MAPPING THE MIND

THE TOWNS AND cities of wartime Britain were a world turned upside down. Craters appeared where buildings had stood the day before. Wallpapers and fittings of what had been homes were exposed on the walls of terraces like dystopian dolls' houses. The living sought shelter deep underground.

In the midst of the chaos artists were at work, drawing because it was the most effective way to record the shocking reconfigurations in the immediate aftermath of bomb strikes before sites were cleared and made safe. Nothing about their task was easy, and artists worried that the act of sketching in the face of death and destruction risked appearing detached and unfeeling. When the medieval Coventry Cathedral was targeted one terrible night during the Blitz of autumn 1940, Kenneth Clark, the chairman of the War Artists' Advisory Committee, sent John Piper (1903–1992) there the following morning to record the still-smoking ruins as bodies were recovered from the surrounding rubble. Piper, reluctant to take out his sketchbook in the shell of the cathedral, decided to take advantage of a solicitors' office overlooking the site, where he sat by the window to make preparatory drawings for a painting.[1] Two months earlier, the sculptor Henry Moore (1898–1986) and his wife Irina had been waiting on a platform of the Underground until a bombing raid above passed, when he realised that many Londoners were preparing to spend the night sheltering there. He visited more stations, simultaneously horrified and fascinated by the sight of parallel rows of sleeping figures swaddled in blankets – like 'hundreds of Henry Moore Reclining Figures stretched along the platforms', he later reflected – but delayed making sketches until he was back in his studio because he did not want to intrude on the sleepers' privacy.[2] There was another reason: the time lag between witnessing the scene and putting recollections down on paper allowed his imagination to interact with his memories.[3] As he sat down to frame the chaotic scenes he had witnessed on the pages of his sketchbooks he introduced clarity and order, but also distilled his sense of the fear and danger and used it to charge his work with existential horror. From these sketches, he worked up large-scale drawings: one, of sleepers sheltering in the Liverpool Street extension to the Underground, conveys a Piranesian horror of incarceration, with humpy, huddled figures lining the tunnel, hardly differentiated (fig. 86). The pallor of Moore's clammy wax crayon resist, which preserves the whiteness of the paper when watercolour washes are painted over the top, turns blankets into shrouds and evokes the chill of dead flesh.

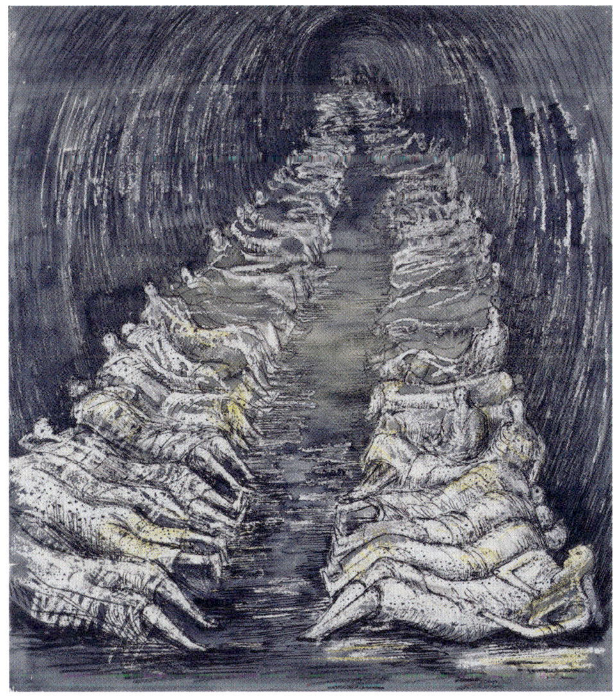

86. Henry Moore, *Tube Shelter Perspective*, 1941. Graphite, ink, wax and watercolour.

Drawing had a job to do during the Second World War. It was busy and needed. But what was its role after the war had ended and the urgency of recording the devastation had slackened? After the unspeakable horror of the concentration camps had come to light and the atomic bomb had been deployed as a weapon of war in Hiroshima and Nagasaki, it seemed to many impossible to continue as before. In the aftermath of the war, artists began to feel that art itself had to be rethought and rebuilt from scratch. The end of the war in Europe, midnight on 8 May 1945, was given the name 'zero hour', or *Stunde Null*, to mark an absolute break with the past and to signal a new beginning; the same word, zero, began to be used by artists' groups around the globe as they asked how it was possible to respond with creativity to a world that still reverberated with trauma.[4] Drawing, because of its immediacy and modesty of means, was at the forefront of their experiments.

Many artists turned their attention inwards to explore their psychological states, whether they were disturbed by the conditions of war or troubled by other factors. But how was this internal topography to be visualised and expressed? In New York, where she had lived since 1938 when she married and left Paris, Louise Bourgeois (1911–2010) watched for the visual thoughts that drifted into her conscious mind, and hurried to get them down on paper before they vanished. She had to be quick, so would reach for whatever surface was nearest: if there was no drawing paper she used envelopes, graph paper or cardboard.[5] She called these deeply personal emanations from her unconscious mind *pensées-plumes*, feather-thoughts; 'Drawing is essential,' she said, 'because all these ideas that come up, you have to catch them like flies when they pass, and then what do you do with the flies or the butterflies, you keep them and use them.'[6]

Bourgeois's drawings describe the shifting patterns of her mindscape like an intimate psychological diary. Many are constructed of dense parallel lines, recalling the threads that were a ubiquitous part of the tapestry-repair workshop that her parents ran and in which the young Louise would work. A drawing of 1944, *Throbbing Pulse*, also seems to liken the human body to the ocean that separated her from France by imagining the pulse as a series of waves surging spikily from a dense and heaving mass – not so much the rhythmic and comforting proof of life promised by the title as an unpredictable

　　　　　　　　　　　　　　THE STORY OF DRAWING

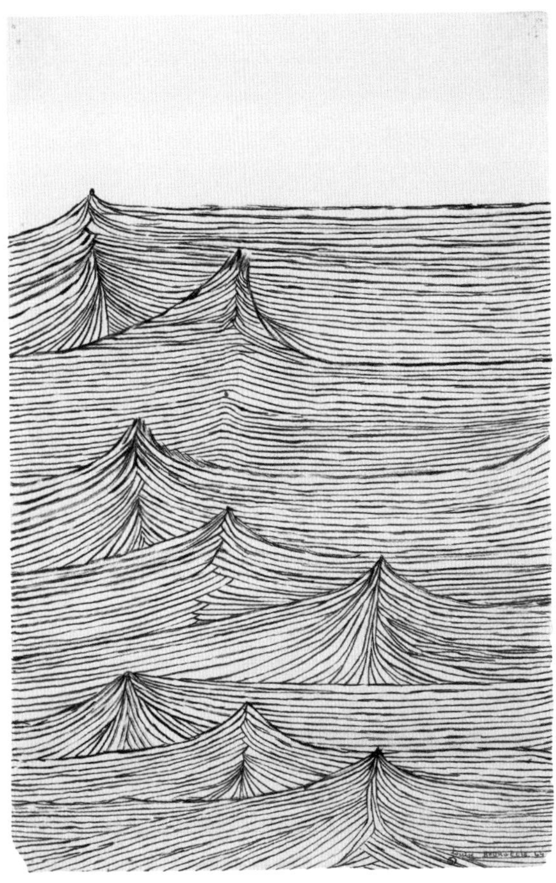

87. Louise Bourgeois,
Throbbing Pulse,
1944. Pen and ink.

disturbance (fig. 87). Some of these private and spontaneous drawings eventually formed the basis for sculptures, while others remained unexplored, put away by the artist and rarely shown – visual thoughts pulsing quietly with potential.

When Yayoi Kusama (b. 1929) was a young girl in Matsumoto City in central Japan she began to suffer from distressing hallucinations in which 'things would be flashing and glittering all around me. So many different images leaped into my eyes that I was left dazzled and dumbfounded.'[7] These recurrent experiences haunted her and she sought to exercise some control over them by drawing and painting obsessively, 'piling up a tremendous number of works in stacks that spiralled to the ceiling'.[8] While she was in her twenties and still living in US-occupied Japan, she continued to paint and draw as a form of therapy, creating hundreds of works that she destroyed before moving to North America in 1957 with the intention of starting again from scratch, piling them up and burning them in the stony riverbed behind her family home.[9] Among those to survive is a drawing of 1951, *Infinity Nets*, that appears to show a section of something bigger: there is no margin at the top or bottom of the sheet, as though the net depicted might extend exponentially (fig. 88). Yet within this implied enormity is intricate detail, obsessive and repetitive, as each space between vertical lines is divided by horizontals. It is a discomfiting image, and tiring to look at. It evokes captivity both in its structure of individual cells, each one divided by an unbroken line, and in a net's connotations of catching and constraining. The eye does not travel easily over the

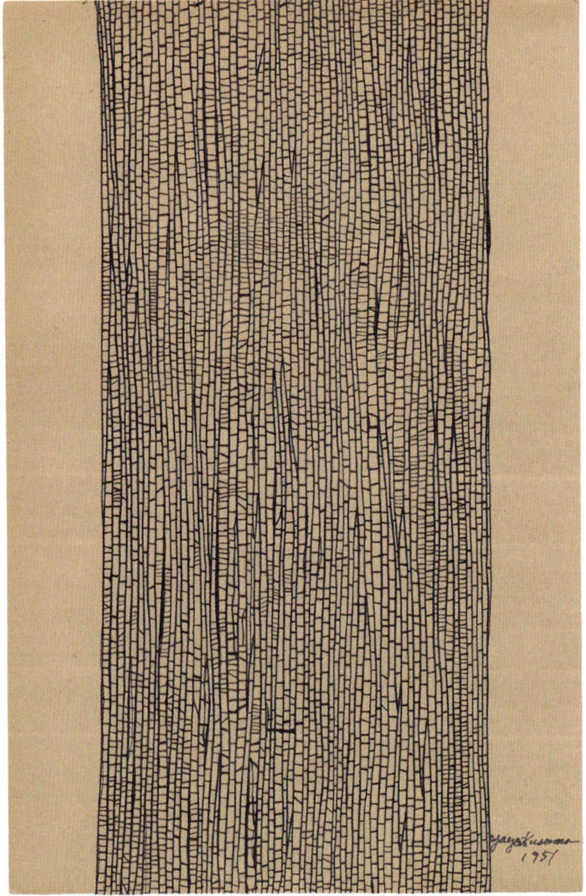

88. Yayoi Kusama, *Infinity Nets*, 1951. Ink on paper.

THE STORY OF DRAWING

drawing but seems repeatedly to snag as though caught in the net, and has to make an effort to free itself and move on.

Did Kusama draw nets in order to capture her frightening visions, to pin them down and stop them getting out of control? Many artists at this time did the opposite, searching instead for ways of opening their minds to the forces of chaos and chance, as though internalising and replaying the recent trauma of war. In Paris, Henri Michaux (1899–1984) had long focused not on the physical world around him but on an imaginary dimension of dreams, nightmares and ghosts, painting, in the late 1930s, a series of strange beings that he called 'phantomisms' in vivid gouache on black backgrounds. After the sudden death of his wife in 1948 he channelled his emotional energy into making hundreds of visionary drawings and watercolours. His interest in the role of spontaneity and chance in art led to his involvement in a movement known as Art Informel, a loose association of international artists committed to redefining what art could be. They were inspired by the automatic drawing that had been practised in the 1920s by the leader of the Surrealist movement André Breton (1896–1966) and later taken up by fellow Surrealists André Masson (1896–1987) and Joan Miró (1893–1983). Breton had encountered the phenomenon of autonomism, which involved drawing without preconceived subject or conscious control, as a form of psychological therapy when he was a medical student during the First World War. Artists associated with Art Informel created abstract images with impulsive gestures, the less premeditated the better, in order to access the potent well of creativity they believed to be located in the subconscious mind. Watery, spillable media such as ink suited works of art that were apparently driven by random and unknowable forces.

In the mid-1950s Michaux took deeper plunges into his unconscious mind when he began to experiment with the hallucinogenic drug mescaline, making drawings while under its influence. He diligently recorded his sensations as he experienced them. One day he accidentally swallowed six times his normal dose, and saw a vision of:

> Lines, more and more lines, which I am not sure I really see, though already distinct and fine (which I feel?) which I begin to see (how tenuous they are this time!) and how ample their

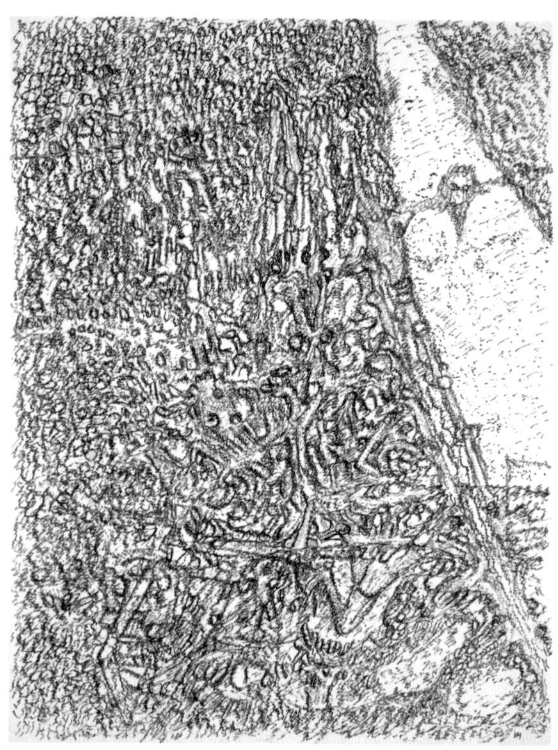

89. Henri Michaux,
Dessin mescalinien,
1959. Pen and ink.

curves, so very ample! I notice that at moments they disappear and again their amplitude, really extraordinary compared with their thinness, and I know that the colour white, which I am soon going to see, will be slightly violet, though I can still see nothing but the light, light gray of the spidery threads which boldly, rhythmically, incessantly stride over empty space.[10]

One drawing, simply called *Dessin mescalinien*, at first glance resembles a map, but look closer: what you might have taken for streets go nowhere (fig. 89). They are dead ends, repeated again and again. The sheet is covered with manic, scribbled lines that confuse and baffle the eye, reminding us of how profoundly the mind is conditioned to a search for order and control, pattern and design – and how disturbing it is when those factors are virtually absent.

There were other ways of pushing the conscious mind out of the way. 'When I am painting I am not much aware of what is taking

                                    THE STORY OF DRAWING

place,' declared Jackson Pollock (1912–1956). 'It is only after a sort of "getting acquainted" period that I see what I have done.'[11] His way of tapping into the subconscious was to involve his whole body in creating large-scale works of art with energetic gestures in a way that had hardly been done since Katsushika Hokusai stood on a vast sheet of paper and dipped a broom in a bucket of ink. In 1947 Pollock laid his brushes aside, as though they were weighed down with history and too greatly associated with control and premeditation, and he began instead to apply paint directly onto the paper or canvas. He poured and pooled, spilled and spattered. Sometimes he used unconventional tools to push the pigment around: sticks, or the handle of a paintbrush.

With this radical break from traditional methods, even from the innovations made by artists of the Art Informel movement, Pollock created a hybrid form of art that was hard to define. Was it painting – or drawing? The directness and spontaneity of his lines suggest drawing; but through repetition and layering many works acquired the substance of paintings. The artist Lee Krasner (1908–1984),

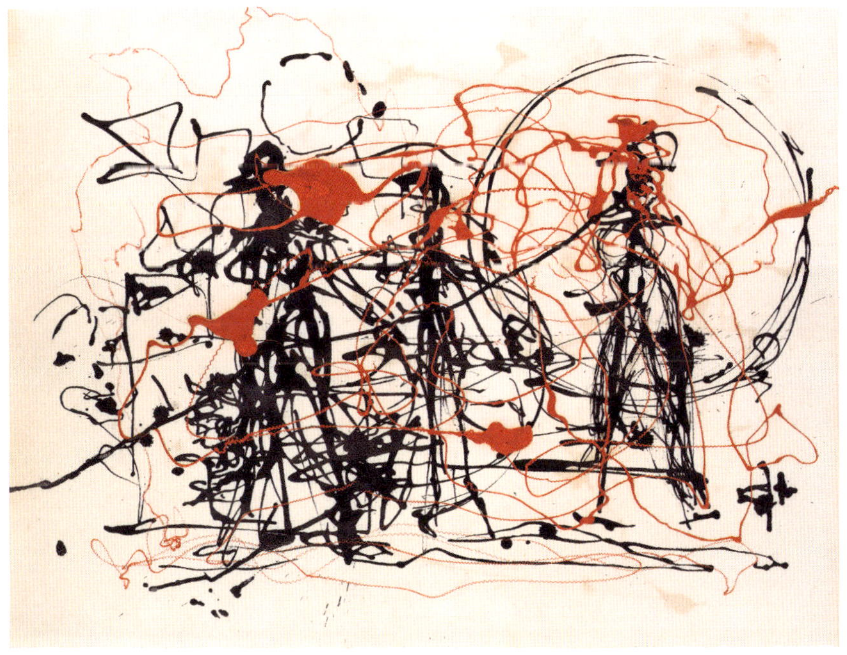

90. Jackson Pollock, *Untitled*, *c.* 1948–9. Dripped ink and enamel on paper.

who became Pollock's wife, remarked that his works 'seemed like monumental drawing, or maybe painting with the immediacy of drawing – some new category'.[12]

Pollock had found a way of expressing ideas and emotions without using conventional visual language, like a singer vocalising phonetic sounds rather than recognisable words. In a work on paper of the late 1940s he began by dripping black ink, establishing three emphatic forms at the heart of the composition: perhaps three standing figures (fig. 90)? As though it has absorbed the dynamic gestures of its making, the drawing resembles a dance, its lines and dashes syncopated rhythms, its arcs and circles whirls and pirouettes. The enamel paint that Pollock applied later than the black ink – blood red, pooling authoritatively over earlier lines – introduces a further dimension: implying the passing of time, perhaps, or even commenting on the first part of the drawing. Just as Pollock was trying to get around his conscious mind and tap into his unconscious, viewers of his works can also find themselves responding intuitively to the rhythms of his dancing, flowing lines.

   THE STORY OF DRAWING

CHAPTER 19

THE HUMAN SPAN

A FELLOW ARTIST once suggested to Jackson Pollock that he should try working directly from nature. 'I *am* nature,' he replied.[1] The pugnacious egotism of his response can also be felt in his compositions. If his canvases can on occasion express the graceful movements of a dance, they can also resemble the floor of a boxing ring after a bout, spattered with the blood, sweat and saliva of a violent struggle. By the time of Pollock's untimely death in a drunken car accident of 1956, however, artists were proposing alternative relationships to the world: more reflective, less fuelled by machismo. Lee Krasner's idea of a 'new category' had been prophetic: during the 1960s and 1970s, a time of huge social change, drawing became a fully independent medium. It took its place alongside other art forms – painting and sculpture, performance art and video art – and became a medium for exploring some of the most fundamental questions: how to express one's sense of self, one's place in the world or, indeed, in nature? How to communicate with others about the human condition?

Works by Pollock's contemporary Agnes Martin (1912–2004), who was born in Canada but moved to the United States when she was twenty, could hardly be more different – as orderly and contained as his were impulsive. Around 1960, while living in a block of artists' lofts in Lower Manhattan, Martin devised a hybrid form of her own that took elements from both painting and drawing: she began by staining the canvas with a wash, often subtly coloured, and then covered it with an even grid, drawn in delicate, ruled pencil lines. While Kusama's nets seem to catch and snag the eye, Martin's grids impose order on their environment like a clock ticking gently as it marks the slow passage of time. There is nothing cold or clinical about them, despite an evident attempt on her part to attain precision and to expunge evidence of a momentarily wavering hand in successive works.[2] Although framed in a different visual language from Pollock's extrovert displays, emotion is there too, pulsing quietly away. Martin's intention with these works is a generous one: rather than spilling her state of mind onto the canvas, she invites the viewer to meet her halfway: her works gently solicit a conversation. This refusal to buttonhole the viewer is played out in the subtlety of the drawing's surface: the eye is not detained by the lines but hovers between grid and background.[3] As a result, her works gradually absorb the viewer in a feeling, whether the sensation of a certain time of day or the experience of being in a particular landscape. She later described how, when she created *Morning* (fig. 91), she was:

91. Agnes Martin, *Morning*, 1965. Acrylic paint and graphite on canvas.

painting about happiness and bliss. I had to leave out a lot of things that one expects to see in a painting. Happiness and bliss are very simple states of mind I guess . . . To myself and to some others there is a lot of difference between one work and another – difference in meaning. There are many different happinesses and blisses. *Morning* [represents] a wonderful dawn, soft, and fresh – before daily care takes hold. It is about how we feel.[4]

Despite the apparent simplicity of these meanings, however, Martin's grids unfold them slowly; the longer we, the viewers, give them attention, the more rewarding her works can be. She was an advocate of stillness. And she knew the subtlety of what she was trying to capture, summing it up in a lecture of 1976: 'We are in the midst of reality responding with joy. It is an absolutely satisfying experience but extremely elusive.'[5]

The discipline and reticence of Martin's grids inspired a younger artist, Sol LeWitt (1928–2007). If a drawing could be planned on a mathematical principle, he asked himself, what did that mean for artistic expression? If a work of art could be created according to a formula, could the same work be recreated elsewhere? And did the artist him- or herself even need to touch the art materials, or could others do it? These were radical questions, especially against the background of the uninhibited and visceral disclosures associated with Abstract Expressionism. LeWitt made his first wall drawing in 1968, at the Paula Cooper Gallery in a group exhibition in Manhattan. A wall was the perfect surface for his purposes: it raised awkward questions about ownership and permanence. Using hard, sharpened pencils and a ruler LeWitt drew a series of squares, and within them horizontal, vertical and diagonal lines. But who would be prepared to buy a chunk of a gallerist's wall? Would she even allow it? In the event the work itself was painted over after the show, but it did not matter because for LeWitt the idea for the drawing retained its value. It could be created elsewhere. With this in mind he began to produce clear instructions for the making of his works that could be interpreted by others. *Wall Drawing #91*, for example, was first realised in 1971. And yet it could be created anew today by following his directions: 'A six-inch (15cm) grid covering the wall. Within each square, not straight lines from side to side, using red, yellow and blue pencils. Each square contains at least one line of each color.'[6] LeWitt separated idea from performance, like a composer writing a score that can be performed by musicians anywhere. Graphite particularly appealed to him because of the minimal material traces left by a pencil, especially a regularly sharpened one; as a medium it was less readily associated with bodily fluids than oil paint. Insisting that the idea was of greater importance than the execution, LeWitt recast the artist's role as an essentially cerebral one.

Where, though, did this leave the work's viewer? There was much to be said for the artist's fastidious new role – but was anything being lost in translation? Environment was important. At first, LeWitt devised wall drawings that could be created anywhere, but from the 1970s, thinking about the viewer's sensory experience, he began to tailor works to particular rooms. This sensitivity to the relationship between person, space and work of art was explored further by an artist who fled Nazi Germany in 1939 to settle in Venezuela, Gertrud Goldschmidt, known as Gego (1912–1994).[7] In the 1950s Gego began to experiment with wire, modelling it into three-dimensional *dibujos sin papel* – drawings without paper – which not only created shifting patterns as they were suspended in the air, but also cast slow-moving shadow drawings on walls and ceilings as the light changed. Then, in the summer of 1969, she flipped the relationship between viewer and work of art with an immersive installation in the Museum of Fine Arts in Caracas called *Reticulárea* (fig. 92). This time, viewers had to find their way around a three-dimensional drawing made of articulated stainless steel and aluminium wire, flexible nets mostly constructed of triangle shapes suspended from the ceiling to the floor and extending from wall to wall. Gego thought about the experience of visitors moving between her great volumetric nets like fish at the bottom of a lake of air: she was creating not just a cerebral experience, but one that involved the whole body. Imagine walking into Gego's *Reticulárea*, negotiating the airy, angular shapes that gracefully meet the floor. Look up: with every step you take the wiry nets realign themselves to your vision; hundreds of new linear arrangements hang in space. The wires frame the gaps between, dividing the space into shifting and dynamic sections, making you think of the volume of the air itself, high above your head. On the walls, the work multiplies itself with shadows.

                         THE STORY OF DRAWING

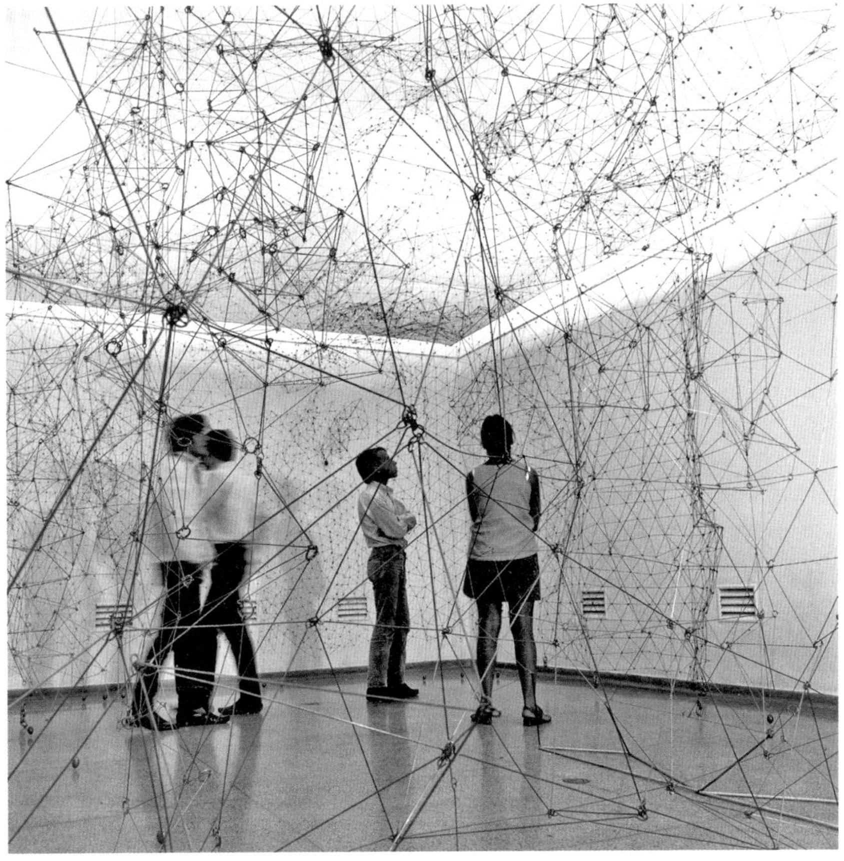

92. Gego (Gertrud Goldschmidt), *Reticularea*, 1969–82.
Installation of modular pieces made of stainless steel and aluminium wire.

Gego chose industrial materials that contrasted with the subtle emotional resonances of her nets – to catch, or to be caught. Artists have continued to explore self-imposed constraints and the state of being messily and imperfectly human, and the things that happen when the two push up against each other. In London, David Connearn (b. 1952) has spent decades exploring the most basic component of a drawing: the line. He normally uses a Rotring pen, designed for technical drawing, on the grounds that the line it produces is more even than that produced by most pens and less capable of expressive flourishes (Goltzius would have hated them). Connearn's method, though rigorous, is apparently simple: he draws a horizontal line near the top of a sheet of paper and tries to make it as straight as

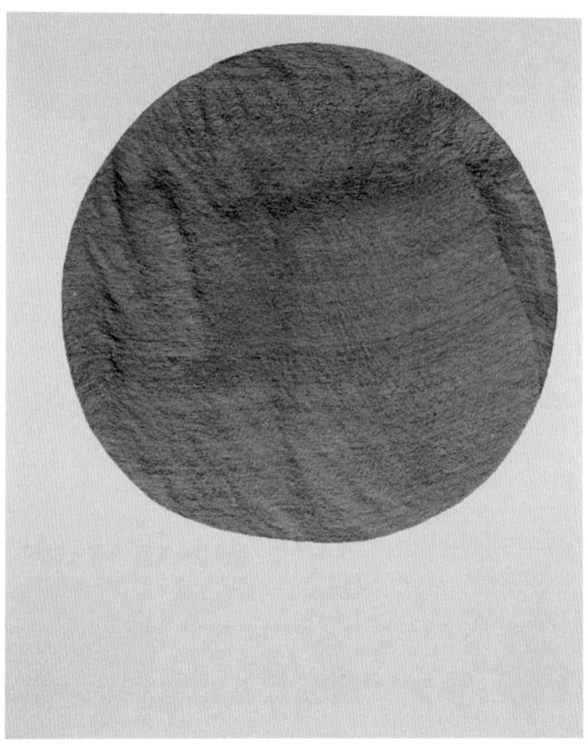

93. (a) David Connearn, *Mappa Mundi: Drawing to
the Extent of the Body*, 1984. Rotring pen.

possible. Then he draws another underneath it, close but not touching. This too he tries to make perfectly straight – although if the
line above has strayed slightly or wobbled, the one below will have
to follow suit: imperfection is as much a constraint as perfection.
And so on, down the sheet, until the drawing is finished. Today we
are conditioned to regard repetition as boring: but think instead of
a poem or a prayer; or the breath; or a day followed by another,
the same and yet different. Each month, each year, ticking by on
the pattern of those that went before. It is a method both humble
and profound. No line is quite the same, because the temperature
or humidity of the day will subtly affect the flow of ink, or some
other influence will cause the artist's hand momentarily to pause or
shake. Connearn strives for perfection but would, I think, acknowl-
edge the backhanded wisdom of Samuel Beckett's instruction, in his
1983 story 'Worstward Ho', to 'Try again. Fail again. Fail better.'[8]

                                     THE STORY OF DRAWING

In 1984 Connearn embarked on a major project, a drawing to which he gave the title *Mappa Mundi: Drawing to the Extent of the Body* (fig. 93). It was intended to reflect a human span, so he stood in front of the sheet with his feet in a fixed spot and reached with his right arm as high as he could to draw the first line. It had not only to be straight but horizontal too, and as a result it was short. Under such physical constraint, the longest straight line could only be achieved halfway down the drawing, and it was finished when he reached his limit with another short line at the bottom of the sheet. Together, the lines form a dense circle, recalling the human span of Leonardo's encircled Vitruvian man. The title suggests a globe. This, it says archaically, is what we know of the world: a subjective and partial vision assuredly, but the only one we have. Imperfections, where kinks have caused a line to buckle, and the error has been repeated and magnified down the sheet, seem to crumple the drawing like fabric.

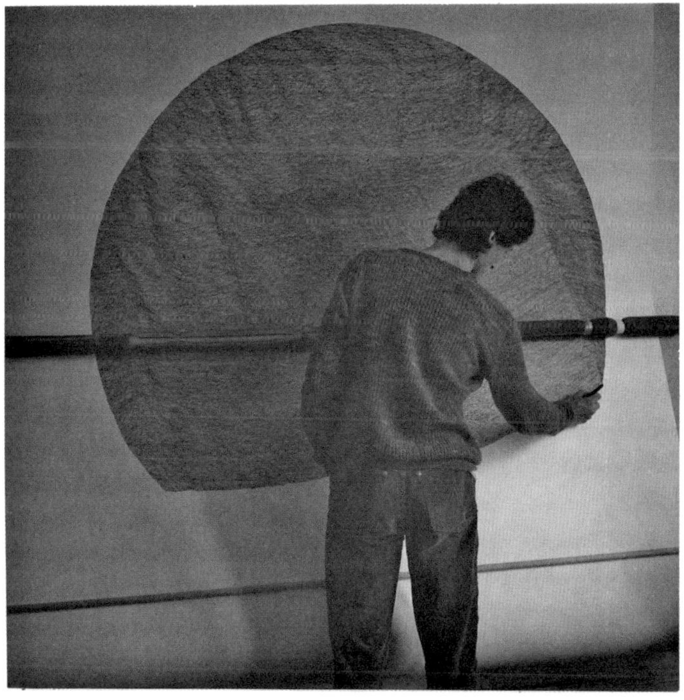

(b) David Connearn drawing *Mappa Mundi*, 1984.

Throughout his career Antony Gormley (b. 1950) has also explored the human span, putting his own body at the centre of his work, both in sculpture and drawing. Like Jonathan Richardson repeatedly scrutinising his own face with candour and courage, Gormley has undertaken a profound and extensive project of self-examination. He has asked: what is it like to be a self, looking out from a body? What are the body's boundaries? What is its relationship to the world it inhabits? Many, if not all, of Gormley's drawings are oblique self-portraits: he has drawn, for example, with his own blood and semen, both life-giving fluids containing his unique DNA (fig. 94). He has made a series of prints by pressing parts of his body, such as hands and knees, mouth and penis, onto prepared plates. Self-imposed constraints, however, direct his vision not inwards but outwards. 'The effect,' he explains, 'is of being inside the body and looking out at the universe.'[9]

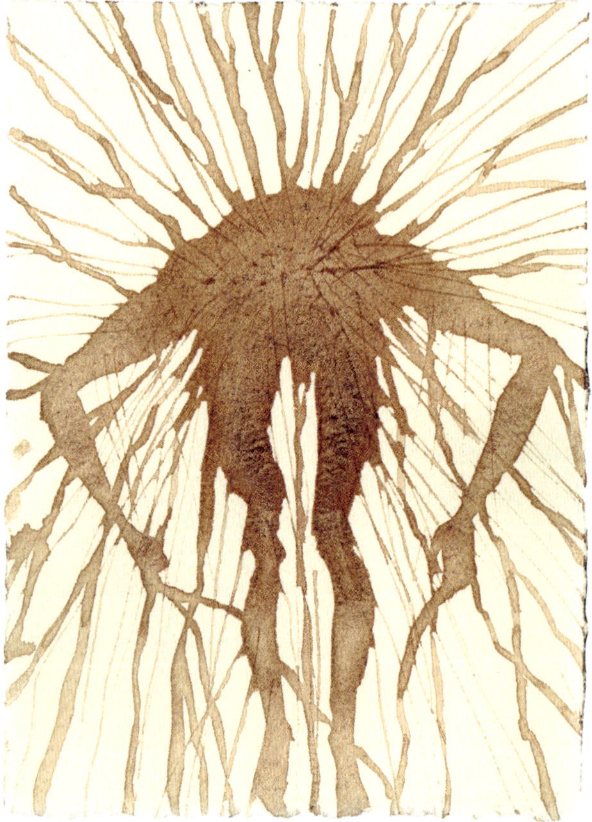

94. Antony Gormley, *7th Blood Field II*, 2020. Blood on paper.

Gestures are an important part of Gormley's work because they explore the paradox that marks made by an individual are both unique and typically human. He made the series *Systole/Diastole* (2008–10) – the title refers to the two pumping actions of the heart – by swinging his arm, sometimes both arms at once, to create swooping ovoids on large sheets of paper, which can be seen as oblique self-portraits. He held an etching tool in his hand to incise marks on sheets of paper coated with casein, a kind of paint that has a matt, velvety texture – creating a modern version of metalpoint. In another series, *Cusp* (2008), he repeatedly swept his arm from left to right, his hand like the mark-making arm of a recording instrument. Recalling the minimalist music of Steve Reich or Philip Glass, these drawings seem to pulse percussively. They share an elemental, ancient quality with all Gormley's drawings. Like anchors dropped through the turbulence of changing times down to the unchanging bedrock of humanity, they connect with the basic acts of breathing and coupling, standing and watching, of being in the world.

Reflections on the condition of being human are one thing. But what about an actual individual, sitting in front of you in all their complexity? Someone ultimately unknowable, even if loved, someone meeting your gaze at this very moment – how does an artist negotiate the immediacy of this encounter and enrich the eye-catching here and now with the quieter depth of experience? For Frank Auerbach (b. 1931), drawing a portrait is a lengthy and exacting exercise of discovery. He might work on one portrait drawing for many hours with charcoal or graphite, erasing, adding and erasing again until the surface is worn and abraded and the work itself has become a palimpsest, accumulations of older, imperfectly effaced marks – what he calls 'ghost drawings' – shadowing newer ones.[10] The process mirrors the layers of memory, emotion and imagination that the artist brings to bear on his subjects. Describing her own approach to drawing portraits, Maggi Hambling (b. 1945) has talked about discovering 'the landscape of a face', and quotes Alberto Giacometti (1901–1966), who 'likened making art to "a blind man groping in the darkness". True. I try to discover exactly the relation between an eye and a nostril, between a chin and a forehead, or an ear and an eyelash. It's venturing into new territory, every time.'[11] An artist of uncompromising candour, Hambling has repeatedly taken her sketchbook to the deathbeds of people to whom she has been close: her mother, father and her muse Henrietta Moraes. 'I'm well known for painting and drawing people long after they're dead,' she remarks wryly, adding, 'Artists are lucky in that they can grieve in a very positive way. I'm trying to make these drawings as alive as possible even though the subject is dead, because they're still alive inside me.'[12] A graphite drawing of her dead mother's face, her head seeming to float in space on a barely indicated pillow, makes her skin almost tangible: Hambling's usually vigorous and emphatic marks are gentle and lyrical here, stroked onto the paper with a tenderness so palpable it makes the viewer half want to look away (fig. 95). Here and there she has subtly shaded eyes, nose and chin by rubbing the surface with her fingers. Last touches, these, but each stroke a renewed connection and an act of remembrance.

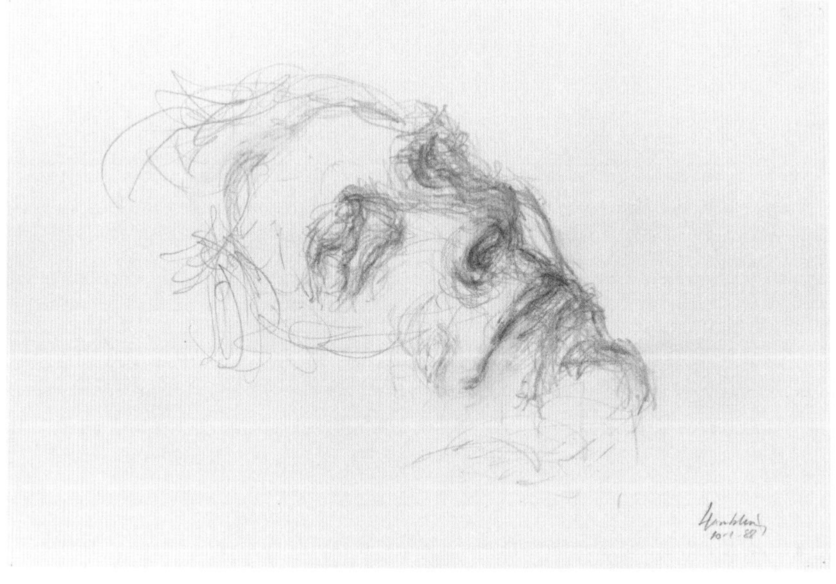

95. Maggi Hambling, *My Mother Dead, VII;
Portrait of the Artist's Mother*, 1988. Graphite.

   THE STORY OF DRAWING

CHAPTER 20

BEARING WITNESS

How can nature be captured at its most swift-moving and nebulous? How, for instance, do you draw a cloud? John Constable thought skies were every bit as important as the land and that artists should take their complexity more seriously. Fascinated by the ever-changing overhead drama, he frequently went 'skying', carrying his oil paints or watercolours out onto Hampstead Heath, choosing a section of cloud and dabbing furiously with his brush to capture the formations before they changed shape, his hand racing the wind. These sketches were never intended to be exhibited as though they were finished works – though these days they are, and audiences love the way they have of catching nature in the act. Tacita Dean (b. 1965) has gone further, choosing to draw clouds with materials that imply erasure: spray chalk on slates once used by children in Victorian schoolrooms, the mute witnesses to countless chalky doings and undoings. Dean was first prompted to make a series of cloud drawings during an eighteen-month stay in Los Angeles, when she noticed how different they were from those that drifted over British skies. There they hung, isolated in vivid blue, criss-crossed by vapour trails, preternaturally white and promising no rain. Dean then added a literary dimension to her drawings by inscribing quotations on the swirling vapour that turn the clouds into the pages of a book. 'The clouds methought would OPEN', proclaims one drawing, quoting Caliban in *The Tempest* (fig. 96). Another bears words from

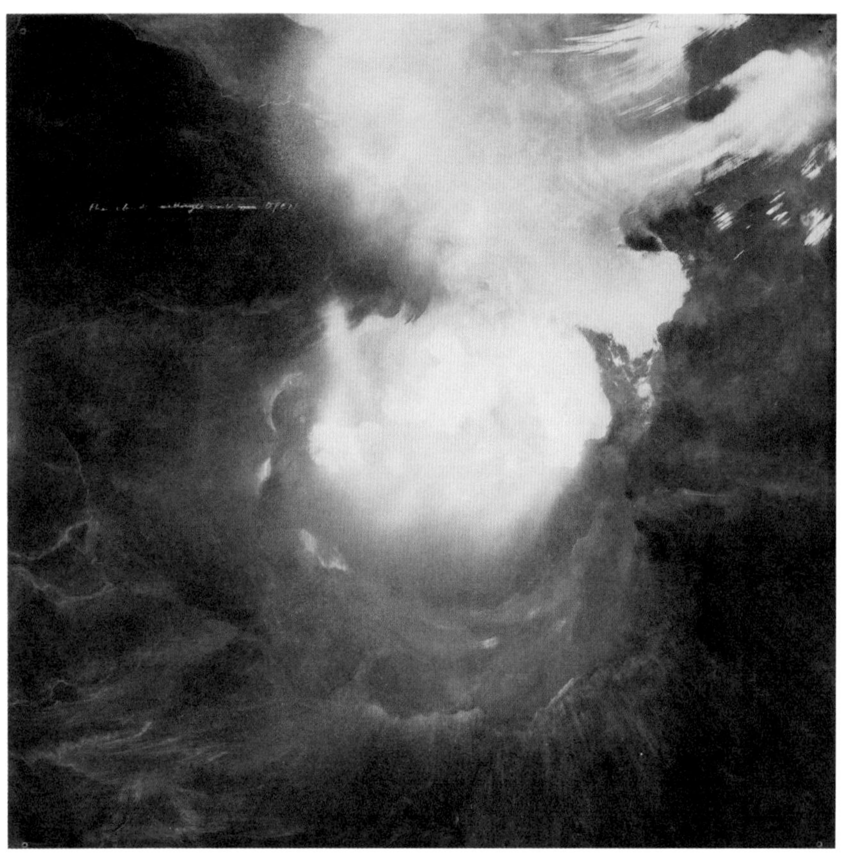

96. Tacita Dean, *The Clouds Me Thought Would Open*, 2015.
Spray chalk, gouache and charcoal pencil on slate.

Titus Andronicus: 'Sometime clouds, when they do hug'. Dean is a charismatic storyteller, casting enigmatic Shakespearean fragments into the skies. The words sit within each of her carefully crafted drawings like incantations, charming us into looking more intently into the drawings' vaporous depths and involving us in the artist's cosmic tale as she unfolds it from slate to slate and from cloud to shifting cloud.

Landscapes – and skyscapes – can be heavy with history. Dean may have seeded her Angeleno clouds with literary allusions, but for many artists today the stories the land itself has to tell are enough. Place, with its emotional resonance of the local and the particular, has taken over from the traditional concept of landscape, and artists are digging there in search of the hidden and the overlooked. Their choice

                    THE STORY OF DRAWING

of humble materials – ink and graphite – is a gesture of solidarity with the ordinary and the anonymous. The Irish artist Miriam de Búrca (b. 1972) became fascinated by the charged places known as *cillíní*, historic burial sites for unbaptised or stillborn babies and others the Catholic Church ruled to be unfit for consecrated ground, such as suicides, executed criminals and nameless bodies washed ashore from shipwrecks, especially after the revelation of the abuse and humiliation inflicted at state-run 'mother and baby homes' that operated between 1922 and 1998.[1] The graves of *cillíní* have no headstones or markers to commemorate the individuals buried, so de Búrca decided to make a series of drawings as a way of paying attention to the forgotten people. She would drive her car to a *cillín*, dig a small and unremarkable chunk of turf from the ground and take it back to her studio where she would draw it, earth, roots, weeds and all, in the kind of unselective detail coupled with extreme finesse that Albrecht Dürer would have relished (fig. 97). I imagine her, not in her studio but drawing at a steel table in a lab coat, so forensic an eye does she bring to the evidence. 'It's about not leaving anything out,' she says

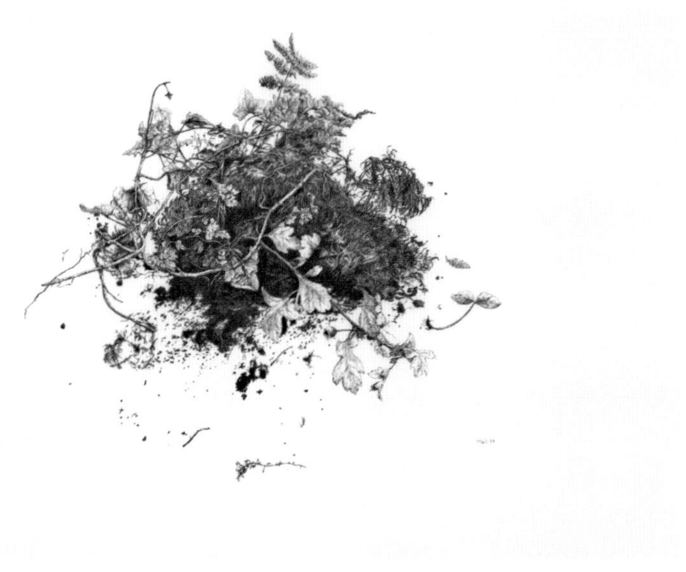

97. Miriam de Búrca, *Long Forgotten in Oughterard*, 2017.
Pen and ink on artificial vellum.

simply. She is aware of how the living grasses and weeds have been nourished by the decomposing, uncoffined bodies beneath, taking on their qualities: 'When I'm drawing the roots, I see hair, I see veins.'[2] As a surface for her turf drawings de Búrca chooses to use artificial vellum, partly because its smooth surface is receptive to fine detail and it is tough enough to withstand intensive working with her fine-nibbed pen; she has described areas in which she wants 'to achieve a sense of endless black'. The other reason is for its association with skin: the drawings embody their subject.[3] Having honoured the turf – and by extension, the lives of those whose bodies lay beneath – with her close attention, de Búrca drives back to the site and replaces it in the ground. The drawings, beautiful and slightly macabre, remain to demand the viewer's attention. They have a tale to tell.

Telling stories that bear witness to those wrongfully killed is at the heart of *Last Seen*, a series of drawings by Catherine Anyango Grünewald (b. 1982).[4] Her starting point is an image of a street or a park, taken from CCTV or mobile phone footage, that either by chance or by design captures the moment of someone's death through a violent attack or police brutality. She copies the image with pencil, a medium she chooses for its anonymity and grey ubiquity, working over the surface until the graphite builds up and begins to bubble and crack: a material echo of the frightening eruption of violence into normal life. The uneven graphite surface catches the light, so that to see the entirety of the drawings we are obliged, as the artist has put it, to 'observe them almost forensically, moving around to catch the light and with it, details and clues'.[5] Anyango Grünewald's drawings dignify grainy images of otherwise unremarkable places, giving them meaning and value, transforming them into modern-day 'history paintings' with titles that suggest nobility, such as *The Death of Trayvon Martin, Florida, 26.2.12*; or *The Death of Mike Brown, Ferguson, 9.8.2014*. Like de Búrca, she honours the victims both by her own investment of time and attention, and by obliging viewers to look with care. Her drawings involve and challenge their viewers, daring them to look away.

Abel Rodríguez (b. 1941), who grew up in the Muinane community near the headwaters of the Cahuinarí River in the Colombian Amazon with the birth name Mogaje Guihu, also recognises the role of drawing in bearing witness and honouring significant places.

But for him, the idea of 'art' is of little significance. 'We don't really have that concept,' he has said, 'but the closest one I can think of is *iimitya*, which in Muinane means "word of power" – all paths lead to the same knowledge, which is the beginning of all paths.' Rodríguez (a name he was given as a baby by Capuchin priests) is an expert on the rainforest, having learned from his uncle, a *sabedor*, or man of knowledge. 'I learned about the forest the hard way,' Rodríguez has said. 'I had to be awake for long hours at night; I had to lend my ears to the elders and make special diets.'[6] Having no system of writing or drawing, he had to learn about cycles of nature, the ecological balance of the forest and the medicinal and nutritional properties of individual plants and trees by heart, until he became known as *el nombrador de plantas*, the namer of plants. In the 1990s, however, he and his family were displaced from their native land by a combination of Colombian armed conflict and the depletion of local resources, and moved to the capital, Bogotá. There he met Carlos Rodríguez, the Director of Tropenbos International Colombia, a non-governmental organisation with a mission to study, understand

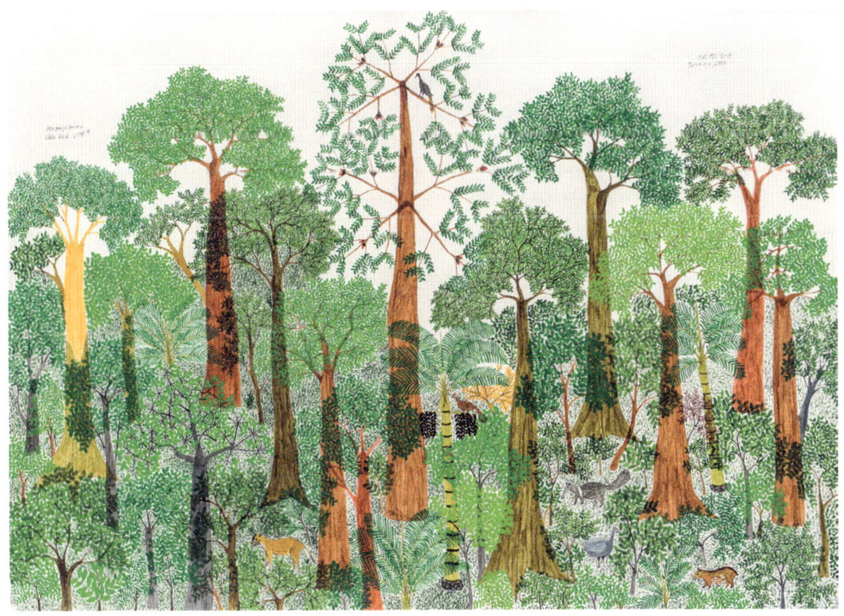

98. Abel Rodríguez, *Terraza Alta II*, 2018. Pen and ink.

and protect forests and their indigenous communities. Carlos became aware not only of the extent and subtlety of Don Abel's knowledge, but also its shamanistic dimension and an emphasis on spirituality that enabled the Muinane and other groups to live in harmony with the forest. He gathered art materials and commissioned Abel to make drawings of the forest from memory. 'I had never drawn before,' recalled Rodríguez; 'I barely knew how to write, but I had a whole world in my mind asking me to picture the plants.'[7]

The resulting drawings, executed in vividly coloured Chinese ink, are absorbing and complex, their precise detail inviting the eye to roam the forest floor, to travel up trunks and linger among leaves (fig. 98). In them, Rodríguez shows us around his forest, pointing out specific trees, and the birds and animals that rely on them; explaining how creatures behave when the rivers flood; revealing the gigantic tree of life that represents the forest's spirit. His are works neither of direct observation nor of the imagination, but instead forest chronicles that give visual expression to their creator's wealth of knowledge and experience. They carry within them a people's entire cosmography.

Protest drawings can be disconcertingly subtle. If you were to walk into a gallery and see a drawing by Imran Qureshi (b. 1972) on the wall, you might at first take it for a Mughal miniature of the seventeenth century (fig. 99).[8] Ah yes: the decorative border, the rich, jewel-like colours, the precision. But approach more closely; there is something wrong with the story. Overhead roll storm clouds, from which hail cascades like bullets from a machine gun. Spike-leaved plants bristle from the ground. Parasitic tendrils grip the lone tree's trunk and wave around its canopy, a menacing aureole. In the most courteous of terms, the miniature describes a catastrophe: a nuclear winter? The results of climate change? The extinction of the human race? We had expected a familiar story of leisure in a well-tended garden, only to find that we are confronting the end of the world.

Qureshi studied traditional miniature painting at the National College of Arts in Lahore, and uses the miniature's traditional role as a political tool to express his own convictions, whether forcefully or playfully (he has, for instance, created a series with a title of finely

   THE STORY OF DRAWING

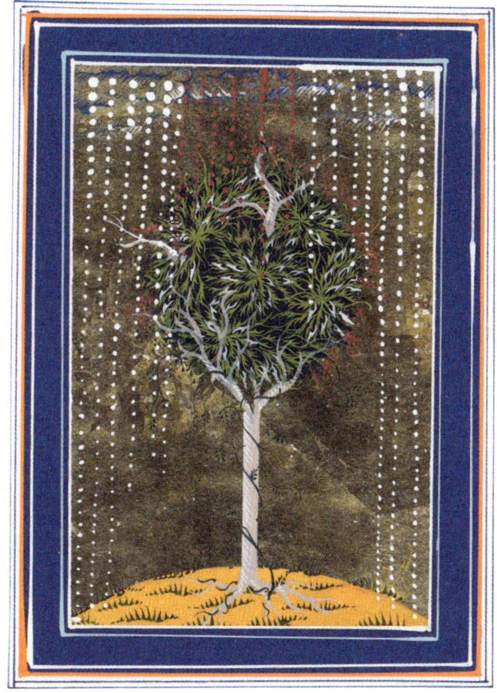

99. Imran Qureshi, detail from the series *Where the Shadows are so Deep*, 2015. Bodycolour and gold leaf on wasli paper.

tuned irony, *Moderate Enlightenment*). His drawings exploit the viewer's surprise when their expectations of the medium are baffled and challenged by the content. In the United States, Kara Walker (b. 1969) also uses a traditional art form to thwart expectations, in her case the cut-paper silhouette, a popular form of portraiture in the eighteenth and early nineteenth centuries and one favoured by middle-class women as a polite artistic accomplishment because of its neatness and delicacy. The world Walker draws so precisely with her scissors is, however, decidedly indelicate, her dark, tangled fables more Goya than Jane Austen, with earthy hints of Bruegel. And her cut-outs cannot be discreetly tucked away in a drawer, but are large enough to fill the walls of an entire room, where they command attention. Walker typically makes cut-paper figures representing black slaves and slave-owners in the plantations of the antebellum South, the absurdly exaggerated contours of the slaves' bodies based on racist stereotypes: she draws cartoon sambos, mammies and pickaninnies. By carefully positioning her cut-out figures and pasting them onto walls, she makes mordant observations on issues of race and gender. Her characters interact in ways that are often violent, sexualised and scatological: ungainly figures caper, tumble and fly; two pairs of legs surreally emerge from the hem of a fine lady's crinoline; a girl winds a key set into an exhausted slave's back. They are hard to look at, and as soon as you do you are swept up in Walker's graphic carnivalesque horror story, guilty by association.

The art of visual storytelling, with which this book begins, is a growing theme in contemporary drawing. It is present in Walker's riddling vignettes and in Qureshi's charged scenarios – present too in the poetry of Dean's clouds and the drama of Anyango Grünewald's CCTV stills. Toyin Ojih Odutola (b. 1985) has brought a new dimension to the genre, partly by the scale and ambition of her narrative drawing sequences and also by her layering of fictions.[9] When she exhibited her series of forty drawings *A Countervailing Theory* in London in 2020, she adopted the guise of an archaeologist to claim that they were not actually drawings at all, but scans of ancient

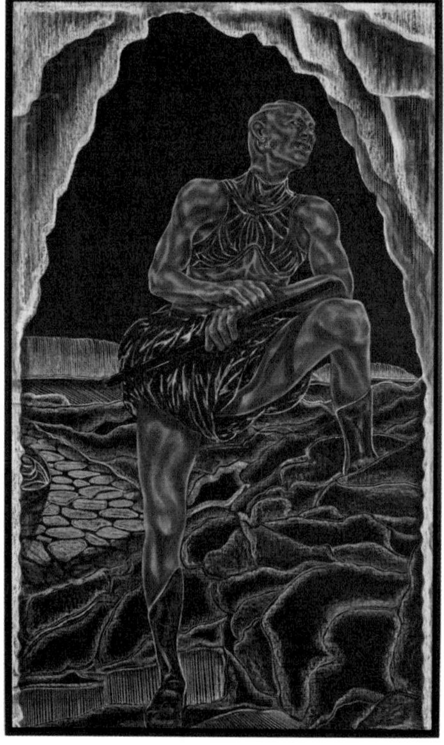

100. Toyin Ojih Odutola, *The Ruling Class (Eshu)* from *A Countervailing Theory*, 2019. Pastel, charcoal and chalk on black linen.

images inscribed onto rock that had recently been discovered at a dig in Riyom in Nigeria (the artist's country of birth), a place of spectacular rock formations. The sequence of images purportedly reveals the existence of an ancient civilisation in the region: they tell of how it was ruled by female warriors called the Eshu, and how they relied for labour on an underclass of manufactured beings resembling adult men, the Koba (fig. 100). They relate how sexual norms were upended too, with homosexuality being compulsory and heterosexuality regarded as deviant. The narrative framing device embeds Ojih Odutola's drawings deeply in time and place: viewers to the exhibition were invited to suspend belief as her story unfolded frame by frame, half-believing in the myth, but half-beguiled by the drawings' striking beauty as physical objects that undermined the premise. The works themselves have a compelling authority, partly due to their vision-filling scale and partly because of the artist's sensitive use of monochromatic pastel, chalk and charcoal on a black background to depict human figures with an almost three-dimensional presence against strange landscapes. Like Rosalba Carriera before her, Ojih Odutola is a master of pastel, able to contrast the roughness of rocks with the lustrous tactility of skin and to bring an uncanny liveliness to the silky, powdery surface.[10]

Enigmatic and immersive, playful and profoundly serious, Ojih Odutola's works seem to push at the boundary between present and future at the same time as they insist on their ancientness. It is an ambiguity that suits drawing itself: a medium that is both as old as humanity and as new as the dawn, always changing and forever constant. It is a medium for now and every age.

* * *

It is November, and the blustery wind that turned umbrellas inside out in the streets on my way to the gallery has suddenly dropped, causing rain clouds to drift off elsewhere, leaving chinks of vivid blue. I have come to see an exhibition of art inspired by the landscape of the English county of Sussex and I am looking down at *Chalk Stones* (2002) by Andy Goldsworthy (b. 1956): a line of seven hefty chalk boulders arranged on the floor, each one scraped around its middle with a flint to expose a stripe, pale against the weathered grey surface. So 'absolutely pristine and pure and white' was the chalk he exposed, said Goldsworthy, that he found it as disorienting as 'finding the sky in the ground'.[11]

As I stand and look, I find the sculpture – or drawing, because it is both – unexpectedly moving. Asking myself why, I realise it is because this unassuming work of art seems to collapse time, connecting deep history with today. When all seven stones are aligned, the stripes form a path from one to the next that suggests a track worn by human feet in a persistent, unending journey over the land. Yet for all that, it is not impersonal: it speaks to me, and it speaks to you. Seven milestones linked by a continuous path: three score years and ten, the natural span of a human life as pronounced by the psalmist. The universal journey. With the humblest of materials and the simplest of means, the artist tells a profound truth that sits at the heart of every human story.

I find myself thinking of the limestone tablet in the British Museum upon which someone scratched images some 13,000 years ago, a stone that also told the tale of its maker and of those who saw it. And then I think of other human stories that artists have told with drawings. I picture Guo Xi sitting down at his pristine table and taking up his brush to draw old friends meeting in a landscape, a scene that still breathes warmth and pathos a thousand years on. I see Michelangelo drawing Adam's torso for the Sistine Chapel ceiling, working out a pose that reverberates with latent power, the red chalk he pressed into the surface of the paper with such conviction bristling with the energy of his touch. And I imagine Antony Gormley, a stylus in each hand, swinging his arms to measure the human span, questioning what it is to be alive in the world today – and communicating what he finds through drawing. As I stand there the gallery suddenly brightens, and the paths scored into *Chalk Stones* gleam with light.

                          THE STORY OF DRAWING

bistre: an ink made from wood soot (often beech), containing tarry material and carbon particles, from which the coarser fragments have been extracted. The refined soot is dissolved in water. Its colour ranges from yellowish brown to dark brown, varying according to the kind of wood. It can be difficult to distinguish bistre from other brown inks, but a bistre wash may have a granular surface, leaving tell-tale particles on the paper. Bistre was mentioned in a treatise on painting of 1431, but was not widely used until the eighteenth century.

black chalk: a naturally occurring material, black chalk is a soft carbonaceous schist that can be cut into drawing sticks. In his technical manual of around 1390, Cennino Cennini described it as follows: 'for drawing, I have come across a certain black stone, which comes from Piedmont; this is a soft stone; and it can be sharpened with a penknife, for it is soft. It is very black. And you can bring it to the same perfection as charcoal. And draw as you want to.'[1] Many years passed, however, before artists began to draw with it at all, and it was not until the early sixteenth century that its potential was widely recognised. At a time when **metalpoint** was generally used for preparatory studies, chalk was a revelation: it was soft enough to create large areas of tone, but still dense enough to be sharpened to an edge or point for fine detail. The introduction of black chalk had a major impact on Renaissance drawing, allowing artists to work with great freedom and at scale.

black lead: see **graphite**

blue paper: from the early sixteenth century blue paper, or *carta azzurra*, made from rags that had originally been dyed blue with indigo or woad, became popular in Venice. Artists such as Vittore Carpaccio (*c.* 1465–1525/6), Titian and Jacopo Tintoretto (1518/19–1594) exploited the rich effects that could be achieved with **black chalk** and **white chalk** on its mid-toned surface. Blue paper has often faded with exposure to light, and taken on a brown, grey or greenish tinge.

bodycolour: also known as gouache, bodycolour is an opaque form of **watercolour** in which a filler such as powdered **chalk**, lead white (see **heightening**) or, after 1834, zinc oxide (patented that year by Winsor & Newton as 'Chinese white') was added to the mix of ground pigment and **gum arabic** that constituted watercolour. Bodycolour has a matt, velvety texture and was extensively used in the medieval period in the illumination of manuscripts.

brushes: in ancient Egypt brushes were made by chewing the ends of reeds to separate and soften the fibres, and as late as 1606 an English drawing manual recommended making a rudimentary brush by cutting a stalk from a shrub and chewing it.[2] Until the nineteenth century, bristles were inserted into quills to hold them tightly together, and used with a wooden or bone handle; the introduction of metal ferrules facilitated a greater variety of brush shapes. Specialist water-colour brushes were traditionally made from the tail fur of animals in the genus *Mustela*, including polecat, ermine, mink and sable, though since around 1980 most good-quality brushes have been made from a mixture of polyester fibres and sable.

carbon ink: a mixture of black, readily available pigment, usually soot or lampblack (the residual soot from burning oil or resinous wood), ground up with gum or animal glue and either moulded into an inkstick or diluted with water and bottled. It produces a black line that does not turn brown or fade. Carbon ink has been made for thousands of years; it was used in ancient Egypt, and was first recorded in China about 2500 BC. It is often called Chinese ink, though it can also be known as Indian ink, probably because from the mid-seventeenth century Europe began importing it from India.

 THE STORY OF DRAWING

cartoon: a preparatory drawing made during the Renaissance to establish the principal outlines of a painting, fresco or tapestry, drawn on the same scale (the name derives from the Italian *cartone*, large sheet of paper). For a large work, several sheets would be needed. The drawn outlines of the composition were perforated, or pricked, with a sharp point so that when the paper was held against the wall or canvas, powdered **chalk** (see **black, red** and **white**), **charcoal** or a similar substance could be pushed or rubbed through the holes, leaving a dotted line. This was a process known as pouncing: a thin, permeable cloth bag containing the pigment would be tapped against the cartoon, causing the colour to pass through the holes. The procedure often damaged the paper, and as a result few cartoons survive. The word acquired its alternative meaning as a humorous drawing in 1843, when a competition was launched to find artists to decorate the newly built Houses of Parliament in London with subjects from British history. The drawings submitted and put on display at Westminster Hall were parodied in the magazine *Punch* as 'Punch's Cartoons'.

charcoal: drawing sticks made by burning wood (often willow, plum, lime, walnut, myrtle and birch) in an airtight container. Cennini suggests filling a casserole dish with them, fixing the lid on tightly and putting it in the baker's oven overnight.[3] The lack of oxygen means that the wood turns to carbon rather than ashes. It has been used since prehistory. Charcoal is a dry, friable material that makes an uneven line and is easily brushed off the drawing surface, and as a result has often been used for preparatory drawing. It can be treated with a fixative to make it adhere more effectively to the drawing surface; soaking it in linseed or olive oil also has this effect, as well as giving it a richer texture.

chiaroscuro: from the Italian *chiaro* (light) and *scuro* (dark), meaning the balance of the two in a composition but generally referring to strong contrasts between light and shade.

Chinese ink: see **carbon ink**

collector's mark: a small inscription or stamp, applied to a drawing or print to signify ownership. This is usually in the form of a monogram or simple initials or occasionally an image. Drawings can acquire several of these marks over time, building up a physical history of provenance. The standard reference work for identifying collectors' marks is Frits Lugt's *Les Marques de collections de dessins & d'estampes*, now available to consult online and regularly updated (marquesdecollections.fr).

Conté crayon: a fabricated pencil originally patented by Nicolas-Jacques Conté in 1795 (see **graphite**). Following various experiments with adapting the original mixture of processed graphite and clay to make it richer, involving the inclusion of lampblack and other oily substances, in 1840 the manufacturers successfully added spermaceti, the waxy substance found in the head of the sperm whale. This resulted in a denser, more fluid line. The suggestive richness of Conté crayon was particularly exploited by artists of the late nineteenth century including Georges Seurat.

counterproof or **offset**: a copy made by dampening a sheet of paper and pressing it against a drawing executed in a friable medium such as **chalk**, thus transferring a portion of its pigment to the second sheet. The resulting image is both fainter and reversed. Making a counterproof was a useful way of reversing a pose in the planning of a composition.

crayon: a term that can refer to a wide range of drawing sticks or cylindrical rods fabricated from pigment and an oily or fatty binder, from **Conté crayon** to **pastel** to compressed **charcoal**. Now it is most often used to describe children's wax crayons.

deckle edge: a feature of hand-made paper. The deckle is a detachable frame that fitted onto a mould (whether for **wove** or **laid paper**), which held the pulp in place as water drained from it. Some pulp would inevitably seep beneath the deckle, creating a thin and irregular 'deckle edge' around the sheet.

drawing paper: see **watercolour paper**

Federkunststück: literally 'quill artwork', a drawing made to emulate the appearance of an engraving, with highly disciplined *hatching* and cross-hatching and lines that swell and taper expressively. Drawings of this kind are virtuoso performances of skill, and are most closely associated with the Dutch artist Hendrick Goltzius.

fibre-tipped pen: invented in Japan in 1962. Water-based ink stored in a fibrous cartridge within the shaft of the pen feeds into a tip made of harder fibre by the process of capillary action. The tips were initially made of bamboo, but later of synthetic fibre.

gouache: see **bodycolour**

graphite: a variety of carbon closely associated, chemically speaking, with diamond. Once known as **plumbago** or black lead because of its perceived similarity to lead (which was also used as drawing material), it was given the name graphite, derived from the Greek word *graphein*, to draw or write, in the 1780s by the German chemist and mineralogist Abraham Gottlob Werner. Other early names for the mineral were wad[d] and iron carbide/carbure of iron. An unprocessed lump of graphite has a slightly greasy feel to the touch because it is composed of hexagonal platelets that slip against each other. A graphite line has a characteristic sheen. In the middle of the sixteenth century a substantial lode of graphite was discovered at Borrowdale in Cumbria in the northwest of England. Used first to mark sheep, its potential as a drawing material was soon realised and by the 1580s a mine was in full operation. The graphite was cut into rods which were either encased in soft wood such as deal and formed into pencils or wrapped in string. Borrowdale graphite was high quality and expensive; it could sell for the price of gold. Other lodes were discovered in Bavaria, the Pyrenees, Flanders, Bohemia and elsewhere. Cheaper, lower-quality graphite could be processed by grinding and combining it with materials such as sulphur, antimony sulphide, fish glue, rosin, tallow and gum tragacanth, although the resulting substance left a weak line and was prone to breakage. A solution arose towards the end of the eighteenth century, when the Borrowdale mine was becoming exhausted and Britain and France were at war. Because of a trade blockade France was unable to import British graphite, so in 1794 Nicolas-Jacques Conté, a French painter and army officer, was tasked with coming up with a solution. He invented a process for grinding low-grade graphite and mixing it with pure clay earths, firing the paste in long, narrow moulds at a high temperature, then inserting the cylinders into grooved wooden batons. He patented his invention in 1795. Adding more or less clay produced a range of results from soft and dark to hard and silvery, resulting in the range of H and B pencils familiar today. Modern pencils are produced with synthetic graphite obtained from carborundum.

ground: see **prepared paper**

gum arabic: a water-soluble gum, usually the sap of the acacia tree, either *Senegalia senegal* (gum arabic, gum acacia or Sudan gum) or *Vachellia seyal* (red acacia). Gum arabic is ground and used as a binding agent for **watercolour** and ink. It causes the pigments to bind to the drawing surface after the water has evaporated.

hatching: even, closely spaced parallel lines used for shading and to create the impression of three-dimensionality. Hatched lines can be strengthened by the addition of another set of parallel lines placed at an angle, known as cross-hatching.

heightening: the application of white or pale highlights over a darker tone. The material used can be dry, such as **white chalk** or **pastel**, or wet, such as **bodycolour** (gouache). In the Renaissance, lead white was often used (a chemical compound formed by mixing lead with weak vinegar fermented in manure or with water and egg yolk), and it is fairly common to find drawings with areas of once white heightening that have turned a disfiguring dark grey because the lead has oxidised.

incising: dots or grooves made on the surface of paper with a metal **stylus** or the point of a compass to create an underdrawing before more visible marks are made. Incising can also be used to transfer the outlines of one drawing onto a second sheet placed beneath.

Indian ink: see **carbon ink**

   THE STORY OF DRAWING

Ingres paper: a **laid** drawing paper of light to medium weight with a distinct texture, or 'tooth', that is particularly receptive to friable media such as pastel, chalk and charcoal. It is produced in a variety of colours. Its name is misleading, because Ingres actually used fine **wove** paper for his graphite drawings. The product is first mentioned in a Winsor & Newton catalogue of 1910, where it is described as 'imitation Michallet'. See **Michallet paper**.

inkstick: see **carbon ink**

inkstone: a mortar, usually made of stone, for grinding **carbon ink** from an inkstick and mixing it with water. An inkstone has a sloping depression in the centre, the shallower part of which, known as the plain, is used for grinding and mixing, and the deeper part, the well, to collect the resulting liquid ink.

iron-gall ink: a mixture of vegetable tannins and iron salts (ferrous sulphate or iron filings), with **gum arabic** as a binder. The tannins are often derived from oak galls (also known as oak apples), round swellings, some 2–4 cm in diameter, that develop on some species of oak. Iron-gall ink was commonly used in Europe between the fifth and the nineteenth centuries, and was valued as a medium for both writing and drawing because of its permanence and intense colour: on oxidising in the air, it became a characteristic purplish black, blue-black or fully black, though over time it fades to deep brown. It is, however, acidic and has a corrosive effect on paper, sometimes eating holes in it. The earliest recipes for oak-gall ink can be found in the writings of Pliny the Elder.

Japanese paper: the most common fibres used in Japanese papers are *kozo* or paper mulberry (*Broussonetia kazinoki*), *mitsumata* (*Edgeworthia chrysantha*) and *ganpi* or *gampi* (*Wikstroemia sikokiana*). *Ganpi* or *gampi* paper is lustrous and translucent while *mitsumata* has a surface that is smooth and soft. Paper was probably introduced to Japan from China, via Korea, in the fourth century AD. Japanese papers were introduced to the Netherlands by the Dutch East India Company, via two shipments in 1643 and 1644. Rembrandt was among the first Western artists to use Japanese paper.

laid paper: before the introduction of smooth **wove** paper in the 1750s, all Western paper was 'laid' paper, made by draining a layer of pulped linen or cotton rags in a mould; the paper pulp would retain the pattern of the mould's mesh, which consisted of closely spaced horizontal 'laid' wires, held in place by widely spaced vertical 'chain' wires (for a fuller description, see **paper**). In the mould, the pulp that lies directly over the wires is slightly thinner, and so the pattern of horizontal and vertical lines shows up as paler than the surrounding paper when held up to the light (see **watermark**). Laid paper has a distinctly ridged texture.

lead pencil: a misnomer of extraordinary longevity arising from the superficial similarity of lead and **graphite**. See also **metalpoint**.

limning: a term used from the fifteenth century for painting in **water-colour**, deriving from the word 'illumination'. Small-scale portraiture developed in the Renaissance from a tradition of manuscript illumi-nation, and portrait miniatures were called 'limnings'.

metalpoint: a stylus with a tip made from silver (usually an alloy of silver and tin), gold, copper or lead. While lead leaves a mark on ordinary paper, gold, silver and copper only leave a visible line on paper that has been prepared with a ground, typically ground eggshell or burnt bone mixed with a binder (see **prepared paper**), to give it sufficient 'tooth' to abrade the metal. Metalpoint lines often oxidise in the air, turning a variety of colours depending on their constituent elements: silver becomes a warm greyish brown, while gold remains grey. Metalpoint was a challenging medium: once made, a line was difficult to erase (think of dragging a key over a wall painted with emulsion); it could be rubbed with a moistened finger, which left a smudge, or covered over with another layer of ground. Metalpoint is relatively unresponsive, as increasing or decreasing pressure does little to affect the strength or thickness of the line. Shading can only be achieved through a build-up of closely placed strokes. It was, however, well suited to sketching because once the surface was prepared the artist could draw without having to stop regularly to refill a pen. Metalpoint was widely used until the beginning of the sixteenth century, when artists turned to the more expressive media of **black chalk** and **red chalk** and metalpoint use went into a sharp decline. There was a revival of metalpoint drawing in late nineteenth-century Britain among artists such as Alphonse Legros (1837–1911).

Michallet paper: a French, hand-made, heavy, cream-coloured drawing paper with a bumpy surface; tiny comma-shaped projections from the surface catch and hold dry media such as **Conté crayon** and **chalk**, creating a rich effect. Georges Seurat favoured Michallet paper for monochrome drawings in Conté crayon.

ostraca: potsherds or flakes of limestone used in ancient Egypt as notepads or sketching surfaces. Because of their ephemeral nature, drawings on ostraca are often informal or satirical.

paper: invented in China in the second or first century BC and spread to Japan in the fourth century. Papermaking mills were established across Europe in the thirteenth and fourteenth centuries. In the West, the process of papermaking involved soaking cotton or linen rags, beating them in order to pulp the fibres and then adding water. A frame or mould made with a mesh – perhaps originally in Asia of cloth and later bamboo slats and, in Europe, closely spaced wires – is dipped into this pulpy solution, from which the excess water is allowed to drain away. The rectangular sheet of wet pulp is tipped onto a woollen felt, and another felt placed on top. When a stack of sheets is produced in this way, they are placed, along with their felts, in a press. When thoroughly pressed and dry, the sheets are dipped into a solution of water-resistant size (usually warm gelatine) to reduce their absorbency and make them suitable for purposes such as writing, drawing and printing. Finally, the sheets are polished, either by pounding with a hammer or by pressing them against a hot metal plate, any imperfections having been removed with a knife. They are then seasoned in the mill for several months so that sudden atmospheric changes do not cause the sheets to cockle or distort. In the nineteenth century wood pulp replaced cotton or linen rags in most commercially produced paper, resulting in a poorer-quality product that discolours and becomes brittle when exposed to light. See also **laid paper**, **wove paper** and **Japanese paper**.

papyrus: a drawing and writing surface made in ancient Egypt from at least the third millennium BC from the pithy stem of the papyrus plant, *Cyperus papyrus*, an aquatic wetland sedge widespread in the swampy areas of the Nile Valley.

parchment: the skin of an animal, usually a calf, sheep or goat, dried and treated to provide a surface for drawing, writing, painting and bookbinding. The younger the animal, the finer the skin; the finest parchment is produced from foetuses. The skins of white-haired animals were particularly valued in the production of manuscripts because they produced the palest surface. In the manufacture of parchment, skins that have first been dried and stretched are softened, often through soaking and agitating them in a vat of lime liquor, then the hair is removed with a knife and the flesh from the other side is scraped away. In the next stage skins are washed, then stretched on a wooden frame to dry. While drying, the skin is 'slicked' with a scraper, a process that removes residual hairs and pigment from the hair side and tissue and fat from the flesh side. The skin can be rendered smoother still by working over the surface with a flat pumice stone, which provides it with a fine nap. For fine parchment made from the skin of a calf, see **vellum**.

pastel: first used in the fifteenth and sixteenth centuries, pastel crayons are formed by grinding together pigment with filler and a binding agent, usually **gum arabic** (the hardened sap of the acacia tree). Water is then added and the damp mixture formed into cakes. Excess moisture is squeezed out and the residue (the *pasta*, or paste, that provided its name) either shaped by a die into long cylinders or rolled by hand. These coloured rods are cut to length, then left on wooden racks to dry for around a fortnight before being packaged for sale. In the seventeenth and eighteenth centuries pastel was most often used for portraiture. Pastel portraits became particularly popular in eighteenth-century France, Switzerland and Italy, notably those by Joseph Vivien (1657–1734), Jean-Étienne Liotard (1702–1789) and Rosalba Carriera respectively, each of whom brought a new liveliness and immediacy to the medium. In the nineteenth century pastel was revived by artists who recognised its potential for swift notations of light and colour, such as Eugène Delacroix, Edgar Degas and the Impressionists.

　　　　　　　　　　　　　　　THE STORY OF DRAWING

Later in the century, Symbolist artists including Odilon Redon were drawn to its chromatic intensity and its propensity for producing a dream-like blurring of edges.

pencil: for the familiar wooden case containing a rod of graphite (real or synthetic) see **graphite**. Confusingly, 'pencil' was once a common term for a paintbrush, particularly, though not exclusively, one associated with fine and delicate work. In a drawing manual of 1672, *Polygraphice*, the physician William Salmon writes that 'Pensils are of all bignesses, from a pin to the bigness of a finger, called by several names, as Ducks quill fitched and pointed . . . Jewelling pensils and bristle Pensils'.[4] As watercolour painting grew in popularity in the last decades of the eighteenth century, it became associated with the tapering brushes used for watercolours. A painting manual of 1859, however, states: 'The smaller kinds of brushes are still sometimes termed "pencils"; but the use of the word "pencil" instead of "brush" as distinctive of and peculiar to water-colour painting, has become obsolete.'[5]

plumbago: a name for the mineral **graphite** before 1789, when it acquired its modern name. Meaning an ore containing lead, the word derives from graphite's superficial similarity to lead. A plumbago can also be a small portrait executed in graphite (and sometimes ink), on **vellum**, like a monochrome portrait miniature. Plumbago portraits were fashionable from the middle of the seventeenth century until the early years of the eighteenth, and were a spin-off of the flourishing print trade in the Netherlands.

porte-crayon: a narrow, tubular metal holder (usually of brass or steel) principally for sticks of **chalk** or **pastel**, though it could also be used for **graphite** and **charcoal**. The ends are usually split and equipped with sliding rings that can be adjusted to hold the crayon tightly in place. The porte-crayon was usually double-ended, so could easily be turned around. It could hold short lengths of material and had the advantage of keeping the hands clean. The instrument was once synonymous with the act of drawing: 'The porte-crayon ought to be for ever in your hands,' urged Sir Joshua Reynolds (1723–1792) in 1769 to students at the newly founded Royal Academy of Arts in London.[6]

pouncing: see **cartoon**

prepared paper: paper that has been coated with a substance consisting of a filler, such as burnt and ground bone or eggshell, and a binder, such as gelatine or **gum arabic**. Several layers would be needed, and the final surface could be polished. A pigment would normally be added to colour the ground, adding another dimension to the drawing and affecting the appearance of the drawing medium. Leonardo da Vinci and Albrecht Altdorfer are both notable for their use of a wide range of rich and subtle colours. Prepared paper has a slight 'tooth' and was often used in conjunction with **metalpoint** (which leaves virtually no trace on ordinary paper), sometimes with the addition of **heightening** in lead white (a compound formed of lead with the addition of weak vinegar fermented in manure or water and egg yolk).

pricked for transfer: see **cartoon**

quill pen: used as a drawing instrument since at least the medieval period and supplanted only in the 1830s by the industrially produced **steel nib**. The most common feathers to be used for quills were those of the crow, duck, goose or swan. A large, strong feather was taken from the wing or tail. The quill would be partly stripped, then the lower part of the shaft placed in hot ashes to harden it and remove the outer membrane. The end was then cut at an angle with a sharp penknife to form a tapering point, and given a central slit which allowed the ink held in the shaft to flow more easily. The tip could be shaped with the knife to be broad or fine, according to the artist's wishes. The quill is an expressive drawing implement, gliding smoothly over the surface of the paper and responding readily to pressure from the artist's hand.

red chalk: also known as sanguine because it was considered to be the colour of blood. A naturally occurring material consisting of clay coloured by red ferrous oxide (also known as haematite, again because of its blood colour). Depending on where it is found, its colour can range from soft light red to reddish brown. Red chalk is an ancient art material, used in prehistoric cave painting and for wall drawing by the ancient Egyptians and the Romans. It was not adopted specifically for drawing, however, until surprisingly late. Leonardo da Vinci was among the first artists to explore its possibilities, and others quickly followed. Use of red chalk in early sixteenth-century Italy coincided with a new artistic focus on the human body as a vehicle for expression, and its colour introduced a new warmth and liveliness to flesh tones in figure studies and faces. Red chalk is usually harder than **black chalk,** so can be sharpened for detailed work. It is a component of the drawing type that came to be known as *trois crayons*.

reed pen: the most ancient of drawing implements, used in ancient Egypt and by the Romans, made from reeds (the shafts of tall, wetland plants) that have been cut into lengths and dried. The pith is removed from the shaft to make a reservoir to hold ink, and a nib is cut and shaped with a central slit. A reed pen is stiff and somewhat stick-like, and does not glide as easily over paper as a **quill pen**. It produces lines that are typically short, because the shaft does not hold much ink and needs regular refilling, and blunt because of its fibrous texture. Its lines tend to be either inky or, when it begins to run out, dryish and speckled in appearance. It was supplanted by the more pliant quill and rarely used by artists in the post-medieval period. Notable exceptions were Rembrandt, Piranesi, Van Gogh, Matisse and George Grosz (1893–1959), all of whom appreciated and exploited the emphatic and unpolished character of its lines. There is some confusion about the flexibility or otherwise of reed pens. Because of the fabled pliancy of living reeds it is often assumed that pens made from reeds are similarly supple. Although there is naturally some difference between reed varieties, when cut and dried reeds become stiff.

Rotring pen: in 1928 the German company Tintenkuli Handels, later renamed Rotring, produced a 'nibless fountain pen' known as the 'Tiku'. It had a narrow steel tube in place of a conventional nib, fitted with a wire to regulate ink flow. The design was patented in 1931. For the first time it was possible to produce a regular ink line that did not vary according to pressure, and as a result the Rotring was often used for technical drawing.

scratching out: a method of adding white highlights to a drawing in **watercolour** or ink wash that involves scratching the dry medium from the paper with a knife or fingernail in order to reveal the paper beneath. Both J.M.W. Turner (1775–1851) and John Constable used the technique.

sepia: although often thought of as a colour, true sepia ink is derived from the dried and pulverised ink sacs of the Mediterranean cuttle-fish and other cephalopods. After the ground sacs are mixed with boiling water and allowed to dry, the resulting sediment is mixed with **gum arabic** and a few drops of candy sugar to form a paste. Sepia has a cool, violet-brown colour and is prone to fading. It was mentioned by Pliny the Elder, though only became popular as a drawing medium in the nineteenth century.

silverpoint: see **metalpoint**

sinopia: a red or reddish-brown earth pigment that has been used as a drawing material since antiquity. Found in Egypt, the Balearic Islands and Cappadocia in Turkey, it acquired its name from the Turkish town of Sinop, on the Black Sea, where it was taken and sold. Pliny recorded that sinopia was among the four colours used by the Greeks. The pigment was commonly used to sketch the outlines of a mural directly onto stone or plaster. It was eventually replaced by the paper **cartoon**. These underdrawings, many of which have been discovered and restored in recent years, are known as sinopie.

Solander box: a box made of rigid board or wood in which draw-ings are stored. It has a hinged lid that fits snugly on the base so that dust is kept out and a stable environment is maintained within: the contents are shielded from sudden changes of temperature and humidity. The interior is lined with acid-free paper and the exterior is normally covered in cloth. When the lid is fully open the box lies flat. It is named after Daniel Solander, a Swedish naturalist who invented the box while cataloguing natural history specimens at the British Museum between 1763 and 1782. Solander boxes are made in standard sizes: Half Imperial, Royal, Imperial, Atlas, Elephant and Antiquarian.

steel nib: metal nibs have a long history – one was even found at Pompeii – and in the sixteenth century pens with gold or silver nibs were prized. The advantage of metal was that the tip remained sharp and did not need to be frequently re-cut and eventually replaced like a **reed** or **quill**. This was outweighed, however, by problems with corrosion and inflexibility. Nibs made of steel began to be produced industrially in the 1820s, but the first fully successful steel nib was patented in 1831 by Joseph Gillott of Birmingham; it had three slits to make it more flexible. Subsequently, steel nibs, stamped out of sheet metal and then shaped, were manufactured in vast numbers, and quickly supplanted the **quill pen**. They were available in a wide range of gauges, from wide to fine – the finest were called 'mapping pens'.

stump: an implement made from blotting paper or chamois leather, tightly rolled and tapering to a point at both ends. It is used for blending dry media such as chalk and charcoal, creating a soft effect.

stylus: a metal implement with a hard, pointed tip used for **incising** scored lines as preliminary guides in the planning of a drawing, before the addition of other media; it was also used to copy the contours of a drawing onto a sheet placed beneath.

trois crayons: drawing *aux trois crayons* refers to a combination of red, black and white chalk, often with the foil of a buff-coloured paper. The resulting lively interplay of colours is particularly associated with Antoine Watteau. Drawing *aux quatre crayons* refers to the use of black, white and two shades of red chalk.

vellum: the skin of a calf, dried and treated for use as a support for writing, drawing and painting. Vellum is of particularly fine quality. For animal skin (including the skins of kids and lambs) as a generic drawing support, see **parchment**.

wash: a generic term for a liquid pigment such as **bistre, carbon ink** or **watercolour** applied with a brush to provide tone.

watercolour: pigment ground with water-soluble binder, typically **gum arabic**. It is diluted with water and usually used on paper.

Watercolour pigment is translucent so that when the light passes through washes of colour and bounces off the paper it creates a slightly luminous effect. Traditional pigments were derived from natural materials: earths such as sienna, burnt umber, yellow ochre and terre verte, minerals such as azurite and ultramarine, and plant-based substances such as gamboge and rose madder. From the late eighteenth century onwards new synthetic pigments increased the range of colours. Artists originally ground their own pigments from materials that could be purchased in apothecaries' shops. In 1781 William Reeves invented small ready-made cakes of ground pigment and binder in a range of colours for which portable watercolour boxes were adapted. In the 1830s Winsor & Newton began to produce more malleable moist colours, first in porcelain pans and, from 1846, in metal tubes.

watercolour paper: towards the end of the eighteenth century a wide range of specialist **wove** watercolour papers began to be produced by firms like Whatman with varying degrees of 'tooth' or texture, from distinctly bumpy to smooth, and colours from bright white to tinted. This was originally known as drawing paper; the term watercolour paper only began to be used towards the end of the nineteenth century.

watermark: a distinctive emblem, word or decorative device identifying the mill or papermaker, formed from wire and attached to the mould. Its lines are transferred to the paper in the same way as the laid and chain lines and have the same translucency.

wax: used as a resist and applied to the drawing surface before **watercolour** or another wet medium is brushed over the top, so that the white of the paper is retained. It is particularly associated with drawings of the mid-twentieth century by artists including Henry Moore, John Piper and Graham Sutherland (1903–1980).

wax crayon: see **crayon**

white chalk: a naturally occurring material, usually calcite or calcium carbonate, a soft, brilliant white that leaves a powdery mark.

White chalk has often been used in conjunction with other drawing materials, particularly **black chalk** and/or **red chalk**, for highlights, often on coloured paper. It is a component of *trois crayons*.

wove paper: thought to have been invented around 1750 when the English printer John Baskerville asked the Whatman Turkey Mill in Maidstone, Kent, to produce more finely textured paper, though not widely produced and marketed as drawing paper until the 1780s. In the manufacture of wove paper, the pulp is dried on a fine wire mesh that gives it an even texture, eliminating the prominent pattern of parallel and crossing lines characteristic of **laid paper**. Wove paper enabled drawing media to flow unimpeded over the sheet, rather than bumping over the ridges and pooling in the hollows. 'I . . . could cry my Eyes out to see those furrows,' exclaimed Thomas Gainsborough to the man who sent him laid paper instead of the smooth drawing paper he had requested.[7]

The literature on drawing is uncontainably vast, and as a result a conventional bibliography, even one qualified by the word 'selective', would be too extensive to be of much practical use to readers. So instead I have placed details of particularly useful monographs on the drawings of individual artists or groups in the endnotes, where I suspect they are more likely to be found.

Because I have spent so much time over the years consulting shelves of books on drawing, I have imagined the following suggestions for further reading in the form of an ideal bookcase containing a capsule library of the volumes I have found to be the most useful and inspiring.

The first shelf is devoted to books that tackle the wider subject of drawing in terms of history, theory and practice: Joseph Meder's classic text *The Mastery of Drawing*, trans. Winslow Ames (New York: Abaris, 1978); Egbert Haverkamp-Begemann with Carolyn Logan, *Creative Copies: Interpretative Drawings from Michelangelo to Picasso* (London: Philip Wilson/Sotheby's, 1988); Diana Dethloff (ed.), *Drawing: Masters and Methods, Raphael to Redon* (London: Philip Wilson/Royal Academy of Arts, 1992); John Berger, *Berger on Drawing*, ed. Jim Savage (Cork: Occasional Press, 2005); Melanie Holcomb, *Pen and Parchment: Drawing in the Middle Ages*, exh. cat. (New York: Metropolitan Museum of Art, 2009); Deanna Petherbridge's magisterial *The Primacy of Drawing: Histories and Theories of Practice* (New Haven, CT, and London: Yale University Press, 2010); Stacey Sell and Hugo Chapman, *Drawing in Silver and Gold: Leonardo to Jasper Johns*, exh. cat. (Washington, DC: National Gallery of Art/London: British Museum, 2015); and Isabel Seligman's excellent *Lines of Thought: Drawing from Michelangelo to Now* (London: British Museum/Thames & Hudson, 2016).

On the next shelf the focus turns to recent and contemporary drawing: Laura Hoptman, *Drawing Now: Eight Propositions* (New York: Museum of Modern Art, 2002); Emma Dexter, *Vitamin D: New Perspectives in Drawing* (London: Phaidon, 2005); Tania Kovats (ed.), *The Drawing Book: A Survey of Drawing, the Primary Means of Expression* (London: Black Dog, 2007); Colin Perry, Marina Cashdan and Carina Krause, *Vitamin D2: New Perspectives in Drawing* (London: Phaidon, 2013); Katharine Stout, *Contemporary Drawing: From the 1960s to Now* (London: Tate, 2014); Roger Malbert, *Drawing People: The Human Figure in Contemporary Art* (London: Thames & Hudson, 2015); Isabel Seligman, *Pushing Paper: Contemporary Drawing from 1970 to Now* (London: British Museum/ Thames & Hudson, 2019); Julian Bell, Julia Balchin and Claudia Tobin, *Ways of Drawing: Artists' Perspectives and Practices* (London: Thames & Hudson/Royal Drawing School, 2019); Kelly Chorpening and Rebecca Fortnum (eds), *A Companion to Contemporary Drawing* (Hoboken, NJ: Wiley-Blackwell, 2020); *Vitamin D3: Today's Best in Contemporary Drawing* (London: Phaidon, 2021); and Claire Gilman and Roger Malbert, *Drawing in the Present Tense* (London: Thames & Hudson, 2023).

Books on drawings from particular regions begin with Italy with Francis Ames-Lewis and Joanne Wright, *Drawing in the Italian Renaissance Workshop*, exh. cat. (Nottingham: University Art Gallery, 1983); Carmen Bambach, *Drawing and Painting in the Italian Renaissance Workshop: Theory and Practice, 1300–1600* (Cambridge: Cambridge University Press, 1999); and Hugo Chapman and Marzia Faietti, *Fra Angelico to Leonardo: Italian Renaissance Drawings*, exh. cat. (London: British Museum/Florence: Galleria degli Uffizi, 2010–11). Progressing to Northern Europe, we come to John Rowlands and Giulia Bartrum, *The Age of Dürer and Holbein: German Drawings 1400–1550*, exh. cat. (London: British Museum, 1998); Mark Evans with Elania Pieragostini, *Renaissance Watercolours: From Dürer to Van Dyck* (London: Victoria & Albert Museum, 2020); Emily J. Peters and Laura Ritter, *Tales of the City: Drawing in the Netherlands from Bosch to Bruegel* (New Haven, CT, and London: Yale University Press, 2022); and An Van Camp, *Bruegel to Rubens: Great Flemish Drawings*, exh. cat. (Oxford: Ashmolean Museum, 2024). France is represented by Perrin Stein with *French Drawings from the British Museum: Clouet to Seurat*, exh. cat. (London: British Museum/New York: Metropolitan Museum of Art, 2005) and Christopher Lloyd, *Impressionist and Post-Impressionist Drawings* (London: Thames & Hudson, 2019); and England by Lindsay Stainton and Christopher White, *Drawing in England from Hilliard to Hogarth* (London: British Museum, 1987) and Kim Sloan and Stephen Lloyd, *The Intimate Portrait: Drawings, Miniatures and Pastels from Ramsay to Lawrence*, exh. cat. (London: British Museum, 2008).

The final shelf is devoted to books on drawing materials and techniques. The volume for which I have probably reached most often is the magnificent work by Carlo James, Caroline Corrigan, Marie Christine Enshaian and Marie Rose Greca, *Old Master Prints and Drawings: A Guide to Preservation and Conservation*, ed. and trans. Marjorie B. Cohn (Amsterdam: Amsterdam University Press, 1997). Of great value, and a good read in itself, is James Watrous, *The Craft of Old-Master Drawings* (Madison, WI: University of Wisconsin Press, 1957). Also here are Susan Lambert, *Drawing: Technique and Purpose* (London: Trefoil Press, 1984), John Krill's absorbing cultural history *English Artists' Paper: Renaissance to Regency* (New Castle, DE: Oak Knoll Press, 2001), Julian Brooks, *Master Drawings Close-Up* (London: British Museum Press, 2010) and Henry Petroski, *The Pencil: A History of Design and Circumstance* (London: Faber & Faber, 1989). Hugo Chapman and Marzia Faietti's *Fra Angelico to Leonardo* (2010–11) contains extremely useful passages on drawing materials. When compiling the glossary, as well as each of the above I have drawn on the detailed and extensive essays in *Grove Art Online* on particular subjects, such as parchment, paper, pens and ink.

Notes

Introduction

1 Grayson Perry, 'Grayson Perry Lassos Thoughts with a Pen', *Guardian*, 19 September 2009.
2 Web page introducing *Another Tradition: Drawings by Black Artists from the American South*, Morgan Library & Museum, New York, 2021 <www.themorgan.org/exhibitions/another-tradition> [accessed 7 May 2023].
3 Andy Needham et al., 'Art by firelight? Using experimental and digital techniques to explore Magdalenian engraved plaquette use at Montrastruc (France)', *Plos One*, 20 April 2022 <www.journals.plos.org/plosone/article?id=10.1371/journal.pone.0266146> [accessed 19 June 2023].
4 Neil MacGregor, *A History of the World in 100 Objects* (2010; London: Penguin Books, 2012), p. 17.
5 Deanna Petherbridge writes of the 'futility of attempting such a task' in *The Primacy of Drawing: Histories and Theories of Practice* (New Haven, CT, and London: Yale University Press, 2010), p. 16.
6 David Erdman, *The Notebook of William Blake* (Oxford: Oxford University Press, 1973), fol. N44, transcript.

1. Scribes, saints and sinners

1 See Guillemette Andreu-Lanoë (ed.), *L'Art du contour: le dessin dans l'Égypte ancienne*, exh. cat. (Paris: Musée du Louvre, 2013), pp. 144–5.
2 Anon., *Book of the Dead: The Final Judgement Scene*, c. 940 BC, British Museum, 1910,0509.1.80.
3 The authorship of the drawing is discussed in Melanie Holcomb, *Pen and Parchment: Drawing in the Middle Ages*, exh. cat. (New York: Metropolitan Museum of Art, 2009), pp. 50–2.
4 Holcomb, *Pen and Parchment*, p. 5; see also Melanie Holcomb, 'The Scribe as Draftsman', Metropolitan Museum blog, 11 August 2009 <blog.metmuseum.org/penandparchment/2009/08/11/the-scribe-as-draftsman/#more-1185> [accessed 25 May 2022].
5 See Martin Kauffmann, 'Scriptorium', *Grove Art Online*, 2003, rev. 2015 <https://doi.org/10.1093/gao/9781884446054.article.T077202> [accessed 25 May 2022].

6 Closing lines of Prior Petrus's MS of Beatus of Liébana's 'Commentary on the Apocalypse', British Library Add. MS 11695, here quoted from André Grabar and Carl Nordenfalk, *Early Medieval Painting from the Fourth to the Eleventh Century* (Lausanne: Skira, 1957), p. 168.
7 Steph Yin, 'In an Ancient Nun's Teeth: Blue Paint', *New York Times*, 9 January 2019; see also Amy Jeffs, 'The Nun with Lapis Lazuli in Her Teeth Is a Great Story – But She Wasn't Alone', *Apollo*, 21 January 2019 <www.apollo-magazine.com/the-nun-with-lapis-lazuli-in-her-teeth-is-a-great-story-but-she-wasnt-alone> [accessed 25 May 2022].

2. The wide world

1 Quoted in Arthur Waley, 'Chinese Philosophy of Art – IV. Kuo Hsi [Guo Xi] (Part I)', *Burlington Magazine for Connoisseurs*, vol. 38, no. 218 (1921), pp. 244–7 (at p. 247).
2 Mary S. Lawton, updated by Henning von Mirbach, 'Guo Xi [Kuo Hsi; zi Shunfu], *c*.1020–*c*.1090', *Oxford Dictionary of National Biography*, 2003/2021.
3 Quoted on the web page for the exhibition *Streams and Mountains without End: Landscape Traditions of China*, Metropolitan Museum of Art, New York, 2019 <www.metmuseum.org/exhibitions/listings/2017/streams-and-mountains/exhibition-themes> [accessed 21 July 2022].
4 Online catalogue entry for Guo Xi, *Old Trees, Level Distance*, *c*. 1080, Metropolitan Museum of Art, New York, 1981.276 <www.metmuseum.org/art/collection/search/39668> [accessed 21 July 2022].
5 On medieval diagrams, see M.W. Evans, *Medieval Drawings* (London, New York, Sydney and Toronto: Paul Hamlyn, 1969), pp. 11–13, and Holcomb, *Pen and Parchment*, pp. 20–2.
6 On the drawings of Matthew Paris, see Suzanne Lewis, *The Art of Matthew Paris in the Chronica Majora* (Aldershot: Scolar Press, 1987).
7 On Matthew Paris's itineraries, see Daniel K. Connolly, 'Imagined Pilgrimage in the Itinerary Maps of Matthew Paris', *Art Bulletin*, vol. 81, no. 4 (1999), pp. 598–622 (at pp. 598–9).
8 See Holcolmb, *Pen and Parchment*, pp. 25–6.
9 Villard de Honnecourt's model book is now in the Bibliothèque Nationale de France, MS Fr. 19093 <gallica.bnf.fr/ark:/12148/btv1b10509412z> [accessed 30 May 2022].
10 Translations from <www.medievalists.net/2018/12/medieval-sketches-villard-de-honnecourt> [accessed 1 June 2022].

3. In the Renaissance workshop

1 For a representation of pigments being ground in the workshop, see Parmigianino, *A Painter's Assistant Grinding Pigments*, *c*. 1530s, red chalk, Victoria and Albert Museum, D.989-1900.
2 Cennino Cennini, *The Craftsman's Handbook, 'Il Libro dell' Arte'*, trans. Daniel V. Thompson (New York: Dover Publications, 1960), p. 4.
3 Ibid., pp. 4–5.
4 Ibid., p. 8.

5 Raimondo Sassi, catalogue entry to Filippino Lippi, 'Two Male Nudes', in Hugo Chapman and Marzia Faietti, *Fra Angelico to Leonardo: Italian Renaissance Drawings*, exh. cat. (London: British Museum/ Florence: Galleria degli Uffizi, 2010–11), p. 236. On the function, survival, technique, development and legacy of fifteenth-century Italian drawings, see Hugo Chapman in Chapman and Faietti, *Fra Angelico to Leonardo*, pp. 15–75.

6 A comparable book containing ninety-three drawings by Jacopo Bellini, though on vellum rather than paper, is in the Louvre. See Hugo Chapman, catalogue entry to Jacopo Bellini, 'A Tournament: From an Album of 99 Folios', in Chapman and Faietti, *Fra Angelico to Leonardo*, pp. 122–9.

7 Doris Oltrogge, Robert Fuchs and Oliver Hahn, '*Finito* and *Non finito* Drawing and Painting Techniques in Botticelli's *Divine Comedy*', in *Sandro Botticelli: The Drawings for Dante's Divine Comedy*, exh. cat. (Berlin: Ausstellungshallen am Kulturforum/Rome: Scuderie Papali al Quirinale/London: Royal Academy of Arts), 2000–1, pp. 334–41 (at pp. 334–5). On Botticelli as a draughtsman, see Furio Rinaldi, *Botticelli Drawings* (New Haven, CT, and London: Yale University Press, 2023).

8 See catalogue entry to *The Empyrean: Beatrice and Dante in the River of Light, Paradiso XXX*, in *Sandro Botticelli: The Drawings for Dante's Divine Comedy*, pp. 282–3.

4. *Discoveries*

1 Giorgio Vasari, *Lives of the Painters, Sculptors and Architects*, ed. David Ekserdjian and trans. Gaston du C. de Vere, 2 vols (London: David Campbell Publishers, 1996), I, pp. 280–2. See also Maria Maddalena Rook, catalogue entry to Paolo di Dono called Paolo Uccello, 'Study of a Chalice', in Chapman and Faietti, *Fra Angelico to Leonardo*, p. 120.

2 Martin Kemp, *Leonardo da Vinci: Experience, Experiment and Design*, exh. cat (London: Victoria and Albert Museum, 2006), p. 2. On Leonardo as a draughtsman, see ibid.; Martin Clayton, *Leonardo da Vinci: A Life in Drawing* (London: Royal Collection Trust, 2018); and Carmen Bambach, *Leonardo da Vinci Rediscovered*, 4 vols (New Haven, CT, and London: Yale University Press, 2019).

3 The drawing is in the British Museum, inventory number 1875,0612.17.

4 Quoted in Kemp, *Leonardo da Vinci*, p. 51; the words are inscribed on a drawing in the Royal Collection, RCIN 919097v. On Leonardo's anatomical drawings, see Martin Clayton and Ron Philo, *Leonardo da Vinci: The Mechanics of Man* (London: Royal Collection Trust, 2010) and Martin Clayton, *Leonardo da Vinci: Anatomist* (London: Royal Collection Trust, 2014).

5 Martin Clayton, 'Leonardo in 1510: The Anatomical Manuscript A', in Clayton and Philo, Leonardo da Vinci: *The Mechanics of Man*, pp. 8–30 (at p. 8).

5. *Shows of emotion*

1 Vasari, *Lives of the Painters, Sculptors and Architects*, I, p. 306.
2 Ibid., II, p. 736; Hugo Chapman, *Michelangelo Drawings: Closer to the Master* (London: British Museum Press, 2005), p. 27.
3 Vasari, *Lives of the Painters, Sculptors and Architects*, II, p. 736.
4 A group of Michelangelo's écorché drawings is in the Teylers Museum in Haarlem.
5 See Chapman, *Michelangelo Drawings*, pp. 27 and 130.
6 Vasari, *Lives of the Painters, Sculptors and Architects*, II, p. 737. *The Punishment of Tityus* is now in the British Royal Collection; *Jupiter and Ganymede* is in the Fogg Art Museum, Cambridge, MA.
7 Both drawings are now in the British Royal Collection, RCIN 912766 and RCIN 912777.
8 Quoted in Chapman, *Michelangelo Drawings*, p. 278.
9 On Raphael's drawings, see Catherine Whistler and Ben Thomas, *Raphael: The Drawings*, exh. cat. (Oxford: Ashmolean Museum, 2017).
10 John Shearman, *Raphael in Early Modern Sources*, 2 vols (New Haven, CT, and London: Yale University Press, 2003), I, pp. 385–6; see also *The Art of Italy in the Royal Collection: Renaissance and Baroque*, exh. cat. (London: Queen's Gallery, 2007), p. 84.
11 Frederika H. Jacobs, 'Woman's Capacity to Create: The Unusual Case of Sofonisba Anguissola', *Renaissance Quarterly*, vol. 47, no. 1 (1994), pp. 74–101 (at p. 95).

6. *Close encounters*

1 Albrecht Dürer, *Self-Portrait, Study of a Hand and a Pillow*, 1493, pen and ink, Metropolitan Museum of Art, New York, 1975.1.862; Albrecht Dürer, *Self-Portrait*, 1521, pen and ink, Kunsthalle, Bremen, 1851/50 Z; Albrecht Dürer, *Nude Self-Portrait*, *c.* 1499; pen and ink with grey wash white bodycolour on blue paper, Weimar, Klassik Stiftung, KK 106. On Dürer's drawings, see Christof Metzger, *Albrecht Dürer* (Munich: Prestel, 2019), and Giulia Bartrum (ed.), *Albrecht Dürer and His Legacy: The Graphic Work of a Renaissance Artist* (Princeton, NJ: Princeton University Press, 2003).
2 See, for instance, Quinten Massys's *An Old Woman ('The Ugly Duchess')*, *c.* 1513, National Gallery, London, NG5769. Leonardo da Vinci also made many drawings of grotesque heads, usually of elderly men and women.
3 Alexander Browne, 'An Appendix to the Art of Painting or Limning', in *Ars Pictoria: or an Academy Treating of Drawing, Limning, Painting, Etching* (London, 1675), pp. 28–9.
4 Lauren Porter, 'Collecting Old Master Drawings', in *Charles II: Art & Power*, exh. cat. (London: Queen's Gallery, 2017), pp. 289–319 (at p. 293).
5 Hans Holbein, *An Unidentified Woman*, *c.* 1526–8, black and coloured chalks, Royal Collection Trust, RCIN 912273. I should like to pay tribute to the inspiring scholarship of the late Jane Roberts, formerly Royal Librarian, who showed me how to look at the details.

6 Matthias Grünewald, *Study for an Apostle (James or John) in the Frankfurt Transfiguration*, c. 1510–11, charcoal, fixed, partially heightened with white, Kupferstich-Kabinett, Staatliche Kunstammlungen Dresden, C1910-42.

7. *Enchanted landscapes*

1 Charles Talbot, 'Altdorfer Family', *Grove Art Online*, 2003, p. 1 <www.doi.org/10.1093/gao/9781884446054.article.T002094> [accessed 2 October 2023].

8. *Virtuoso performances*

1 See, for example, a drawing in the Courtauld Gallery, London, commissioned to celebrate the Holy Roman Emperor Charles V's entry into Genoa in 1533: <courtauld.ac.uk/gallery/exhibitions/past-exhibitions/perino-triumphal-arch/> [accessed 6 December 2022].
2 See online caption to the drawing in the Metropolitan Museum of Art by Carmen C. Bambach, <https://www.metmuseum.org/art/collection/search/395485?sortBy=Relevance&what=Drawings&ft=Perino+del+Vaga+(Pietro+Buonaccorsi)&offset=0&rpp=40&pos=1> [accessed 6 December 2022]; and Bernice F. Davidson, 'The Furti di Giove Tapestries Designed by Perino del Vaga for Andrea Doria', *Art Bulletin*, vol. 70 (1988), pp. 424–50 (at pp. 437–9). Davidson aptly describes the 'atmosphere enveloping the figures' in this drawing as 'clouded and dense, almost palpable, so that the forms appear suspended in liquid, illuminated by soft light drifting down through some watery realm' (p. 437).
3 E.K.J. Reznicek, 'Hendrick Goltzius', *Grove Art Online*, 2003, <www.doi.org/10.1093/gao/9781884446054.article.T033104> [accessed 9 December 2022]; see also Lawrence W. Nichols, 'The "Pen Works" of Hendrick Goltzius', *Philadelphia Museum of Art Bulletin*, vol. 88 (1992), pp. 4–56.
4 On Goltzius as a draughtsman during the period 1587 to 1614, see Huigen Leeflang and Ger Luijten, *Hendrick Goltzius (1558–1617): Tekeningen, Prenten en Schilderijen*, exh. cat. (Amsterdam: Rijksmuseum/New York: Metropolitan Museum of Art/Toledo, OH: Toledo Museum of Art, 2003), pp. 235–63.
5 Christopher White, Catherine Whistler and Colin Harrison, *Old Master Drawings from the Ashmolean Museum* (Oxford: Ashmolean Museum/Oxford University Press, 1992), p. 124.
6 John M. Gash, 'Michelangelo Merisi da Caravaggio', *Grove Art Online*, 2003, rev. 2015, pp. 23–4, <https://doi.org/10.1093/gao/9781884446054.article.T013950> [accessed 1 December 2022].
7 Carlo Cesare Malvasia, *Felsina Pittrice: Vite de' pittori bolognesi*, ed. Giovanni Pietro Zanotti and Vicente Victoria, 2 vols (1678; Bologna: Tipografia Guidi all'Ancora, 1841), I, p. 187; here quoted from Clare Robertson, 'The Carracci as Draughtsmen' in Clare Robertson and Catherine Whistler, *Drawings by the Carracci from British Collections*,

exh. cat. (Oxford: Ashmolean Museum, 1996–97), pp. 27–35. On the Carracci as draughtsmen, in addition to Robertson's essay see Babette Bohn, *Ludovico Carracci and the Art of Drawing* (London: Harvey Miller, 2005) and Catherine Loisel Legrand et al., *The Drawings of Annibale Carracci* (London: Lund Humphries, 2000).

8 See Gail Feigenbaum, 'Practice in the Carracci Academy', *Studies in the History of Art*, vol. 38 (1993), pp. 58–76.

9 Eve Straussman-Pflanzer and Oliver Tostmann (eds), *By Her Hand: Artemisia Gentileschi and Women Artists in Italy 1500–1800*, exh. cat. (Hartford, CT: Wadsworth Atheneum Museum of Art/Detroit, MI: Detroit Institute of Arts, 2021), pp. 34–5.

10 Babette Bohn, 'Elisabetta Sirani and Drawing Practices in Early Modern Bologna', *Master Drawings*, vol. 42 (2004), pp. 207–36 (at p. 208). See also Babette Bohn, *Women Artists, Their Patrons, and Their Publics in Early Modern Bologna* (University Park, PA: Pennsylvania State University Press, 2021).

11 The nineteen portrait drawings, mounted in an album of the early eighteenth century, are now in the Morgan Library, New York <www.themorgan.org/drawings/item/263862> [accessed 28 January 2023]. See Bohn, *Women Artists*, pp. 175–8; Straussman-Pflanzer and Tostmann, *By Her Hand*, p. 89. On the drawings of Lavinia Fontana see also Aoife Brady, *Lavinia Fontana, Trailblazer, Rule Breaker*, exh. cat. (Dublin: National Gallery of Ireland, 2023).

12 Malvasia, *Felsina Pittrice*, II, pp. 388 and 402. Translation by Babette Bohn in Bohn, *Women Artists*, p. 57.

13 Malvasia, *Felsina Pittrice*, II, p. 402. Translation by Babette Bohn in Bohn, *Women Artists*, p. 173.

14 Bohn, *Women Artists*, p. 183; Straussman-Pflanzer and Tostmann, *By Her Hand*, p. 147.

15 Bohn, *Women Artists*, p. 186.

9. *Culture and colonisation*

1 On individual drawings by John White, see <www.britishmuseum.org/collection/term/BIOG50964> [accessed 14 December 2022], which incorporates text from Kim Sloan, *A New World: England's First View of America*, exh. cat. (London: British Museum, 2006).

2 Quoted in A. Rogers and H. Beveridge (eds and trans), *The Tuzuk-i-Jahangiri or Memoirs of Jahangir*, 2 vols (London: Royal Asiatic Society, 1909 and 1914), I (1909), p. 215.

3 Ustad Mansur's drawing of a chameleon is in the Royal Collection, RCIN 912081. See <www.rct.uk/collection/912081/a-chameleon> [accessed 15 December 2022].

4 Quoted in *The Indian Heritage: Court Life & Arts under Mughal Rule*, exh. cat. (London: Victoria and Albert Museum, 1982), p. 39. See also Asok Kumar Das, *Wonders of Nature: Ustad Mansur at the Mughal Court* (Mumbai: Marg Foundation, 2012), pp. 86–8.

5 The curators of the Museum Rembrandthuis in Amsterdam have recreated Rembrandt's *kunstkammer* in one of the rooms.

6 Andries Pels, *Gebruik én Misbruik des Tooneels*, ed. Maria A. Schenke-veld-van der Dussen (Culemborg: Tjeenk Willink/Noorduijn, 1978), p. 78; quoted in Stephanie Schrader (ed.), *Rembrandt and the Inspiration of India*, exh. cat. (Los Angeles: J. Paul Getty Museum, 2018), p. 5. As Stephanie Schrader has put it of Rembrandt, 'the world came to him in Amsterdam' (ibid., p. 6).

7 Schrader aptly describes this group of drawings as 'creative copies' in *Rembrandt and the Inspiration of India*, p. 2.

8 Schrader identifies the subject of fig. 43 as Prince Daniyal, Jahangir's brother, and cites Rembrandt's source as Manohar's late sixteenth-century miniature of the prince in the Metropolitan Museum of Art, New York (accession no. 1955,55.121.10.32); Schrader, *Rembrandt and the Inspiration of India*, pp. 43–59.

9 Elisabeth Rücker and William T. Stearn, *Maria Sibylla Merian in Surinam: Commentary to the Facsimile Edition of Metamorphosis Insectorum Surinamensium (Amsterdam, 1705) Based on Original Watercolours in the Royal Library, Windsor Castle* (London: Pion, 1982), p. 85. On Merian's drawings, see also Kurt Wettengl (ed.), *Maria Sibylla Merian 1647–1717: Artist and Naturalist*, exh. cat. (Frankfurt am Main: Historisches Museum/Haarlem: Teylers Museum, 1998–9); Ella Reitsma, *Maria Sibylla Merian & Daughters*, exh. cat. (Amsterdam: Rembrandt House Museum/Los Angeles: J. Paul Getty Museum, 2008); and Bert van de Roemer et al. (eds), *Maria Sibylla Merian: Changing the Nature of Art and Science* (Tielt: Lannoo, 2022).

10 Rücker and Stearn, *Merian in Surinam*, p. 117 (caption accompanying plate 36).

11 Ibid.; and Reitsma, *Merian & Daughters*, p. 183.

12 This is one of the puzzles of Merian's book, as scientists have never found evidence that lantern flies are capable of emitting light and the story seems to be based on a fable. See Reitsma, *Merian & Daughters*, p. 206.

13 Maria Sibylla Merian to Johann Georg Volkammer, 8 October 1702; quoted in Rücker and Stearn, *Merian in Surinam*, pp. 64–5 (at p. 65).

10. *Peculiar ground*

1 Anne-Marie Logan has been able to infer that 'more definitely once existed' and has suggested that in the past summary landscape sketches were not appreciated by collectors and as a result were not preserved. Anne-Marie Logan and Michiel C. Plomp, *Peter Paul Rubens: The Drawings*, exh. cat. (New York: Metropolitan Museum of Art, 2005), p. 286.

2 See 'curator's comments', <www.britishmuseum.org/collection/object/P_Gg-2-229> [accessed 19 December 2022].

3 'De boomen wederschyn [en] In het Waeter bruynder / ende veel perfect-er In het Waeter als de boomen selvde.'

4 On Rembrandt as a draughtsman, see Seymour Slive, *The Drawings of Rembrandt* (London: Thames & Hudson, 2019).

5 Nicholas Turner and Carol Plazzotta, *Drawings by Guercino from British Collections*, exh. cat. (London: British Museum, 1991), p. 191.

6 See, for example, <www.rct.uk/collection/902717/a-landscape-with-a-three-arched-bridge-over-a-river-in-the-centre> [accessed 20 December 2022]; Turner and Plazzotta, *Drawings by Guercino*, pp. 199–200.

7 Jon Whiteley, *Claude Lorrain: Drawings from the Collections of the British Museum and the Ashmolean Museum* (London: British Museum Press, 1998), pp. 28–30.

8 Ibid., p. 100; see also Martin Sonnabend and Jon Whiteley, *Claude Lorrain: The Enchanted Landcape*, exh. cat. (Oxford: Ashmolean Museum, 2011), p. 76.

9 Wen Fong, 'Zhu Da [Chu Ta; Chuanqi; hao Bada Shanren, Pa-ta Shen-jen]', *Oxford Art Online*, 2003, pp. 1–3 <https://doi.org/10.1093/gao/9781884446054.article.T093469> [accessed 22 December 2022]. See also Mae Anna Pang, 'Zhu Da: The Mad Monk Painter', *Art Bulletin of Victoria*, no. 25 (2014) <www.ngv.vic.gov.au/essay/zhu-da-the-mad-monk-painter> [accessed 21 December 2022].

11. *Searching for the self*

1 Jonathan Richardson, *Two Discourses: An Essay on the Whole Art of Criticism and An Argument in Behalf of the Science of a Connoisseur* (London, 1719), p. 45; Jonathan Richardson, *An Essay on the Theory of Painting* (London, 1715), p. 179.

2 On Jonathan Richardson's self-portrait drawings, see Susan Owens, *Jonathan Richardson by Himself*, exh. cat. (London: Courtauld Gallery, 2015).

3 Ibid., pp. 44–5 and 26–9.

4 Rosalba Carriera, *Lettere, Diari, Frammenti*, ed. Bernadina Sani (Florence: Olschki, 1985), p. 390; see also Bruce Redford, *Venice and the Grand Tour* (New Haven, CT, and London: Yale University Press, 1996), p. 93.

5 On the drawings of Antoine Watteau, see Alan Wintermute et al., *Watteau and His World: French Drawing from 1700 to 1750* (London: Merrell Holberton/American Federation of Arts, 1999), and Pierre Rosenberg and Louis-Antoine Prat, *Watteau: The Drawings*, exh. cat. (London: Royal Academy of Arts, 2011).

6 Quoted in Marianne Roland Michel, *Watteau: An Artist of the Eighteenth Century*, trans. Richard Wrigley and Jennifer Wanklyn (London: Trefoil, 1984), p. 93.

7 Ibid., pp. 75–80.

8 See Wintermute, *Watteau and His World*, p. 33.

9 Quoted in Malcolm Cormack, *The Drawings of Watteau* (London: Hamlyn, 1970), p. 30.

12. *Places of the mind*

1 Antonio Maria Zanetti [the younger], *Della pittura veneziana e delle opere pubbliche de' veneziani maestri* (Venice, 1771), p. 462; and see Martin Clayton, *Canaletto in Venice*, exh. cat. (London: Queen's Gallery, 2005), p. 22.

2 On the drawings of Piranesi, see Sarah Vowles, *Piranesi Drawings: Visions of Antiquity*, exh. cat. (London: British Museum, 2020); and John Marciari, *Sublime Ideas: Drawings by Giovanni Battista Piranesi*, exh. cat. (New York: Morgan Library & Museum, 2023).

3 Johann Wolfgang von Goethe, *Italian Journey*, ed. Thomas P. Saine and Jeffrey L. Sammons, trans. Robert R. Heitner (New York: Suhrkamp, 1989), p. 363.

4 John Wilton-Ely, *Piranesi*, exh. cat. (London: Hayward Gallery, 1978), pp. 72–3.

5 Thomas De Quincey, *Confessions of an English Opium Eater*, ed. Alethea Hayter (1821; London: Penguin, 1971), p. 106.

6 Wilton-Ely, *Piranesi*, p. 73; Vowles, *Piranesi Drawings*, p. 21.

7 On the drawings of Alexander Cozens, see Kim Sloan, *Alexander and John Robert Cozens: The Poetry of Landscape* (New Haven, CT, and London: Yale University Press, 1986).

8 Alexander Cozens, *A New Method of Assisting the Invention in Drawing Original Compositions of Landscape* (London, 1785–6), pp. 4–7.

9 On the drawings of Thomas Gainsborough, see Marco Simone Bolzoni, *Thomas Gainsborough: Experiments in Drawing*, exh. cat. (New York: Morgan Library & Museum, 2018).

10 Philip Thicknesse, *A Sketch of the Life and Paintings of Thomas Gainsborough, Esq.* (London, 1788), p. 6.

11 <www.hsm.ox.ac.uk/moon-pastel-and-selenographia#listing_578786_0> [accessed 14 January 2023].

13. *Marbles and models*

1 The degrees of involvement in Italian art academies permitted to women in the seventeenth and eighteenth centuries are discussed by Sheila Barker in 'Art as Women's Work: The Professionalisation of Women Artists in Italy, 1350–1800', in Straussman Pflanzer and Tostmann, *By Her Hand*, pp. 46 51.

2 Kauffman's sketchbook is in the Victoria and Albert Museum, London, nos E.345 to 481-1927: <www.collections.vam.ac.uk/search/?page=1&page_size=15&q=Angelica+Kauffman+sketchbook> [accessed 29 March 2024].

3 On Rome as a centre for the study of antique sculpture in the eighteenth century, see Adriano Aymonino, ' "Nature Perfected": The Theory and Practice of Drawing after the Antique', in Adriano Aymonino and Anne Varick Lauder, *Drawn from the Antique: Artists & the Classical Ideal*, exh. cat. (Haarlem: Teylers Museum/London: Sir John Soane's Museum, 2015), pp. 15–67 (at pp. 52–7).

4 Peter Walch, in 'An Early Neoclassical Sketchbook by Angelica Kauffman', *Burlington Magazine*, vol. 119 (1977), pp. 98–111, remarks that this drawing is 'A rapid outline sketch. Much freer than the other studies of antique statues' (at p. 111).

5 On this particular point see Walch, 'An Early Neoclassical Sketchbook', p. 107. See also Wendy Wassyng Roworth, 'Kauffman and the Art of Painting in England', in Wendy Wassyng Roworth (ed.), *Angelica*

Kauffman, A Continental Artist in Georgian England (London: Reaktion, 1992), pp. 11–95 (at pp. 17–19).

6 Johan Joseph Zoffany, *The Academicians of the Royal Academy* (1771–1). Oil on canvas, 101.1 × 147.5 cm. Royal Collection Trust; <www.rct.uk/collection/400747/the-academicians-of-the-royal-academy> [accessed 28 November 2023].

7 John Thomas Smith, *Nollekens and His Times*, 2 vols (London, 1828), I, p. 69.

8 Remark recorded by Miette de Villars in *Mémoires de David, peintre et député à la Convention* (Paris, 1850); here quoted from Anita Brookner, *Jacques-Louis David* (London: Thames & Hudson, 1980), p. 49.

9 Quoted in Perrin Stein (ed.), *Jacques Louis David: Radical Draftsman*, exh. cat. (New York: Metropolitan Museum of Art, 2022), p. 78.

10 On the significance of David's Roman albums and drawings, see Benjamin Perronet in Stein, *Jacques Louis David*, pp. 90–8 (at pp. 97–8).

11 On Flaxman's drawing, see David Bindman, 'Line into Contour: John Flaxman's Drawing in Practice and Theory', *Art UK*, 2016 <www.artuk.org/discover/stories/line-into-contour-john-flaxmans-drawing-in-practice-and-theory> [accessed 20 January 2023].

12 From Fuseli's *Aphorisms on Art*, compiled in the late 1780s but not published until John Knowles's *Life and Writing of Henry Fuseli* in 1831. Here quoted from Aymonino and Lauder, *Drawn from the Antique*, p. 182.

13 Suggested by Adriano Aymonino and Eloisa Dodero in their catalogue entry to Fuseli's drawing, *Drawn from the Antique*, pp. 180–4 (at p. 184).

14. Observation and imagination

1 On the drawings of this group of artists in 1770s Rome, see Nancy L. Pressly, *The Fuseli Circle in Rome: Early Romantic Art of the 1770s*, exh. cat. (New Haven, CT: Yale Center for British Art, 1979).

2 On Fuseli's erotic drawings, see Ketty Gottardo and David H. Solkin (eds), *Fuseli and the Modern Woman: Fashion, Fantasy, Festishism*, exh. cat. (London: Courtauld Gallery, 2022–3).

3 On Goya's drawings and prints, see Mark McDonald, *Goya's Graphic Imagination*, exh. cat. (New York: Metropolitan Museum of Art, 2021).

4 William Blake to William Hayley, 23 October 1804; *The Letters of William Blake*, ed. Geoffrey Keynes (Oxford: Clarendon Press, 1980), p. 101.

5 Allan Cunningham, *The Lives of the Most Eminent British Painters, Sculptors and Architects*, 6 vols (London, 1829–33), II, pp. 165–6.

6 Charles Robert Leslie, *Memoirs of the Life of John Constable, Composed Chiefly of His Letters*, ed. Jonathan Mayne (1951; London: Phaidon, 1995), p. 239.

7 John Constable to Maria Bicknell, 27 August 1815; *John Constable's Correspondence*, ed. R.B. Beckett, 6 vols (Ipswich: Suffolk Records Office/HMSO, 1962–70), II (1964), p. 149. On Constable's drawings, see Ian Fleming-Williams, *Constable: A Master Draughtsman*, exh. cat. (London: Dulwich Picture Gallery, 1994).

8 Leslie, *Memoirs of the Life of John Constable*, p. 174.

9 See Gary Tinterow and Philip Conisbee (eds), *Portraits by Ingres: Image of an Epoch*, exh. cat. (London: National Gallery/Washington, DC: National Gallery of Art/New York: Metropolitan Museum of Art, 1999), p. 111. One version of the anecdote is related in Auguste Jean Boyer d'Agen (ed.), *Ingres d'après une correspondance inédite* (Paris, 1909), p. 26.

10 Réné Longa, *Ingres inconnu: 129 reproductions de croquis à la plume du Musée de Montauban* (Paris: Librarie Rombaldi, 1942), p. 10.

11 On Constable's late drawings, see Matthew Hargraves, 'Majestic Darkness: Constable's Late Drawings', in Anne Lyles, *Late Constable*, exh. cat. (London: Royal Academy of Arts, 2021–2), pp. 53–63.

12 Wilhelm von Kügelgen, *Jugenderinnerungen eines alten Mannes*, ed. Adolf Stern (Leipzig, 1903), p. 151, here quoted from Sabine Rewald (ed.), *The Romantic Vision of Caspar David Friedrich: Paintings and Drawings from the USSR*, exh. cat. (Chicago: Art Institute of Chicago/ New York: Metropolitan Museum of Art, 1990–1), p. 92.

13 On Delacroix as a draughtsman, see Ashley E. Dunn, *Delacroix Drawings: The Karen B. Cohen Collection*, exh. cat. (New York: Metropolitan Museum of Art, 2018).

14 Ibid., p. 137.

15 Eugène Delacroix, *Journal*, 19 January 1847, ed. Michele Hannoosh, 2 vols (Paris: José Corti, 2009), I, pp. 326–7; English translation quoted from Dunn, *Delacroix Drawings*, p. 25.

15. *New subjects, new methods*

1 Masato Naitō, 'Katsushika Hokusai', *Oxford Art Online*, 2003 <www. doi.org/10.1093/gao/9781884446054.article.T046003> [accessed 8 February 2023]. I have drawn on articles and talks published on the British Museum website on pages relating to their exhibition *Hokusai: The Great Picture Book of Everything*, 30 September 2021–30 January 2022, <www.britishmuseum.org/exhibitions/hokusai great-picture-book-everything> [accessed 8 February 2023]; see also Timothy Clark, *Hokusai: The Great Picture Book of Everything* (London: British Museum Press, 2021).

2 Michel Melot, 'Honoré Daumier', *Oxford Art Online* <www.doi.org/ 10.1093/gao/9781884446054.article.T021507> [accessed 11 February 2023].

3 On the Pre-Raphaelites and drawing, see Colin Cruise, *Pre-Raphaelite Drawing* (London: Thames & Hudson, 2011) and Christiana Payne, *Pre-Raphaelites: Drawings & Watercolours* (Oxford: Ashmolean Museum, 2021).

4 A favourite term of abuse for the Pre-Raphaelites, and inscribed on drawings Rossetti made of Hunt and Millais talking (both Birmingham Museums & Art Gallery); the word appears in a speech bubble coming out of Millais's mouth, while Hunt replies: 'Of course!' See Cruise, *Pre-Raphaelite Drawing*, pp. 25–6.

5 See Julian Treuherz, Elizabeth Prettejohn and Edwin Becker, *Dante Gabriel Rossetti*, exh. cat. (Amsterdam: Van Gogh Museum/Liverpool: Walker Art Gallery, 2004,) no. 68, p. 171.

6 See Susan Owens, *Imagining England's Past: Inspiration, Enchantment, Obsession* (London: Thames & Hudson, 2023), pp. 165–73.

7 Fiona Mann, 'Navigating the "Many Botherations of a Picture": The Techniques and Materials of George Price Boyce, Dante Gabriel Rossetti and Edward Burne-Jones', in Payne, *Pre-Raphaelites*, pp. 29–49 (at pp. 38–9).

16. *Mediums of modern life*

1 Paul Mantz, 'L'Exposition des peintres impressionistes', *Le Temps*, 22 April 1877.

2 George Moore, 'Degas: The Painter of Modern Life', *Magazine of Art*, November 1890, p. 421.

3 'Il faut copier et recopier les maîtres, et ce n'est qu'apres avoir donné toutes les preuves d'un bon copiste qu'il pourra raisonnablement vous être permis de faire un radis d'après nature.' Ambroise Vollard, *Degas (1834–1917)* (Paris: Editions G. Crès et Cie, 1924), p. 64. On Degas and drawing, see Christopher Lloyd, *Edgar Degas: Drawings and Pastels* (London: Thames & Hudson, 2017); and on drawing and Impressionist artists more generally see Ann Dumas, Leïla Jarbouai, Christopher Lloyd and Harriet Stratis, *Impressionists on Paper: Degas to Toulouse-Lautrec*, exh. cat. (London: Royal Academy of Arts, 2023–4).

4 Related by Gustave Geffroy in *Claude Monet: Sa vie, son temps, son oeuvre* (Paris: Editions G. Grès et Cie, 1922), p. 197.

5 On Cézanne and drawing, see Jodi Hauptman and Samantha Friedman (eds), *Cézanne Drawing*, exh. cat. (New York: Museum of Modern Art, 2021), and Carol Armstrong, *Cézanne in the Studio: Still Life in Water-colours*, exh. cat. (Los Angeles: J. Paul Getty Museum, 2004–5).

6 Vincent van Gogh to Paul Gauguin, 17 October 1888; *Vincent van Gogh: The Letters*, ed. Leo Jansen, Hans Luijten and Nienke Bakker (Amsterdam: Van Gogh Museum, 2009) <www.vangoghletters.org/vg/letters/let706/letter.html> [accessed 30 June 2023]. On Van Gogh and drawing, see Colta Ives et al., *Vincent van Gogh: The Drawings*, exh. cat. (New York: Metropolitan Museum of Art, 2005); and Christopher Lloyd, *The Drawings of Vincent van Gogh* (London: Thames & Hudson, 2023).

7 Vincent van Gogh to Theo van Gogh, 5 June 1888 <www.vangoghletters.org/vg/letters/let620/letter.html> [accessed 30 June 2023].

8 I should like to thank the artists' suppliers L. Cornelissen & Son for their advice on reed pens, and Magnus Sigurdsson of Cutting Edge History for sharing his expertise on their manufacture and use with particular reference to *Arundo donax*, the giant reed that grows in southern France. On Van Gogh's use of reed pens see Susan Alyson Stein, 'Drawing in Arles: Reed Pen in Hand' in Ives et al., *Vincent van Gogh: The Drawings*, p. 146; and James Watrous, *The Craft of Old-Master Drawings* (Madison, WI: University of Wisconsin Press, 1957), p. 56.

9 Odilon Redon, *A soi-même: journal 1867–1915* (1922; Paris: Librairie José Corti, 1979), p. 28. On Redon, see Rodolphe Rapetti, *Odilon Redon: Prince du Rêve*, exh. cat. (Paris: Grand Palais/Montpellier: Musée Fabre, 2011), and Jodi Hauptman, *Beyond the Visible: The Art of Odilon Redon*, exh. cat. (New York: Museum of Modern Art, 2005). See also Lee Hendrix (ed.), *Noir: The Romance of Black in 19th-Century French Drawings and Prints*, exh. cat. (Los Angeles: J. Paul Getty Museum, 2016), pp. 118–20.

10 Redon, *A soi-même*, p. 22; here quoted from Hauptman, *Beyond the Visible*, p. 31.

11 On Seurat's drawings, see Jodi Hauptman (ed.), *Georges Seurat: The Drawings*, exh. cat. (New York: Museum of Modern Art, 2007), and Hendrix, *Noir*, pp. 95–7, 120–2.

17. *Rethinking the body*

1 Aubrey Beardsley, 'The Art of the Hoarding', in Stephen Calloway and David Colvin (eds), *In Black and White: The Literary Remains of Aubrey Beardsley* (London: Cypher, 1998), pp. 117–20 (at p. 119).

2 On Beardsley and drawing, see Stephen Calloway and Caroline Corbeau-Parsons (eds), *Aubrey Beardsley*, exh. cat. (London: Tate Britain, 2020).

3 On Klimt, see Marian Bisanz-Prakken, *Gustav Klimt: The Magic of Line*, exh. cat. (Los Angeles: J. Paul Getty Museum, 2012), and *Klimt / Schiele: Drawings from the Albertina Museum, Vienna*, exh. cat. (London: Royal Academy of Arts, 2018).

4 See Marian Bisanz-Prakken, 'The New Message of Line', in *Klimt / Schiele*, pp. 18–29 (at p. 22).

5 Arthur Roessler to Egon Schiele, 4 January 1911, in Christian M. Nebehay, *Egon Schiele: Leben, Briefe, Gedichte* (Salzburg: Residenz, 1979), no. 169.

6 Photolithographs of fifteen of Klimt's drawings were published in Franz Blei's German translation of Lucian's *Dialogues of the Courtesans* (Leipzig, 1907).

7 Käthe Kollwitz, diary entry for 4 January 1920, in *The Diary and Letters of Kaethe Kollwitz*, ed. Hans Kollwitz, trans. Richard and Clara Winston (Evanston, IL: Northwestern University Press, 1988), p. 96.

8 On Picasso and drawing, see Christopher Lloyd, *Picasso and the Art of Drawing* (London: Modern Art Press, 2018). The anecdote about Picasso asking for a 'piz' or 'lápiz' (pencil) with his first words is recorded in Roland Penrose, *Picasso: His Life and Work* (1958; London: Penguin, 1971), p. 13.

9 Lloyd, *Picasso and the Art of Drawing*, p. 13.

10 See Christopher Lloyd, 'Picasso and Drawing', in *Picasso and Paper*, exh. cat. (London: Royal Academy of Arts/Cleveland, OH: Cleveland Museum of Art, 2020), pp. 36–41 (at p. 36).

11 Elizabeth Cowling (ed.), *Visiting Picasso: The Notebooks and Letters of Roland Penrose* (London: Thames & Hudson, 2006), p. 122. See also Penrose, *Picasso: His Life and Work*, pp. 360–3.

12 See Emilia Philippot, 'Picasso: A Dictionary of Paper', in *Picasso and Paper*, pp. 22–35 (at p. 33).

13 Quoted in Lloyd, *Picasso and the Art of Drawing*, p. 17.

14 On Matisse and drawing, see John Elderfield, *The Drawings of Henri Matisse* (London: Thames & Hudson, 1985); and Christopher Lloyd, *Matisse and the Joy of Drawing* (London: Modern Art Press, 2022).

15 Louis Aragon, *Henri Matisse: A Novel*, trans. Jean Stewart, 2 vols (London: Collins, 1972), I, p. 129.

16 Quoted in John Elderfield with Beatrice Kernan, *Henri Matisse: A Retrospective*, exh. cat. (New York: Museum of Modern Art, 1992), p. 413.

18. *Mapping the mind*

1 See Frances Spalding, *John Piper, Myfanwy Piper: Lives in Art* (Oxford: Oxford University Press, 2009), p. 180.

2 Philip James (ed.), *Henry Moore on Sculpture* (London: Macdonald, 1966), pp. 212, 216.

3 See Andrew Causey, *The Drawings of Henry Moore* (Farnham: Lund Humphries, 2010), p. 104.

4 Samantha Friedman, 'Drawing, from a Starting Point of Zero', *MoMA Magazine*, 21 May 2021 <www.moma.org/magazine/articles/569> [accessed 4 May 2023]. See also *Degree Zero: Drawing at Midcentury* <www.moma.org/calendar/exhibitions/5223> [accessed 4 May 2023]. Friedman's excellent online text relating to this MoMA exhibition held in 2020–1 has helped to shape my thinking on the subject.

5 Marie-Laure Bernadac, in *Louise Bourgeois: Dessins/Pensées-Plumes*, exh. cat. (Paris: Centre Georges Pompidou, 1995), p. 1. On Louise Bourgeois and drawing, see Ann Coxon, *Louise Bourgeois* (London: Tate Publishing, 2010).

6 'Le dessin est indispensible, parce que toutes ces idées qui viennent, il faut les attraper comme des mouches quand elles passent, et puis alors, que fait-on des mouches ou des papillons, on les conserve et on s'en sert.' Louise Bourgeois in an interview with Marie-Laure Bernadac, in *Louise Bourgeois: Dessins/Pensées-Plumes*, p. 1.

7 Yayoi Kusama, *Infinity Net: The Autobiography of Yayoi Kusama*, trans. Ralph McCarthy (London: Tate Publishing, 2011), p. 62.

8 Ibid., p. 71.

9 Ibid., p. 84.

10 Henri Michaux, *Miserable Miracle: Mescaline*, trans. Louise Varèse and Anna Moschovakis (1972; New York: New York Review of Books, 2002), p. 113.

11 Jackson Pollock, draft statement for *Possibilities*, 1947, quoted in Francis O'Connor and Eugene Thaw (eds), *Jackson Pollock: A Catalogue Raisonné of Paintings, Drawings and Other Works*, 4 vols (New Haven, CT, and London: Yale University Press, 1978), I, p. 230.

12 Quoted in Bernard Harper Friedman, *Jackson Pollock: Energy Made Visible* (New York: McGraw-Hill, 1972), p. 182.

19. *The human span*

1 Lee Krasner, 'Interview with Bruce Glaser' [1967], in Kirk Varnedoe and Pepe Karmel (eds), *Jackson Pollock* (New York: Museum of Modern Art, 1998), p. 28. The artist was Hans Hofmann.

2 See Anna Lovatt, 'In Pursuit of the Neutral: Agnes Martin's Shimmering Line', in Frances Morris and Tiffany Bell (eds), *Agnes Martin*, exh. cat. (London: Tate Modern, 2015), pp. 99–106 (at pp. 101–2.)

3 Rachel Barker describes how 'The effect of this grid superimposed on the white field offers the viewer a dazzling sensory experience, a very particular sublimation of visual cues.' Barker, '*Morning*, 1965', in Morris and Bell (eds), *Agnes Martin*, pp. 88–92 (at p. 90).

4 Agnes Martin in 1975, quoted in Ronald Alley, *Catalogue of the Tate Gallery's Collection of Modern Art Other than Works by British Artists* (London: Tate Gallery/Sotheby Parke-Bernet, 1981), p. 488.

5 From a lecture by Martin, 'We Are in the Midst of Reality Responding with Joy', delivered at Yale University, New Haven, CT, in 1976, here quoted from Dieter Schwarz (ed.), *Agnes Martin: Writings* (Winterthur: Kunstmuseum Winterthur, 1992), p. 93.

6 Instructions for Sol LeWitt, *Wall Drawing #91*, 1971, Yale University Art Gallery <www.artgallery.yale.edu/collections/objects/179947> [accessed 14 May 2023].

7 On Gego's drawings, see Geaninne Gutiérrez-Guimarães and Pablo León de la Barra, *Gego: Measuring Infinity*, exh. cat. (New York: Solomon R. Guggenheim Museum, 2023).

8 Samuel Beckett, *Worstward Ho* (London: John Calder, 1983), p. 7.

9 Antony Gormley, 'Body and Soul, 1990' <www.antonygormley.com/works/drawing/prints/body-and-soul> [accessed 22 May 2023]. On Antony Gormley's drawings, see *Antony Gormley*, exh. cat. (London: Royal Academy of Arts, 2019).

10 On the drawings of Frank Auerbach, see Kate Aspinall, 'Occluded Depths: Frank Auerbach and Drawing', in Mark Hallett and Catherine Lampert (eds), *Frank Auerbach: Drawings of People* (New Haven, CT, and London: Paul Mellon Centre for Studies in British Art), pp. 113–37; and Barnaby Wright and Colm Tóibín, *Frank Auerbach: The Charcoal Heads*, exh. cat. (London: the Courtauld Gallery, 2024).

11 Interview between Jennifer Ramkalawon and Maggi Hambling, 2015; quoted in Jennifer Ramkalawon, *Maggi Hambling: Touch: Works on Paper* (London: Lund Humphries/British Museum, 2016), p. 16.

12 Maggi Hambling in conversation with Hugo Chapman about her retrospective exhibition *Touch: Works on Paper* (British Museum, London, 2016–17) <www.britishmuseum.org/blog/maggi-hambling-life-death-and-drawing> [accessed 22 May 2023].

20. *Bearing witness*

1 On Miriam de Búrca's drawings, see *Vitamin D3: Today's Best in Contemporary Drawing* (London: Phaidon, 2021), pp. 72–3.

2 Interview with Miriam de Búrca, March 2019, Anna McNay for *Studio International* <www.studiointernational.com/index.php/miriam-de-burca-protest-and-remembrance-video-interview> [accessed 31 May 2023].
3 Private correspondence with Miriam de Búrca, 7 June 2023.
4 On Catherine Anyango Grünewald's drawings, see *Vitamin D3*, pp. 30–1, and Isabel Seligman, *Pushing Paper: Contemporary Drawing from 1970 to Now* (London: British Museum/Thames & Hudson, 2019), p. 44.
5 Catherine Anyango Grünewald, 'Last Seen', artist's website <www.catherine-anyango.com/#/violentcrimes/> [accessed 1 June 2023].
6 Abel Rodríguez, quoted in exhibition text to accompany *Abel Rodríguez*, Baltic Plus, 2020 <www.balticplus.uk/abel-rodriguez-interpretation-guide-c33759/> [accessed 31 May 2023].
7 Ibid.
8 On this group of drawings by Imran Qureshi, see Imran Qureshi, Mohsin Hamid and Eleanor Nairne, *Where the Shadows are so Deep* (London: Ridinghouse, 2016).
9 On the drawings of Toyin Ojih Odutola, see Lotte Johnson (ed.), *Toyin Ojih Odutola: A Countervailing Theory*, exh. cat. (London: Barbican Art Gallery, 2020); and *Vitamin D3*, pp. 180–1.
10 See Cora Gilroy-Ware, 'Master Class: A Fictional Civilisation Makes Its Mark at the Barbican', *Apollo*, 17 September 2020; and Amy Tobin, 'A Countervailing Theory, A Parable', exhibition review in *Burlington Contemporary*, 22 December 2020; <www.contemporary.burlington.org.uk/reviews/reviews/a-countervailing-theory-a-parable> [accessed 6 June 2023].
11 Quoted by Andrew Graham-Dixon in 'Chalk Stones Trail by Andy Goldsworthy', *Sunday Telegraph*, 18 August 2002; here quoted from Alexandra Harris, *The Rising Down: Lives in a Sussex Landscape* (London: Faber & Faber, 2024), p. 134.

Glossary

1 Cennini, *The Craftsman's Handbook*, p. 20.
2 Henry Peacham, *The Art of Drawing with the Pen* (London, 1606), p. 11.
3 Cennini, *The Craftsman's Handbook*, p. 19.
4 William Salmon, *Polygraphice, or the Art of Drawing, Engraving, Etching, Limning, Painting, Washing, Varnishing, Colouring and Dying in Three Books*, 3 vols (London: Richard Jones, 1672), III, p. 165.
5 Thomas John Gullick and John Timbs, *Painting Properly Explained* (London, 1859), p. 295.
6 Joshua Reynolds, 'Discourse II', in *Discourses on Art*, ed. Robert R. Wark (New Haven, CT, and London: Yale University Press, 1975), p. 33.
7 Quoted in John Hayes, *The Drawings of Thomas Gainsborough*, 2 vols (New Haven, CT, and London: Yale University Press, 1971), I, p. 21; see also John Krill, *English Artists' Paper: Renaissance to Regency* (London: Trefoil, 1987), p. 83.

1. Engraved plaquette found at Montastruc, France, *c.* 11,000 BC. Stone, 10.7 × 16.3 cm. British Museum London. © The Trustees of the British Museum.
2. Palette belonging to the scribe Amenmes, Egypt, 1279–1213 BC (front and back). Wood, 40.2 × 7.5 cm. Musée du Louvre, Paris. RMN-Grand Palais / Dist. Photo SCALA, Florence Franck Raux.
3. Ostracon figure of a cat and a mouse, *c.* 1295–1075 BC. Limestone and ink, 8.9 × 17.3 cm. Brooklyn Museum, New York. Charles Edwin Wilbour Fund, 37.51E. Photo: Brooklyn Museum; Gavin Ashworth.
4. Christ and St Dunstan in St Dunstan's Classbook, England, probably Glastonbury, *c.* 950. 27 folios (fol. 1r), 27 × 18 cm. Bodleian Library, Oxford. Photo: © Bodleian Libraries, University of Oxford.
5. Zoomorphic initial from the Corbie Psalter, France, early ninth century. 144 folios, 29.2 × 18.5 cm. Bibliothèques d'Amiens Métropole, Amiens.
6. Psalms 122–4 from the Utrecht Psalter, Reims/Hautvillers, *c.* 820–45 (fols 1–92), Wearmouth-Jarrow in Northumbria, *c.* 700 (fols 94–105). 105 folios (fols 72v–73r), 33 × 25.5 cm. Utrecht University Library Special Collections.
7. Guo Xi, *Old Trees, Level Distance*, *c.* 1080. Handscroll; ink and watercolour on silk, 35.6 × 104.4 cm. Metropolitan Museum of Art, New York.
8. Cosmological representation of the annual cycle, from *Annals*, Zwiefalten, Swabia, *c.* 1162. 153 folios (fol. 17v), 31.5 × 22 cm. Württembergische Landesbibliothek, Stuttgart.
9. The Aspidochelone, in a bestiary, England, twelfth century. 74 folios (fol. 54v), 28 × 19 cm. Cambridge University Library. © Cambridge University Library.
10. Matthew Paris, *Map of Palestine*, final section of itinerary map of route between London and the Holy Land, *c.* 1250–9. 8 folios (fols 4v–5r). British Library, London. Bridgeman Images.

11. Villard de Honnecourt, *Lion and Porcupine*, *c.* 1240. Leadpoint, pen and ink on parchment, 23.2 × 15.2 cm. 75 folios (fol. 15v). Bibliothèque Nationale, Paris.

12. Filippino Lippi, *Two Nude Men*, *c.* 1485–8. Silverpoint (left figure) and leadpoint (right figure), heightened with white (partly discoloured), over blind stylus, on grey prepared paper, 25.9 × 18.5 cm. British Museum, London. © The Trustees of the British Museum.

13. Pisanello, *Hare*, *c.* 1430–2. Watercolour over black chalk, 13.7 × 22.3 cm. Musée du Louvre, Paris. RMN-Grand Palais / Dist. Photo SCALA, Florence / Christian Jean.

14. Jacopo Bellini, *The Raising of Lazarus* from the Jacopo Bellini album, *c.* 1440–70. Leadpoint, 41.5 × 33.6 cm. 99 folios (fol. 56). British Museum, London. © The Trustees of the British Museum.

15. Sandro Botticelli, *The Empyrean: Beatrice and Dante in the River of Light*, *Paradiso* XXX, drawing for Dante's *Divine Comedy*, *c.* 1480s. Pen and ink and leadpoint on parchment, 32 × 47 cm. Staatliche Museen zu Berlin, Kupferstichkabinett. Photo Scala, Florence / bpk, Bildagentur fuer Kunst, Kultur und Geschichte, Berlin / Philipp Allard.

16. Paolo Uccello, *Study of a Chalice*, *c.* 1450–70. Pen and ink over ruled stylus and compass, 34.9 × 24.3 cm. Gabinetto Disegni e Stampe degli Uffizi, Florence. Photo Scala, Florence – courtesy of the Ministero Beni e Att. Culturali e del Turismo.

17. Andrea Mantegna, studies for *Christ at the Column*, early to mid-1460s. Pen and ink, 23.7/23.5 × 14.5 cm. Courtauld Gallery, London. Photo © The Courtauld / Bridgeman Images.

18. Leonardo da Vinci, *Studies of the Virgin and Child with a Cat*, *c.* 1475–82. Pen and ink over black chalk and leadpoint, 28 × 19.7 cm. British Museum, London. © The Trustees of the British Museum.

19. Leonardo da Vinci, *The Skull Sectioned*, 1489. Traces of black chalk, pen and ink, 19 × 13.7 cm. Royal Collection Trust, Windsor. Royal Collection Trust / © His Majesty King Charles III 2024.

20. Leonardo da Vinci, *A Deluge*, *c.* 1517–18. Black chalk, 16.1 × 20.7 cm. Royal Collection Trust, Windsor. Royal Collection Trust / © His Majesty King Charles III 2024.

21. Michelangelo, studies for the figure of Adam in the fresco *The Creation of Man* on the vault of the Sistine Chapel, *c.* 1511. Red chalk over stylus underdrawing, 19.3 × 25.9 cm. British Museum, London. © The Trustees of the British Museum.

22. Michelangelo, *Christ on the Cross with the Virgin and St John*, *c.* 1560–4. Black chalk and white heightening, 38.2 × 21 cm. Royal Collection Trust, Windsor. Royal Collection Trust / © His Majesty King Charles III 2024.

23. Raphael, *The Three Graces*, *c.* 1517–18. Red chalk over some stylus underdrawing, 20.3 × 25.8 cm. Royal Collection Trust, Windsor. Royal Collection Trust / © His Majesty King Charles III 2024.

24. Sofonisba Anguissola, *Asdrubale Bitten by a Crayfish*, *c.* 1554. Black chalk and charcoal with white heightening, reinforced by a later hand in ink, on oxidised blue paper, 38.5 × 33.6 cm. Museo di Capodimonte, Naples. Su concessione del MiC – Museo e Real Bosco di Capodimonte, Napoli.

25. Albrecht Dürer, *Self-Portrait at the Age of Thirteen*, 1484. Silverpoint on prepared paper, 27.3 × 19.5 cm. Albertina, Vienna. Bridgeman Images.

26. Albrecht Dürer, *Portrait of the Artist's Mother at the Age of Sixty-Three*, 1514. Charcoal, 42.1 × 30.3 cm. Staatliche Museen zu Berlin, Kupferstichkabinett. Photo Scala, Florence / bpk, Bildagentur fuer Kunst, Kultur und Geschichte, Berlin.

27. Hans Holbein the Younger, *Sir Thomas More*, *c.* 1526–7. Black and coloured chalks, the outlines pricked for transfer, 39.8 × 29.9 cm. Royal Collection Trust, Windsor. Royal Collection Trust / © His Majesty King Charles III 2024.

28. Matthias Grünewald, *Study of the Virgin for a Painting of the Annunciation*, *c.* 1512–14. Black chalk, heightened with white, 20.7 × 21 cm. Staatliche Museen zu Berlin, Kupferstichkabinett. Photo Scala, Florence / bpk, Bildagentur fuer Kunst, Kultur und Geschichte, Berlin.

29. Albrecht Altdorfer, *Dead Pyramus*, *c.* 1511–13. Pen and black ink, heightened with white, on blue prepared paper, 21.6 × 15.7 cm. Staatliche Museen zu Berlin, Kupferstichkabinett. Photo Scala, Florence / bpk, Bildagentur fuer Kunst, Kultur und Geschichte, Berlin.

30. Wolfgang Huber, *Infernal Castle in a Ravine*, 1552. Pen and ink with grey wash, 21.3 × 33.3 cm. UCL Art Collection, University College London. UCL Art Collection, London / Bridgeman Images.

31. Pieter Bruegel the Elder, *The Temptation of St Antony*, 1556. Pen and ink, 21.6 × 32.6 cm. Ashmolean Museum, Oxford. © Ashmolean Museum.

32. Titian, *Pastoral Scene*, *c.* 1565. Pen and ink over black chalk, heightened with white gouache, 19.5 × 30.2 cm. Getty Center, Los Angeles. The J. Paul Getty Museum.

33. Perino del Vaga, *Jupiter and Juno*, study for the *Furti di Giove* tapestries, *c.* 1532–5. Pen and dark brown ink with brown and grey wash, heightened with white gouache. Metropolitan Museum of Art, New York. Met, NY (Purchase, Acquisitions Fund and Annette and Oscar de la Renta Gift, 2011).

34. Niccolò dell'Abate, *Masquerade Costume: The Frog Man*, *c.* 1552–71. Pen with brown ink and wash, 35.5 × 24.8 cm. Nationalmuseum, Stockholm. Foto Hans Thorwid / Nationalmuseum 2012.

35. Hendrick Goltzius, *Head of Mercury*, 1587. Pen and ink, 44.4 × 36.5 cm. Ashmolean Museum, Oxford. © Ashmolean Museum.

36. Agostino Carracci, *River Landscape with Figures and Boats*, *c.* 1572–1602. Pen and grey ink, 34 x 25.2 cm (left sheet); 33 x 25.2 cm (right sheet). British Museum, London. © The Trustees of the British Museum.

37. Annibale Carracci, *A Young Man Pulling on a Sock*, *c.* 1585–90. Red chalk, 29.2 × 37.2 cm. British Museum, London. © The Trustees of the British Museum.

38. Lavinia Fontana, *Nun or Young Woman with a Veil*, *c.* 1577–95. Red and black chalk, 7.9 × 6.8 cm. Morgan Library & Museum, New York.

39. Elisabetta Sirani, *Study for Allegory of Justice, Charity and Prudence*, *c.* 1664. Brush and brown wash over traces of red chalk, 13.5 × 18.7 cm. Rhode Island School of Design, Providence. Courtesy of the RISD Museum, Providence, RI.

40. Riza-yi 'Abbasi (attrib.), *Portrait of a Man*, *c.* 1600. Ink, bodycolour and gold on paper, 21.3 × 13.3 cm. Metropolitan Museum of Art, New York. MET / NY Gift of Alexander Smith Cochran, 1913.

41. John White, *A Native American 'Werowance' or Chief*, *c.* 1585–93. Watercolour and graphite, touched with bodycolour and gold, 26.3 × 15 cm. British Museum, London. © The Trustees of the British Museum.

42. Ustad Mansur, *A Zebra*, 1621. Bodycolour and gold, 26.9 × 38.7 cm. Victoria and Albert Museum, London. © Victoria and Albert Museum, London.

43. Rembrandt van Rijn, *A Mughal Nobleman (Prince Daniyal) after a Mughal Miniature*, *c.* 1656–61. Pen and brown ink with grey and brown wash, touched with red chalk and white heightening, 18.4 × 11.2 cm. British Museum, London. © The Trustees of the British Museum.

ILLUSTRATIONS

44. Maria Sibylla Merian, *Swamp Immortelle with Giant Silk Moth*, 1702–3. Watercolour and bodycolour with gum arabic on vellum, 35.9 × 28.5 cm. Royal Collection Trust, Windsor. Royal Collection Trust / © His Majesty King Charles III 2024.

45. Peter Paul Rubens, *Trees Reflected in Water at Sunset*, c. 1635–8. Black, red and orange chalks, heightened with white, on buff paper, 27.6 × 45.4 cm. British Museum, London. © The Trustees of the British Museum.

46. Rembrandt van Rijn, *The Grain Mill 'De Bok' on the Bulwark 'Het Blauwhoofd'*, c. 1645. Pen and brown ink and wash, 11.6 × 19.8 cm. Fondation Custodia, Collection Frits Lugt, Paris.

47. Claude Lorrain, *Landscape with a Figure by a Group of Trees*, c. 1640. Pen and brown ink and wash on blue paper, 19.1 × 25.7 cm. British Museum, London. © The Trustees of the British Museum.

48. Bada Shanren (Zhu Da), *Fish and Rocks*, 1699. Hanging scroll; ink on paper, 135.3 × 61 cm. Metropolitan Museum of Art, New York.

49. Huang Xiangjian, *Searching for my Parents*, 1656. Handscroll; ink and colour on silk, 35.5 × 553.7 cm. Metropolitan Museum of Art, New York / Gift of Julia and John Curtis, 2015.

50. Jonathan Richardson, *Self-Portrait*, 1735. Black chalk heightened with white on blue paper, 32.7 × 26.7 cm. National Portrait Gallery, London. © National Portrait Gallery, London.

51. Rosalba Carriera, *Gustavus Hamilton (1710–1746), Second Viscount Boyne, in Masquerade Costume*, c. 1730–1. Pastel on paper, laid down on canvas, 56.5 × 42.9 cm. Metropolitan Museum of Art, New York / Purchase, George Delacorte Fund Gift, in memory of George T. Delacorte Jr., and Gwynne Andrews, Victor Wilbour Memorial, and Marquand Funds, 2002.

52. Rosalba Carriera, *Antoine Watteau*, 1721. Pastel, 55 × 43 cm. Museo Civico Luigi Bailo, Treviso.

53. Antoine Watteau, *Three Studies of a Young Man*, c. 1718. Black, red and white chalks with grey wash, 24.3 × 27 cm. Musée du Louvre, Paris. RMN-Grand Palais / Dist. Photo SCALA, Florence.

54. Canaletto, *A Capriccio of a Ruined Arch on the Shores of a Lagoon*, c. 1740–60. Pen and ink, with bluish-grey wash, over graphite, 19.8 × 27.8 cm. Royal Collection Trust, Windsor. Royal Collection Trust / © His Majesty King Charles III 2024.

55. Giovanni Battista Piranesi, *An Imaginary Prison*, 1755–61. Pen, brown ink and wash over black chalk, 21.7 × 25.2 cm. National Galleries Scotland, Edinburgh.

56. Alexander Cozens, *'Blot' Landscape*, c. 1750–86. Brush and black ink, 18.3 × 23.7 cm. Victoria and Albert Museum, London. © Victoria and Albert Museum, London.

57. Thomas Gainsborough, *Wooded Landscape with Castle*, c. 1785–8. Black chalk and stumping with white chalk on light blue paper faded to buff, 26.4 × 32.7 cm. Yale Center for British Art, Paul Mellon Collection, New Haven, CT.

58. John Russell, *Moon*, 1795. Pastel, 152.4 × 152.4 cm (approx.). History of Science Museum, Oxford. © History of Science Museum, University of Oxford.

59. Angelica Kauffman, page from a sketchbook used in Rome: *Apollo Belvedere* (fol. 87), c. 1762–6. Graphite and black chalk, 29.3 × 38.8 cm. Victoria and Albert Museum, London. © Victoria and Albert Museum, London.

60. Jacques-Louis David, *A Roman Cuirass, Copied from a Colossal Statue of Mars in the Capitoline Museum, Rome*, c. 1775–80. Black ink and grey wash, 31.9 × 23.7 cm. Musée du Louvre, Paris. RMN-Grand Palais / Dist. Photo SCALA, Florence / Michèle Bellot.

61. Jacques-Louis David, *Marie-Antoinette, Queen of France, Led to Execution*, 1793. Pen and brown ink, 14.8 × 10.1 cm. Musée du Louvre, Paris. Photo Josse / Scala, Florence.

62. Henry Fuseli, *The Artist Moved by the Grandeur of Antique Fragments*, c. 1778–9. Pen and sepia ink, wash and red chalk, 42 × 35.2 cm. Kunsthaus, Graphische Sammlung, Zürich. Bridgeman Images.

63. Francisco Goya, *The Sleep of Reason Produces Monsters*, c. 1796–7. Pen and iron-gall ink, 22.9 × 15.5 cm. Museo del Prado, Madrid. © Photographic Archive Museo Nacional del Prado.

64. William Blake, *Satan Arousing the Rebel Angels*, 1808. Pen and ink and watercolour, 51.8 × 39.3 cm. Victoria and Albert Museum, London. © Victoria and Albert Museum, London.

65. John Constable, page from a sketchbook of ninety pages, c. 1813–15. Graphite, 8.9 × 12.1 cm. Victoria and Albert Museum, London. © Victoria and Albert Museum, London.

66. John Constable, *Elm Trees in Old Hall Park, East Bergholt*, 1817. Graphite, with slight grey and white washes, 59.1 × 49.5 cm. Victoria and Albert Museum, London.

67. Jean-Auguste-Dominique Ingres, *Mr and Mrs Joseph Woodhead and Mr Henry Comber in Rome*, 1816. Graphite, 30.4 × 22.4 cm. Fitzwilliam

Museum, Cambridge. Photograph © The Fitzwilliam Museum, University of Cambridge.

68. Caspar David Friedrich, *Rocky Beach with Moonrise*, *c.* 1835–7. Brush and brown ink over graphite, 23.2 × 35.7 cm. Kupferstich-Kabinett, Staatliche Kunstsammlungen, Dresden. Photo Scala, Florence / bpk, Bildagentur fuer Kunst, Kultur und Geschichte, Berlin.

69. Eugène Delacroix, *Crouching Tiger*, 1839. Pen and brush and iron-gall ink, 13.1 × 18.7 cm. Metropolitan Museum of Art, New York. Metropolitan Museum of Art / Gift from the Karen B. Cohen Collection of Eugène Delacroix, in honor of Sanford I. Weill, 2013.

70. Katsushika Hokusai, *Daoist Master Zhou Sheng Ascends a Cloud-Ladder to the Moon*, 1820s–40s. Pen, brush and ink, 15.2 × 10.5 cm. British Museum, London. © The Trustees of the British Museum.

71. Jean-François Millet, *Women Carrying Faggots*, *c.* 1858. Charcoal heightened with white gouache on grey-blue paper, 34.3 × 27.6 cm. Metropolitan Museum of Art, New York. Robert Lehman Collection, 1975.

72. Theodor Rehbenitz, *Self-Portrait*, 1817. Graphite, 19.6 × 16 cm. Kupferstich-Kabinett, Staatliche Kunstsammlungen, Dresden. Photo Scala, Florence / bpk, Bildagentur fuer Kunst, Kultur und Geschichte, Berlin.

73. Dante Gabriel Rossetti, *Mary Magdalene at the Door of Simon the Pharisee*, 1858. Pen and ink, 50.8 × 45.7 cm. Fitzwilliam Museum, Cambridge. Photograph © The Fitzwilliam Museum, University of Cambridge.

74. Berthe Morisot, *A Woman and Child Seated on the Grass*, 1875. Watercolour over graphite, 16.4 × 22.1 cm. Morgan Library & Museum, New York.

75. Edgar Degas, *Ballet*, *c.* 1876–7. Pastel on monotype, 58.4 × 42 cm. Musée d'Orsay, Paris. RMN-Grand Palais / Dist. Photo SCALA, Florence / Photographer: Hervé Lewandowski.

76. Paul Cézanne, *Still Life with Carafe, Bottle and Fruit*, 1906. Watercolour and graphite on pale buff paper, 48 × 62.5 cm. Henry and Rose Pearlman Collection, New York.

77. Vincent van Gogh, *La Crau Seen from Montmajour*, 1888. Graphite, pen and reed pen with light brown and dark brown ink, 49 × 61 cm. Van Gogh Museum, Amsterdam. Princeton University Art Museum / Art Resource NY / Scala, Florence.

78. Odilon Redon, *Eye-Balloon*, 1878. Charcoal and chalk, 42.2 × 33.3 cm. Museum of Modern Art, New York (Gift of Larry Aldrich). Digital image: The Museum of Modern Art, New York / Scala, Florence.

79. Georges Seurat, *Madame Seurat, the Artist's Mother*, c. 1882–3. Conté crayon on Michallet paper, 30.5 × 23.3 cm. Getty Center, Los Angeles. The J. Paul Getty Museum, Los Angeles, 2002.51.

80. Aubrey Beardsley, *The Abbé*, 1895. Pen, ink and wash, 25 × 17.5 cm. Victoria and Albert Museum, London. © Victoria and Albert Museum, London.

81. Gustav Klimt, *Reclining Woman*, c. 1916–17. Graphite, 34.8 × 56.7 cm. Albertina, Vienna. © Albertina, Wien.

82. Egon Schiele, *Self-Portrait*, 1916. Graphite and bodycolour, 29.5 × 45.8 cm. Albertina, Vienna. © Albertina, Wien.

83. Käthe Kollwitz, *Self-Portrait*, 1911. Black chalk, heightened with violet and grey chalk, on grey-brown paper, 35.9 × 30.8 cm. Kupferstich-Kabinett, Staatliche Kunstsammlungen, Dresden. Photo Scala, Florence/ bpk, Bildagentur fuer Kunst, Kultur und Geschichte, Berlin.

84. Pablo Picasso drawing, film still from Henri-Georges Clouzot's *Le Mystère Picasso*, 1956. © Succession Picasso / DACS, London 2024, Gjon Mili / The LIFE Picture Collection / Shutterstock.

85. Henri Matisse, *Blue Nude (III)*, 1952. Gouache on paper, cut and pasted, 103.8 × 86 cm. Musée National d'Art Moderne / Centre Georges Pompidou, Paris. © Succession H. Matisse / DACS 2024. Photo: RMN-Grand Palais / Dist. Photo SCALA, Florence.

86. Henry Moore, *Tube Shelter Perspective*, 1941. Graphite, ink, wax and watercolour, 48.3 × 43.8 cm. Tate, London.

87. Louise Bourgeois, *Throbbing Pulse*, 1944. Pen and ink, 48.9 × 31.8 cm. Museum of Modern Art, New York. Digital image: The Museum of Modern Art, New York / Scala, Florence © DACS © The Easton Foundation / VAGA at ARS, NY, London 2024.

88. Yayoi Kusama, *Infinity Nets*, 1951. Ink on paper, 39.4 × 25.7 cm. Museum of Modern Art, New York. © YAYOI KUSAMA. Digital image: The Museum of Modern Art, New York / Scala, Florence.

89. Henri Michaux, *Dessin mescalinien*, 1959. Pen and ink, 32 × 24 cm. Musée National d'Art Moderne / Centre Georges Pompidou, Paris. © ADAGP, Paris and DACS, London 2024. Photo © Centre Pompidou, MNAM-CCI, Dist. RMN-Grand Palais / Photo SCALA, Florence.

90. Jackson Pollock, *Untitled*, *c.* 1948–9. Dripped ink and enamel on paper, 56.8 × 76.2 cm. Metropolitan Museum of Art, New York. © The Pollock-Krasner Foundation ARS, NY and DACS, London 2023 / Metropolitan Museum of Art, New York / Scala, Florence.

91. Agnes Martin, *Morning*, 1965. Acrylic paint and graphite on canvas, 182.6 × 181.9 cm. Tate, London. © Agnes Martin Foundation, New York / DACS 2023. Photo Tate Images.

92. Gego (Gertrud Goldschmidt), *Reticularea*, 1969–82. Installation of modular pieces made of stainless steel and aluminium wire, first installed in the Museo de Bellas Artes, Caracas. Photo by Paolo Gasparini. © Fundación Gego. All rights reserved.

93. (a) David Connearn, *Mappa Mundi: Drawing to the Extent of the Body*, 1984. Rotring pen, 225 × 183 cm. Victoria and Albert Museum, London. © Victoria and Albert Museum, London.
(b) David Connearn in the process of drawing *Mappa Mundi*, 1984. Black and white photograph, 19 × 19.1 cm.

94. Antony Gormley, *7th Blood Field II*, 2020. Blood on paper, 19.1 × 14.1 cm. © Antony Gormley. Courtesy of the Artist and White Cube.

95. Maggi Hambling, *My Mother Dead, VII; Portrait of the Artist's Mother*, 1988. Graphite, 19.6 × 29.5 cm. British Museum, London. Reproduced by permission of the artist © The Trustees of the British Museum.

96. Tacita Dean, *The Clouds Me Thought Would Open*, 2015. Spray chalk, gouache and charcoal pencil on slate, 121.4 × 121.9 cm. Marian Goodman Gallery, New York. Photo Cathy Carver.

97. Miriam de Búrca, *Long Forgotten in Oughterard*, 2017. Pen and ink on artificial vellum, 49.8 × 69.8 cm. Courtesy Miriam de Búrca and Cristea Roberts Gallery, London. © Miriam de Búrca.

98. Abel Rodríguez, *Terraza Alta II*, 2018. Pen and ink, 70 × 100 cm. Instituto de Visión, Bogotá. Permission granted by Abel Rodríguez.

99. Imran Qureshi, detail from the series *Where the Shadows are so Deep*, 2015. Bodycolour and gold leaf on wasli paper, 41.5 × 33.6 cm. Reproduced by permission of the artist. © The Trustees of the British Museum.

100. Toyin Ojih Odutola, *The Ruling Class (Eshu)* from *A Countervailing Theory*, 2019. Pastel, charcoal and chalk on black linen, 213.4 × 127 cm. Jack Shainman Gallery, New York. © Toyin Ojih Odutola. Image Jack Shainman Gallery, New York.

I N D E X

References to figures are shown in *italics* and glossary terms are in **bold**.

Abbas I, Shah of Persia, 84, 90
Academie de France, 125
Academie Royale de Peinture et de
    Sculpture, 109
Academy of the Progressives, 80
Accademia del Disegno, 122
Altdorfer, Albrecht, 67–8, *68*, 71
Ancient Egypt
    drawings on papyrus, 9
    ostraca (fragments), 9–10, *9*, **207**
    outline scribes, 7–9
    wooden palette, 7, *8*
ancient world
    echoed in Renaissance art, 54
    figure drawing, 33
    Neo-classicism, 126–7, 130
    sculpture, 123–5, *123*, *126*,
        127–9, 130, 145
    Titian's *poesie*, 71
Ancients, the, 145
Anguissola, Sofonisba, 56–7, *57*
Anyango Grünewald, Catherine,
    192, 196
architecture
    in medieval drawing, 28
    in Piranesi's drawing, 114–16,
        116
    in Renaissance drawing, 36

    Renaissance villas, *54–5*
    Venetian scenes, 113–14, *115*
Art Informel movement, 175, 177
Auerbach, Frank, 187
autonomism, 175

Bada Shanren (Zhu Da), 101–3,
    102
Barocci, Federico, 82
Baroque, 98–9
Batoni, Pompeo, 107
Beardsley, Aubrey, 160–2, *161*,
    163
Bellini, Jacopo, 35–6, *35*, 40
bestiaries, 23–4, *24*, 87
bistre, **199**
black chalk, **199**
Blake, William, 6, 132–4, *133*
blue paper, **200**
bodycolour, **200**
Bosch, Hieronymus, 70
Botticelli, Sandro, 36–8, *37*
Boucher, François, 125, 151
Bourgeois, Louise, 2, 172–3, *173*
Boyne, Gustavus Hamilton, 2nd
    Viscount, 108, *109*
Breton, André, 175
Bruegel, Pieter, 69–71, *71*

brushes, **200**
Búrca, Miriam de, 191–2, *191*
Burne-Jones, Edward, 148

Canaletto (Giovanni Antonio
    Canal), 113, *115*
Caravaggio, Michelangelo Merisi
    da, 79
carbon ink, **200**
Carracci, Agostino, 79–80, *79*, 81,
    82
Carracci, Annibale, 79–80, *80*, 84
Carracci, Ludovico, 79–81, 82
Carriera, Rosalba
    career as a portraitist, 106,
        107–8, 108–9, *109*, *110*
    friendship with Watteau, 109–
        10, *110*
    use of pastels, 108, *109*, *110*,
        120, 197, 208
cartoon, **201**
Catherine of Bologna, 82
Cennino Cennini, 30, 31–2, 199
Cézanne, Paul, 152–4, *153*, 165
chalks
    black chalk, **199**
    Leonardo da Vinci's use of, 46–7
    Michelangelo's use of, 51
    red chalk, 46–7, 51, **210–11**
    white chalk, **214–15**
charcoal, 46, *59–60*, 156–7, **201**
Chardin, Jean Siméon, 151
chiaroscuro, **201**
Chinese handscrolls, 19–21, *21*
Cock, Hieronymus, 70
collector's mark, **201–2**
colonialism
    circulation of goods, 88–93, *90*
    limners, 87–8
Connearn, David, 183–5, *184*, *185*
Constable, John
    landscape drawings, 134–5, *135*,
        136, 138, 189
    use of graphite pencils, 135–6,
        136

Conté, Nicolas-Jacques, 158, 202,
    203–4
Conté crayons, 144, 158–9, **202**
counterproof (offset), **202**
Cozens, Alexander, 117–18
crayon
    Conté crayons, 144, 158–9, **202**
    definition, **202**
    porte-crayon, **209**
    trois crayons, **213**
Crozat, Pierre, 108–9

Daumier, Honoré, 142–3
David, Jacques-Louis
    Revolutionary art, 125–6, *127*
    study of ancient sculpture, 125,
        126
Dean, Tacita, 189–90, *190*, 196
deckle edge, **202**
Degas, Edgar, 151–2, *152*, 165, 208
Delacroix, Eugène, 1, 138–9, *140*,
    151, 208
dell'Abate, Niccolò, 76, *77*
drawing
    earliest forms of, 2–4, *3*
    within the history of art, 4–5, 198
    as an informal medium, 1–2
    as an intimate medium, 1, 4–5
    painting-drawing hybridity, 177,
        179–80
    term, 1, 5–6
    viewer–artist relationship, 4,
        181–3, *183*
    see also materials
Dunstan, Saint, 12–13, *13*
Dürer, Albrecht
    inspiration for the Nazarenes, 146
    landscapes, 66–7
    portraiture, *59–60*, *60*
    the Pre-Raphaelites and, 147
    self-portraits, 58–9, *59*

emotion
    in antique sculpture, 128–9
    expressed through drawing, 5

engraving, 2–3, *3*, 77–8, 127, 133
erotica, 130–1
Eyck, Jan van, 146–7

Federkunststück (quill artwork),
   77–8, **202–3**
fibre-tipped pen, **203**
figure, the
   anatomy, 44–5, *44*, 50
   antique sculptures, 123–5, *123*,
      126, 127–9, 130, 145
   draperies/clothing, 32, 42, 84–6,
      85, 123
   in early twentieth-century
      drawing, 160–3, *163*
   female models, *44*, *55*, 123
   in Gormley's works, 186–7, *186*
   in medieval landscapes, 16–18,
      17, 20–1, *21*
   naturalistic representations, *80*,
      81
   in Renaissance drawing, 32–3,
      40–2, *41*, 50–1, *51*, 56–7, *57*
   women's access to models and
      anatomical study, 81, 83,
      122–5
Flaxman, John, 126–7, 130, 134,
   148
Fontana, Lavinia, 82
Francis I, 47, 76
French court, 47–8, 76
Friedrich, Caspar David, 138, *139*
Fuseli, Henry
   emotional impact of antique
      sculpture, 127–9, *128*
   erotica, 130–1

Gainsborough, Thomas, 118–19,
   119, 215
Gaugin, Paul, 154
Gego (Gertrud Goldschmidt),
   182–3, *183*
Gellée, Claude (Claude Lorrain)
   landscapes, 99–100, *101*
   libro di verità, 100

Gentileschi, Artemisia, 81, 82
Giacometti, Alberto, 187
Goldsworthy, Andy, 5, 197–8
Goltzius, Hendrick, 76–8, *78*
Gormley, Antony, 186–7, *186*, 198
gouache, **200**
Goya, Francisco, 131–2, *131*
Grand Tour
   portraits, 106–9, *109*
   Venetian scenes, 113–14, *115*
graphite (plumbago), 135–6, *136*,
   203–4, **209**
Grünewald, Matthias, 63–5, *64*
Guercino (Giovanni Francesco
   Barbieri), 98–9
gum arabic, 66, 149, 200, **204**
Guo Xi, 20–1, 198

Hambling, Maggi, 187–8, *188*
hatching, **204**
heightening, **204**
Henry VIII, 61, 62, 63
history
   anti-urban movements, 145–6
   bearing witness, 190–4
   honoured through drawing,
      141–5
   medieval histories and chronicles,
      24–5
   protest drawings, 194–6
   records of the Second World
      War, 170–2, *171*
Hockney, David, 5
Hokusai, Katsushika, 141–2, *143*,
   145, 177
Holbein the Elder, Hans, 61, *62*
Holbein the Younger, Hans, 61–3,
   62
Huang Xiangjian, 103–4, *103*
Huber, Wolfgang, 68–9, *69*
Hunt, William Holman, 146, 148

imagination
   Claude Gellée's landscapes,
      99–100, *101*

Cozens's 'Blot' landscapes,
    117–18, *118*
decorative art, 75–6, *75*
Gainsborough's landscapes,
    118–19, *119*
grotesques, 75
images of the moon, 120–1, *121*
knowledge of the wider world,
    25–7, 141–2
Mannerism, 74–9
Piranesi's *Carceri* images,
    115–16, *116*
representations of human
    suffering, 41–2, 53, 132, 164–5
Symbolism, 156
the visionary world of the
    eighteenth-century, 130–40
see also psychology
Impressionism, 2, 149–56, 208
incising, **204**
Ingres, Jean-Auguste-Dominique,
    136–7, *137*
Ingres paper, **205**
inkstone, **205**
iron-gall ink, **205**

Jahangir, Mughal Emperor, 89–90
Japanese paper, 92, **205**

Kauffman, Angelica, 122–5, *123*
Klimt, Gustav, 162–3, *163*
Kollwitz, Käthe, 2, 164–5, *165*
Krasner, Lee, 177, 179
Kügelgen, Wilhelm von, 138
Kusama, Yayoi, 173–5, *174*, 180

laid paper, **206**, 215
landscapes
    Baroque, 98–9
    Bronze Age White Horse of
        Uffington, 10–11
    in Chinese handscrolls, 19–21, *21*
    of Claude Gellée, 99–100, *101*
    in Constable's sketchbooks,
        134–5, *135*, *136*, 138, 189

Cozens's 'Blot' landscapes,
    117–18, *118*
of Dürer, 66–7
in European art, 67–72, *68*
figures in, 16–18, *17*, 20–1, *21*
as a medium for drawing, 10–11
Nazca geoglyphs, 11
of the Qing dynasty, 100–4, *102*,
    103
Rembrandt's drawings, 98, *99*
Rubens's drawings, 96–8, *97*
rural labourers, 143, *144*
skyscapes, 189–90
spiritual drawings, 138
Venetian scenes, 112, 113–14,
    115
watercolours, 148
lead pencil, **206**
Leonardo da Vinci
    anatomical studies, 44–5, *44*, 50
    artistic techniques, 43, 45–7
    drawing collections, 49
    drawing practices, 1, 42–4, *43*,
        54, 117
    the natural world, 46–8, *47*
    Virgin and Child composition,
        42–3, *43*, 54
LeWitt, Sol, 181–2
libro di verità, 100
Lippi, Filippino, 32–3, *32*
Long, Richard, 2, 10

Malvasia, Carlo Cesare, 82–3
Mannerism, 74–9
Mansur, Ustad, 89, 90, *90*
Mantegna, Andrea, 40–2, *41*
Mariette, Pierre-Jean, 112
Martin, Agnes, 179–81, *180*
Masson, André, 175
materials
    charcoal, 46, 59–60, 156–7, **201**
    Conté crayons, 144, 158–9, **202**
    for drawing, 2, 5
    graphite pencils, 135–6, *136*,
        203–4

industrial, 183
leadpoint, 27, *28*, *32*, 35, *35*, 36
papyrus, 1, 9, **208**
parchment, 1, 12, 13, 14–15, *28*,
    31, **208**
pastels, 151–2, *152*, **208–9**
pen and ink, 31–2, 43, 44, 148
reed pens, *155*, 156, **211**
tempera, 36
vellum, 33, 148, **213**
watercolours, 66, 148, 149–50,
    213–14
see also chalks; crayon
Matisse, Henri, 168–9, *169*
medieval art
    the annual cycle, *21*, 22–3
    bestiaries, 23–4, *24*, 87
    female scribes, 16
    histories and chronicles, 24–5
    illuminated psalters, 13–14, *15*,
        16–17, 27
    labour of, 15–16
    model books, 27–9, *28*, 33
    monastic scriptoria, 14–15
    pilgrimage routes, 25–7, *26*
    scribes and illuminators, 13–16
    the Utrecht Psalter, 16–18, *17*
Merian, Maria Sibylla, 93–5, *94*
metalpoint, 31, 43, 44–5, 199,
    206–7
Michallet paper, **207**
Michaux, Henri, 2, 175–6, *176*
Michelangelo Buonarroti
    anatomical studies, 50, 56
    on Anguissola's art, 56
    artistic techniques, 51–2
    artist's study of, 54, 74–5
    disegno drawings, 52
    lost drawings, 49, 51, 52
    spiritual drawings, 52–3, *53*
    studies for the figure of Adam,
        50–2, *51*
Millais, John Everett, 146, 148
Millet, Jean-François, 143–4, *144*,
    164

Milton, John, 133
miniatures
    of Imran Qureshi, 194–5, *195*
    Mughal portrait miniatures,
        91–2, *92*
Miró, Joan, 175
model books, 27–9, *28*, 33–5, *34*
Moore, Henry, 170–1, *171*
More, Sir Thomas, 61, *62*
Morisot, Berthe, 149–50, *150*
Moser, Mary, 124

natural world
    colonial explorations of, 89–95,
        90, *94*
    Impressionist drawing *en plein
        air*, 149–51, 154–6
    in Renaissance drawing, 46–8,
        47
Naturalism, *54*, *55*, 79–80
Nazarenes, 146
Nazca geoglyphs, 11
Neo-classicism, 126–7, 130
Neshat, Shirin, 5

offset (counterproof), **202**
Ojih Odutola, Toyin, 196–7, *196*
ostraca (fragments), 9–10, *9*, **207**

Palmer, Samuel, 145
paper
    albums of drawings, 35–6, 40
    blue paper, **200**
    cost, 31
    Ingres paper, **205**
    Japanese paper, 92, **205**
    laid paper, **206**, 215
    manufacture of, 35
    production, **207**
    watercolour paper, **214**
    wove paper, **215**
papyrus, 1, 9, **208**
parchment, 1, 12, 13–15, *15*, *28*,
    31, **208**
Paris, Matthew, 24–7, *26*, 27

Parker, Cornelia, 5
pastels, 151–2, *152*, **208–9**
patronage networks, 4
Pellegrini, Antonio, 108
pencil, **209**
Penrose, Roland, 166–7
performance art, 141
Perino del Vaga (Pietro
    Buonaccorsi), 74–6, *75*
Perry, Grayson, 1
Philip II, 72
Picasso, Pablo, 165–8, *166*
Piper, John, 170
Piranesi, Giovanni Battista,
    114–16, *116*, 123, 129, 211
plumbago, 203, **209**; *see also*
    graphite (plumbago)
political caricatures, 142–3
Pollock, Jackson, 176–8, *177*, 179
porte-crayon, **209**
portraiture
  by Bolognese female artists,
    82–3, *83*
  Dürer's self-portraits, 58–9, *59*
  emotional expression, 63–5
  explorations of the human
    condition, 187–8, *188*
  of the Grand Tourists, 106–9,
    109
  by Holbein, 61–3, *62*
  Mughal portrait miniatures,
    90–2, *92*
  preparatory drawings, 62–3
  Richardson's self-portraits,
    105–6, *107*, 186
  self-portraits, *145*, 146, *165*
  Seurat's *irradiation* technique,
    159, *159*
  use of graphite pencils, 136–7,
    137
pouncing, **210**
prepared paper, **210**
Pre-Raphaelite Brotherhood,
    146–8
pricked for transfer, **210**

print culture
  engraving, 2–3, *3*, 77–8, 127,
    133
  lithography, 143
  monastic scriptoria, 14–15
  political caricatures, 142–3
  zinc plates, 160–1
Pisanello (Antonio Pisano), 34–5,
    34
psychology
  autonomism, 175
  depictions of self, 179–85
  the unconscious mind, 172–7

quill pen, **210**
Qureshi, Imran, 5, 194–5, *195*

Raphael (Raffaello Sanzio da
    Urbino), 54–6, *56*, 63, 75, 146
red chalk, 46–7, **210–11**
Redon, Odilon, 2, 156–8, *157*,
    209
reed pens, *155*, 156, **211**
Rehbenitz, Theodor, *144*, 145
Rembrandt (Harmenszoon van
    Rijn)
  collections, 90–1
  Japanese paper, 92, 205
  landscape drawings, 98, 99
  reed pens, 156, 211
  reproductions of Mughal portrait
    miniatures, 91–2, *92*
  self-portraits, 106
Renaissance drawing
  albums of drawings, 35–6, 40
  the art of drawing, 31–2, 33, 36,
    49
  artist's workshops, 30–1, 33
  Botticelli's illustrations to the
    Divine Comedy, 36–8, *37*
  disegno concept, 52
  figure drawing, 32–3, 40–2,
    50–1, 56–7
  influence on the Nazarenes, 145
  model books, 33–5, *34*

the Pre-Raphaelites and, 146–8
villa frescoes, 54–5
visual innovations, 39–40, *40*
Reynolds, Sir Joshua, 209
Richardson, Jonathan, 105–6, *107*,
  186
Riza-yi 'Abbasi, 84–6, *85*
Rococo, 125
Rodríguez, Abel, 192–3, *193*
Romanticism, 116–17
Rossetti, Dante Gabriel, 146, *147*,
  148
Rotring pen, 183, **211**
Royal Academy of Arts, 124
Royal Academy Schools, 145
Rubens, Sir Peter Paul, 96–8, *97*
Russell, John, 120–1, *121*

Safavid court, Isfahan, 84–6
Schiele, Egon, 162–4, *164*
sciences
  astronomy, 120–1, *121*
  explanatory diagrams, 21–3,
    22
  perspective and geometry,
    39–40, *40*
scratching out, **212**
Secession, Vienna, 162
sepia, **212**
Seurat, Georges, 156, 158–9, *159*
sinopia, **212**
Sirani, Elisabetta, 82–3, *83*, *84*
sketchbooks, 122, *123*
skyscapes, 189–90, *190*
Solander box, 63, **212**
spiritual drawings
  Christ and St Dunstan, 12–13,
    13
  Christ at the Column, 41–2, *41*
  landscapes, 138
  of Leonardo da Vinci, 43–4, *43*,
    54
  of Michelangelo, 52–3, *53*
  Study of the Virgin, 63–4, *64*
  of William Blake, 132–4, *133*

steel nib, 148, **213**
still-life subjects, 152–4, *153*
storytelling, 2–3
stump, **213**
stylus, **213**
Surrealism, 175
Symbolism, 209

Titian (Tiziano Vecellio)
  landscapes, 71–3, *73*
  poesie (classical myth), 71
Tommaso de' Cavalieri, 52, 56
trois crayons, **213**

Uccello, Paolo, 39–40, *40*
Utrecht Psalter, 16–18, *17*

van Gogh, Vincent, 154–6, *155*,
  211
Vasari, Giorgio, 49, 50, 52, 57,
  74
vellum, 33, 148, **213**
Verrocchio, Andrea del, 42
Villard de Honnecourt, 27–9,
  28

Walker, Kara, 195–6
wash, **213**
watercolour, 66, 148, 149–50,
  213–14
watercolour paper, **214**
watermark, **214**
Watteau, Antoine, 109–12, *110*,
  111, 151
wax, **214**
White, John, 87–8, *88*
white chalk, **214–15**
women
  access to anatomical studies, 81,
    83, 122–5
  artists in Bologna, 81–2, 108
  female models, *54*, *55*, 123
wove paper, **215**

Zoffany, Johan, 124

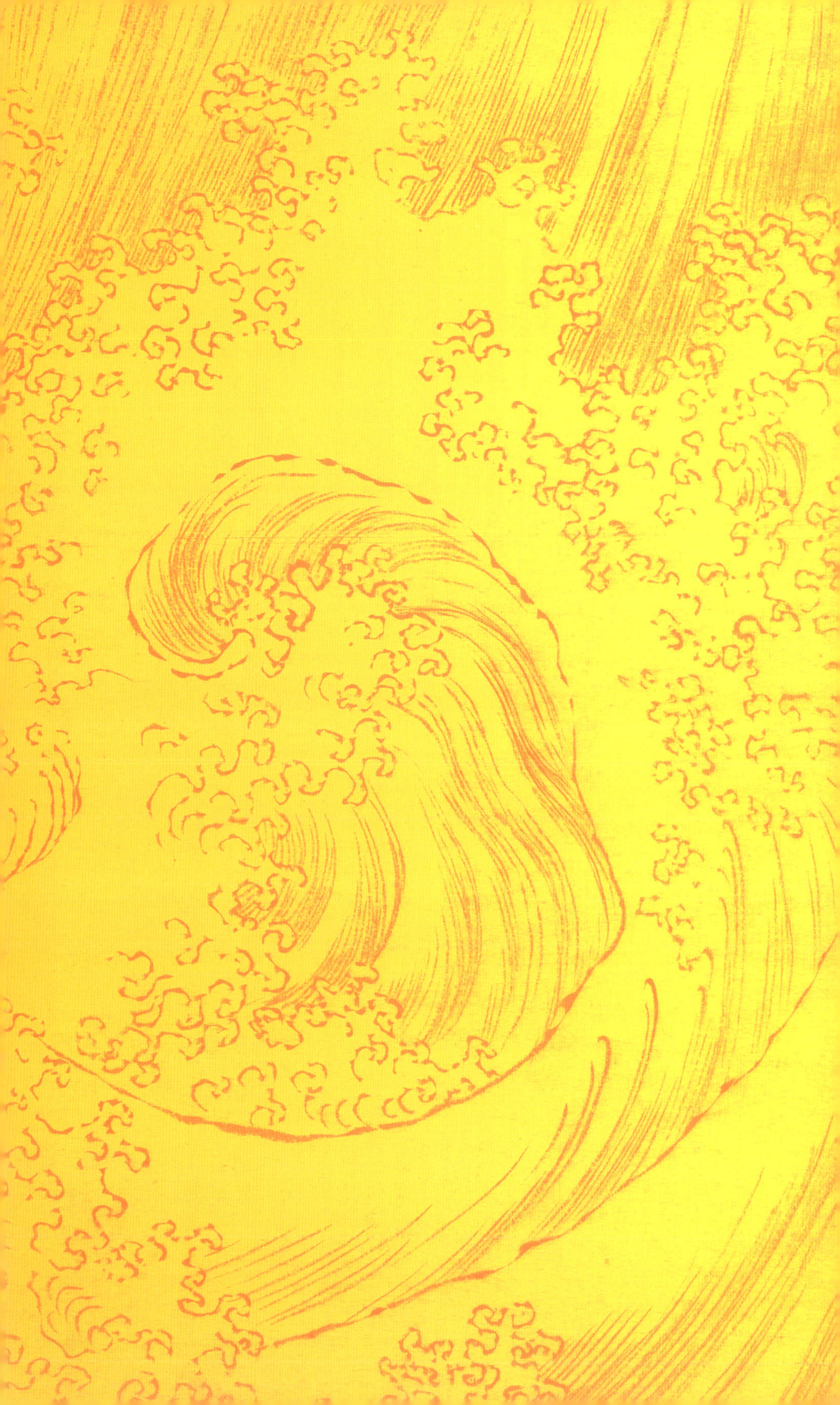

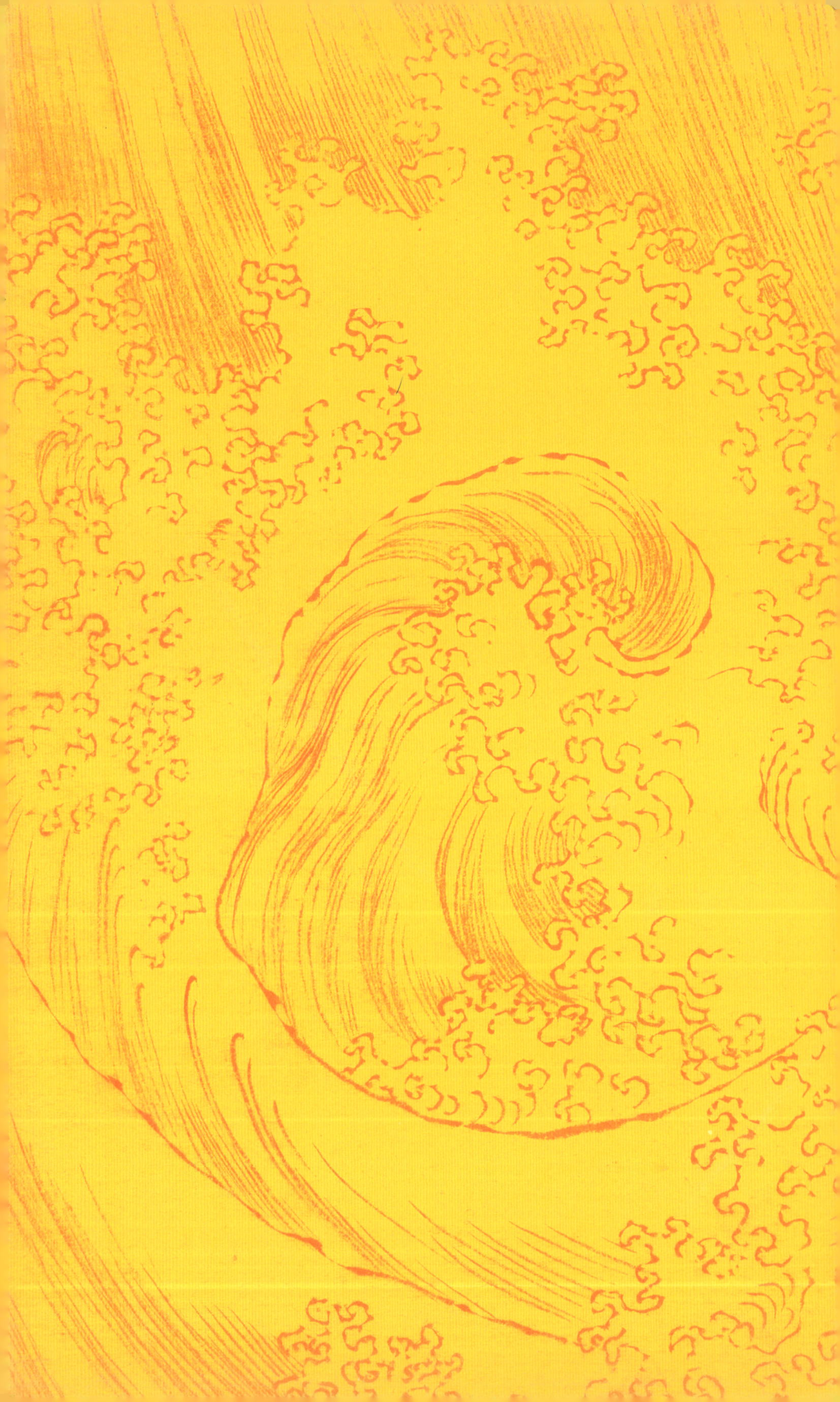